Being Sure of Each Other

Being Sure of Each Other

An Essay on Social Rights and Freedoms

KIMBERLEY BROWNLEE

OXFORD
UNIVERSITY PRESS

Great Clarendon Street, Oxford, OX2 6DP,
United Kingdom

Oxford University Press is a department of the University of Oxford.
It furthers the University's objective of excellence in research, scholarship,
and education by publishing worldwide. Oxford is a registered trade mark of
Oxford University Press in the UK and in certain other countries

© Kimberley Brownlee 2020

The moral rights of the author have been asserted

First Edition published in 2020

Impression: 2

All rights reserved. No part of this publication may be reproduced, stored in
a retrieval system, or transmitted, in any form or by any means, without the
prior permission in writing of Oxford University Press, or as expressly permitted
by law, by licence or under terms agreed with the appropriate reprographics
rights organization. Enquiries concerning reproduction outside the scope of the
above should be sent to the Rights Department, Oxford University Press, at the
address above

You must not circulate this work in any other form
and you must impose this same condition on any acquirer

Published in the United States of America by Oxford University Press
198 Madison Avenue, New York, NY 10016, United States of America

British Library Cataloguing in Publication Data
Data available

Library of Congress Control Number: 2019918190

ISBN 978-0-19-871406-4

Printed and bound in Great Britain by
Clays Ltd, Elcograf S.p.A.

Links to third party websites are provided by Oxford in good faith and
for information only. Oxford disclaims any responsibility for the materials
contained in any third party website referenced in this work.

Contents

Acknowledgements   vii

    Introduction   1

1. Social Beings   7
2. Social Deprivation   39
3. Sustaining Others   75
4. Interactional Freedom   95
5. Dilemmas of Sociability   116
6. Associational Freedom   135
7. Moral Messiness   154
8. Segregation   172

Notes   195
Bibliography   231
Index   241

Acknowledgements

Six years ago, James Nickel, a well-known philosopher of human rights, kindly told me that there might be a book in my thoughts on a human right against social deprivation. I am very grateful to him for that suggestion, and for the support he gave me while I tried to find out if he was right. My heartfelt thanks also go to Anca Gheaus and an anonymous referee for serving as OUP readers for this book, and providing wonderfully detailed, helpful, and challenging comments on the entire manuscript. I also thank Clare Chambers, Rowan Cruft, Fay Niker, Thomas Parr, and Jim Nickel for commenting on the manuscript at a workshop in 2016, funded by the Independent Social Research Foundation, the Warwick Humanities Research Centre, and the Warwick Philosophy Department. I am grateful to the other participants at that workshop for their valuable feedback, and I am particularly grateful to Fay Niker for her organizational work.

Many people kindly commented on specific parts of this work, including Firat Akova, Adrian Blau, Christopher Bennett, Emanuela Ceva, David Coady, Chiara Cordelli, Adam Cureton, Michelle Dempsey, Sarah Fine, Jonathan Floyd, John Gardner, Stuart P. Green, Daniel Groll, Jules Holroyd, Jeffrey Howard, Robert Jubb, Jeff King, Matthew Kramer, Kasper Lippert-Rasmussen, Christopher Mills, Virginia Mantouvalou, Tim Mulgan, Christoph Ortner, Avia Pasternak, Jon Pike, Andrea Sangiovanni, Henry Shue, Walter Sinnott-Armstrong, Adam Slavny, Matthew Soteriou, Zofia Stemplowska, James Stribopoulos, Steven Swartzer, François Tanguay-Renaud, Kartik Upadhyaya, and Laura Valentini. Laura deserves additional thanks for engaging thought-provokingly with me in a symposium on social deprivation at the 2016 Joint Session of the Aristotelian Society and Mind Association. I also wish to thank the students in my *Ethics of Sociability* module at the University of Warwick, who provided very useful feedback on several themes in the book.

I thank the Warwick Law School, Philosophy Department, and Centre for Ethics, Law, and Public Affairs for providing a perfect academic home in which to write this book. I am grateful to the Leverhulme Trust for a Philip Leverhulme Prize, and to the Independent Social Research Foundation for a Fellowship which relieved me from teaching to do the necessary armchair thinking for the book. I am grateful to Monash University, the University of British Columbia, and UCLA for being excellent homes away from home in which to occupy an armchair while on research leave. I thank Patrick Emerton, Jeff Goldsworthy, Dale Smith, and Fleur Morgan for being wonderful hosts during my time in Melbourne.

Ideas in several chapters first came to life in journal articles, but since then have been spliced, bent, reconfigured, and interwoven with new material to form parts of this book. Complete details for the articles that underlie sections of the book are provided in the Bibliography. I am grateful for permission to use this material.

While writing the book, I benefited from the excellent research assistance of Tom Parr, Fay Niker, Kartik Upadhyaya, and Simon Gansinger. I thank them all for their invaluable work. I also thank Simon for his assistance in proofreading the book and producing the index.

Like many other philosophers, I am indebted to Peter Momtchiloff and his editorial team at OUP for patiently shepherding my work into the light. I thank them for supporting me once more.

I thank my dad for painting the cover image and my mom for prodding him to paint four different versions of it to get it right. I thank all the members of my loving family for showing me daily how vital, and wonderful, it is that we can be *sure* of each other. I dedicate this book to them.

Kimberley Brownlee
December 2019

Introduction

In A. A. Milne's *House at Pooh Corner*, Piglet and Pooh have this heart-warming exchange while they are lost in the woods,

> Piglet sidled up to Pooh from behind. 'Pooh?' he whispered.
> 'Yes, Piglet?'
> 'Nothing,' said Piglet, taking Pooh's paw. 'I just wanted to be sure of you.'[1]

This small scene is the inspiration for the title of this book. Piglet and Pooh are the anthropomorphized creations of the imaginative and lonely little boy, Christopher Robin. They are his social surrogates and his social practice partners, as stuffed animals and dolls often are for children. The 'just' in Piglet's expression of relief—'I *just* wanted to be sure of you'—belies how important such assurance is. Being *sure* of each other—being securely connected—is vital to social creatures like us. We need to be persistently sure of at least one other person not just to flourish, but to survive. We also need to be sure of our acceptance within the wider social world, again not just to flourish, but to survive. This book focuses on the *survival* end of our sociability. A companion book, which I aim to write in the medium term, will consider the *flourishing* end of our sociability.

Several philosophers, including notably Martha Nussbaum, Jonathan Wolff, and Avner de-Shalit among others, have done important work to demonstrate that a capability to form and enjoy meaningful interpersonal relationships is a fundamental requirement of basic justice.[2] This book contributes to this justice-oriented discussion of our sociability by analysing our core social needs in the politically potent language of *human rights*. Too little attention has been paid in human rights theory to our *social* rights independent of our economic-welfare rights and civil and political rights.[3] This book goes some way toward rectifying this by arguing that we have a *human right against social deprivation*. In a nutshell, we have a right to have minimally adequate access to decent human contact and connection. In defending this right, this book takes aim at a familiar thought in human rights theory, which is that accounts of human rights must be minimalistic and any credible ranking they give of elemental priorities must rank our social interests far behind our interests in bodily security[4] and our interests in civil and political protections.[5] This book argues that human rights are indeed about the brute moral minimum, but that moral minimum necessarily includes many *positive* protections. Moreover, any credible ranking of elemental priorities must recognize the primacy of our core social needs.[6] These needs are not luxury goods that sit at the debatable end of the human rights spectrum. They are vital both in themselves as constitutive elements of a minimally good human life and as preconditions for securing our other interests, including our bodily security interests and our civil and political interests.

Chapter 1 investigates the nature and normative force of our core social needs. They are the non-contingent, fundamental interpersonal needs we have not just in childhood, but throughout our lives. They include our needs for physical closeness, caring touch, nurturing, good modelling, social-group security, interactional inclusion, interactive play, physical and mental protection, comfort, companionship, persistent association, and meaningful opportunities to sustain the people we care about. One thing this book highlights is that our core social needs include not just our personal relationship needs, which many philosophers make their focus, but also our simpler, interactional needs to have minimally adequate micro-moments of decent interaction with non-associates.[7] Chapter 1 then explains why our core social needs are as vital as, if not more vital than, our core economic-welfare needs for freedom from poverty and for shelter, health, and education, which garner much more attention in distributive justice debates.

Chapter 2 situates this analysis of our core social needs within the conceptual framework of *human rights* and, specifically, within a *moral* conception of *human rights* as claim-rights that, in the first instance, correlate with moral duties and limit moral freedoms. This chapter examines why, despite the importance of our core social needs, human rights debates have paid little attention to these needs. The chapter then fleshes out and defends the human right against social deprivation. We experience social deprivation most obviously when we are placed in long-term coercive isolation such as solitary confinement in prison, isolated immigration detention, or medical quarantine. But we can also experience social deprivation outside of these sites of forced segregation. For instance, we endure social deprivation when our primary social environment is brutal, degrading, or cruel, as many ordinary prison settings are, since these settings deny us minimally adequate access to *decent* social contact. In addition, we endure social deprivation when we are incidentally isolated, that is, when we need some help to stay social and we are left to fend for ourselves, which is the lot of many older people and people with disabilities.

Examining our core social needs and defending the human right against social deprivation yield several more specific conclusions about our sociability.

First, being social is not just about being supported by other people. It's also crucially about being able to support other people. Chapter 3 shows that our core social needs include deep, rights-grounding interests in having the social and material resources necessary to contribute to specific other people's survival and wellbeing. Put simply, we have deep interests in being Pooh Bear in the vignette above—the one whose hand can be safely clasped—and not just in being Piglet—the one who can find a safe hand to clasp. We are not merely disadvantaged when we have few options to support other people. We are also victims of a distinct kind of *social contribution injustice*. This injustice occurs when our social abilities, opportunities, and connections are wrongly compromised in ways that prevent us from meaningfully trying to sustain specific other people. We are also victims of social-contribution injustice when other people are unjustly prejudiced about our potential to be social contributors.

Second, accepting the above claims about sociability and justice has significant implications for our personal freedoms. Liberal thinking tends to assume that, as individuals, we have a largely unqualified right to interact or not with strangers as we please as well as a right to form persistent associations or not with whom we please, at least when we please those who please us. But, this liberal assumption bumps up against our fundamental needs for decent social contact and connection, forcing us to ask the Kantian question: What if *everyone* did that? What if everyone ignored or rebuffed a certain person? What if everyone refused to form an association with a certain type of person? We might say that this is regrettable but not a matter of justice. But suppose the rejected person is a baby, a young child, an older person, a physically or cognitively impaired person, a person who has recently migrated to our society, a person who has recently come out of prison, or a person who has endured significant trauma and suffering. Our answer to the Kantian question can have substantial repercussions both for the rejected person—regardless of who she is—and for all of us. Chapters 4–6 explore this reality.

Chapter 4 examines the fact that our core social needs extend beyond the boundaries of our personal associations to our wider social world, the realm of non-associative interactions. In general, we need to be acknowledged and responded to decently when we make interactional bids to people on whom we have no prior claim. Indeed, our interest in interactional inclusion is strong enough that it gives us some moral rights to general acknowledgement and recognition. Our interests in interactional inclusion conflict, of course, with our competing interests in having some interactional control to decide whether and how to interact with people or not as we wish. The chapter shows that, ultimately, our fundamental interests in acknowledgment, respect, and social connection take priority over our interests in interactional freedom.

The tension between interactional freedom and interactional inclusion also arises, in a magnified form, between our *associational* freedom and our positive social claim-rights which flow out of our right against social deprivation. Recognizing that we have fundamental, positive social human rights has significant implications for the scope of not just our interactional freedom but also our associational freedom. Chapters 5 and 6 show that our freedom to dissociate, like our freedom to rebuff non-associates' interactional bids, is secondary to our positive social claim-rights and must take a back seat when the two conflict. Debates about associational freedom tend to focus on collective and expressive associations, and on the limits of members' rights to be exclusive. This book focuses instead on our intimate associations. It shows that our freedom of association differs from our other personal freedoms with which it is usually listed, such as freedom of expression and freedom of religion, because freedom of association is neither a general moral permission nor a content-insensitive claim-right against interference that gives us an unencumbered sphere in which to act. Instead, our freedom of association is a highly constrained, content-sensitive, form-sensitive, and process-sensitive claim-right against interference. Although we have claim-rights against interference to form some modestly wrongful associations, we do not have broad freedoms to act wrongly in our associative decisions.

Chapter 7 then considers the aftermath of morally problematic associative decisions. Intriguing moral puzzles arise once we make problematic associative decisions, because these decisions change the moral ballgame. Morally problematic associations—such as an under-age marriage to which the spouses become committed—force us to acknowledge that people can have rights to remain in associations that they had no right to form.

Finally, taking our sociability seriously has significant implications for our social and political practices and our political institutions such as prisons, hospitals, and detention centres because, first, these practices and institutions can harm or help us as individuals to support each other as social beings and, second, they are sites of social segregation or connection in their own right. Chapter 8 explores some of the ways—physical and non-physical—in which we segregate people whom we deem to be socially threatening. One powerful but non-obvious way that we segregate people is at the level of personal identity through our use of essentialist language. Labels like 'offender', 'perpetrator', 'alien', 'stranger', and 'patient' can reduce people's lives to a (perceived) threatening feature. We should abandon such language whenever the essentialist image it promotes is not one that its bearers can reasonably reconceive as positive. We also segregate people through various concrete forms of mistreatment, such as giving them criminal sentences they can never spend, detaining them in long-term isolation, and stretching or severing their social bonds (by housing them in 'repellent' settings, limiting their access to outside contact, and holding them miles and miles from their home town and affiliates). The book concludes by recommending changes that we can make to our segregating institutions and social and political practices to better honour the fact that we, human beings, are fundamentally social creatures.

Before proceeding, let me say a word about the focus and argumentative strategy of this book. The book is premised on the idea that sociability is centrally a matter of personal morality. The story this book tells about social rights is, in the first instance, a story about *moral* rights—that is to say, the moral claim-rights that we have in virtue of being fundamentally social creatures. It's also a story about what follows morally from the fact that social resources necessarily rest with us as individuals. There never was nor could be a pool of unowned social resources in the same way there could be a pool of unowned material resources. Consequently, much of the discussion here necessarily focuses on the moral responsibilities that we have as individuals toward each other as social beings, including our responsibilities (1) to attend to each other's core social needs; (2) to make our social resources generally available to the collective social pool if required; (3) to retain our abilities to function socially so that we don't unduly burden the collective social-resource pool and so that we can contribute if needed; (4) to acknowledge the social claims that other people can have on us in virtue of special bonds, legitimate expectations, proximity, and our ability to alleviate their suffering; and (5) to ensure that, when we're not directly involved, the people tasked to meet someone's core social needs are attending to their duty.

All that said, morality is a situated enterprise. We cannot step outside the historical, social, legal, and political set-up within which we're striving to lead morally decent lives. Any set-up is inescapably non-ideal, and often makes our efforts to act well both morally messy and tragic. We can work, of course, to change our particular set-up. But we cannot ignore it when we're determining how we should treat each other. This book comments on the ways that our political, social, and legal set-up can help us or hinder us in our efforts to treat each other as we should as social creatures. The book highlights that political societies through their governments are the primary duty-bearers when it comes to human rights; and the book aims to detail the commitments that we must make as a society if we are to take the ethics of sociability seriously.[8] In short, this book is both a work of moral philosophy and a work of social and political philosophy. Its hybrid nature, and its perfectionism, will no doubt make it appealing to some readers and unattractive to others. But, its vices—or virtues—are ones that it shares with many contributions to political philosophy, and hopefully, in the end, they strengthen its case for the moral urgency of our social human rights.[9] With these preliminaries out of the way, let's investigate who we are as social beings.

1
Social Beings

Introduction

There is a small but growing industry in Japan that allows people to hire surrogates to stand in for their family and friends. People can rent, for impressive rates, not only mourners for a funeral or guests for their wedding, but also stand-in parents, children, in-laws, siblings, fiancé(e)s, spouses, friends, colleagues, and bosses for a variety of one-off occasions or for ongoing social contact. In a 2018 *New Yorker* article on Japan's rent-a-family industry, Elif Batuman tells several stories of people buying social contact. She describes one older couple who hired a man to play their son and listen to the father's hard-luck stories because their real son, who lived with them, wouldn't sit and listen.[1] This couple also hired a surrogate daughter-in-law and baby grandson because their real grandson was no longer an infant, and they missed the touch of a baby's skin. For one three-hour visit with the rented son, daughter-in-law, and grandson, they paid $1,100.

In another example, Batuman presents a widower, Kazushige Nishida, who rented a stand-in wife and adult daughter because he'd become estranged from his real 22-year-old daughter when she moved in with her boyfriend. In his interview with Batuman, Nishida told her that he thought of himself as a strong person, but had realized that 'when you end up alone you feel very lonely.' Nishida met with the stand-in wife and daughter for dinner (for a fee of $375) and told them how his deceased wife and living daughter behaved around him: their flicks of the hair, gestures, and pet names for him. Later, the women visited his home and they ate dinner together. Usually, women don't visit a male client's home, but the women were willing to do so in this case because they were together. (Physical contact beyond hand-holding is forbidden.) After that, Nishida gave their agency his house key and when he returned home from work that day, he found the two women preparing dinner for him. In time, the women began to behave more like themselves. Indeed, the stand-in wife told Nishida about her real husband and he gave her some advice. The stand-in daughter

Being Sure of Each Other: An Essay on Social Rights and Freedoms. Kimberley Brownlee, Oxford University Press (2020). © Kimberley Brownlee.
DOI: 10.1093/oso/9780198714064.001.0001

told him to contact his real daughter to make amends. Eventually, Nishida called his real daughter, and the vignette ends with that daughter having visited his house while he was out.

In a third case, Batuman describes a single mother, Reiko, who, nine years ago, rented an actor, Yūichi Ishii (who also owns the rental agency), to play her ex-husband and the father to her then 10-year-old daughter, Mana, so that Mana wouldn't be bullied at school for having a single mom. At the time that Ishii first visited, Mana was becoming withdrawn, avoiding school, and refusing to leave her room. After a few visits from Ishii, whom Reiko had tasked to respond to Mana with kindness no matter what Mana said or did, Mana crept out of her shell and became a happy child. As of 2018, Yūichi Ishii was still making regular visits to the unsuspecting, now 19-year-old Mana, and Reiko wished to marry him. Apparently, marriage proposals from female clients are a hazard of the job. When an agency detects that a client has become too dependent, they try to wean the client off the surrogate's company by spacing out the visits. Indeed, according to Yūichi Ishii, his agency's aim is, in time, to make itself redundant in clients' lives. Ishii said that his goal is 'to bring about a society where no one needs our service'.

In most, if not all, of Batuman's vignettes, the central figures display genuine emotional connections—indeed, love—for each other. The means through which that love is generated are jarring, since they seem to radiate inauthenticity and often involve deception. But Batuman's *New Yorker* article flirts implicitly with the thought that the way that genuinely caring emotions are generated may not matter that much. Yūichi Ishii reported to Batuman that, when standing in as a bridegroom and planning a wedding with a woman, he often found himself starting to fall for his 'fiancée'. Batuman also noted that, when interviewing Yūichi Ishii alongside Reiko, she could see him visibly toggling between his roles as business owner and husband.

This complex world of purchased sociability exposes some key truths about our need for social connection. To lead minimally good lives, we need certain social goods including: (1) basic social abilities, (2) adequate social opportunities, (3) access to persistent, stable social connections, and (4) the means to contribute directly to other people's survival and well-being (Section 1.1). The rent-a-family stories highlight the lengths to which we will go to be sociable. These stories also support the fourth item on this list of social needs: that we need to have the means to sustain other people in some way, however small. Why else would someone buy time with a stand-in baby grandson?

Three families of arguments undergird my claim that we have these four core social needs. They are: (1) empirical arguments (Section 1.2);

(2) phenomenological arguments (Section 1.3); and (3) respect-based arguments (Section 1.4). Together, they show that all our decent social connections—not just our close relationships—have hefty non-instrumental value in addition to their instrumental value.[2] These arguments pave the road for my claims in Chapters 2 and 3 that we have secure human rights to participate in the world of social connections. The most fundamental of these rights is our human right against social deprivation. Finally, the present chapter closes by distinguishing our non-contingent social needs from our contingent social desires (Section 1.5).

Before proceeding, let me nail down some key terms, starting with *sociability* and *sociality*. *Sociability* has richer connotations than *sociality*. It effuses the scent of virtue. It conjures up images of friendliness, openness to intimacy, geniality, a ready wit, tact, good humour, compassion, respect, empathy, companionability, delight in others' happiness, and pleasure in others' company. Since such virtues lie beyond my focus here, I will leave them for another day. In other words, I will largely ignore the differences between *sociability* and *sociality*, and use these terms interchangeably to denote our basic need to live amicably with other people.

Another key term is *social connections*. Our social connections fall along a spectrum of intimacy and persistence, but they all fortify the web of bonds that makes us human. At the less intimate end of the spectrum, our social connections include everything from our in-person transactional interactions, such as the brief chat we have with a grocery store clerk, to our day-to-day neighbourly relations, our collective and expressive associations in clubs, teams, and unions, and our professional and commercial associations. At the more intimate end of the spectrum, our social connections include our creedal connections in churches, temples, mosques, and synagogues, our ties with friends and family, and our loving relationships with a few people with whom we show mutual investment, intimacy, and care.[3] In what follows, I take the view that all our interactions and bonds that are worthy of the label *social connections* meet a minimal standard of decency. They rise above persistently brutal, degrading, or inhumane treatment.

Despite their minimal decency, our social connections can still fall morally short. Some fall short in modest ways, for instance in the unhappy marriage, the lifelong sibling rivalry, or the bitter friendship. Others fall short in serious ways, such as in a forced but non-abusive marriage or an emotionally fraught marriage. Troubled relations that nonetheless deserve the label 'social connection' can sometimes tread close to brutality, but must keep a discernible distance from it overall. Many social connections are *morally messy* in the technical sense that they defy a principled analysis of their moral qualities. As such, they raise pressing moral questions about associational freedom and positive associational rights, as we will see in Chapters 5, 6, and 7.

Let's begin by fleshing out the nature of our core social needs.

1.1 Social Needs

1.1.1 Contingent and Non-contingent Needs

Not all of our needs are morally urgent. Not all of our needs are even morally acceptable. A *need* is simply a condition necessary for us to achieve some end. To know the moral force of a need, we must look beyond the thing needed to our reason for needing it, which sometimes stands two or three steps away.[4]

Consider the fact that I need water. To get to the heart of this need, Soran Reader and Gillian Brock instruct us to ask the question: 'What for?' My answer might be: 'I cannot wash these dishes without water.' Alternatively, my answer might be: 'I cannot survive without drinking water.' My need for washing-up water is contingent on my desire for clean dishes. My need for drinkable water is independent of any desire I have. It is a non-contingent need that I cannot help but have. Indeed, having drinkable water is a non-contingent, *fundamental* need all humans have that has urgent moral force.

If we are healthy, then we do desire the things that we non-contingently, fundamentally need, such as consumable air, food, and water. But one signal that these needs are non-contingent and fundamental is that we continue to need them even if we cease to desire them. Without them, we cannot persist as needing beings.[5]

This analysis tracks Harry Frankfurt's *principle of precedence*. When a competition arises between a desire and a morally important need, 'the need starts with a certain moral edge'.[6] This is true when a person's need (for food) and her desire (to avoid it) pull in different directions. It's also true, as Frankfurt notes, when one person's need and another person's desire pull in the same direction, but cannot both be met. If Bo desires food, but does not need it to avoid malnourishment, and Jo needs food to avoid malnourishment, then Jo's need has a moral edge over Bo's desire.

With this quick sketch of *needs* on the drawing board, let's investigate non-contingent, fundamental needs in more detail, as this will lead us into the study of social needs.

1.1.2 Non-contingent Needs for a Minimally Good Life

The spectrum of our needs extends from the morally urgent through the trivial to the morally abhorrent. The moral importance of meeting a need or not depends on the moral importance of the end it serves.[7] Many of our non-contingent needs track our non-contingent interests, which are the interests we cannot help but have as the kind of beings we are; and many of our non-contingent interests are vital ends, such as having access to drinkable water, which give rise to morally urgent demands that we should strive to meet.[8] However, some non-contingent needs clash with and threaten non-contingent interests. For instance, a psychologically disturbed person might have a non-contingent need (a need he cannot help but have) to attack other people or to engage in child abuse.[9] Describing his disposition to harm others as a *need* may sound forced, but it highlights the functional nature of the concept of a *need*. His need to harm others is, of course, one that we should thwart.

Our vital ends include our interests in the necessary conditions for a minimally good human life. According to James Nickel, a minimally good life realizes four secure moral claims, where 'secure' means not conditional on group membership, good standing, good behaviour, or productive potential:

1. a secure claim to have a life;
2. a secure claim to lead that life;
3. a secure claim against severely cruel or degrading treatment;
4. a secure claim against severely unfair treatment.[10]

Each claim is centred on a fundamental human interest. What is noteworthy for my purposes, though Nickel does not highlight it, is that each interest is deeply social.

1. *Having a life*. The secure claim to have a life gives us, Nickel says, claims to freedom and protection from murder, indefensible violence, and malicious or negligent harm. These claims give other people negative duties to avoid harming us and positive duties to assist us when we need help to protect ourselves from such threats. The secure claim to have a life also plays a key role in justifying core economic-welfare rights, such as safe food and water, which are necessary to preserve life and health.[11]

Equally, I will argue, our secure claim to have a life justifies our core social rights to develop and maintain our social abilities; to have adequate opportunities for decent social contact; and to be secure within supportive connections during periods of vulnerability (Chapters 2 and 3).

2. *Leading a life.* In Nickel's view, the secure claim to lead a life gives us claims to freedom and protection from slavery, servitude, and the use of our life, time, or body without our consent. It also gives us freedoms in key areas of choice such as our occupation, marriage, associations, movement, and belief. It also 'yields claims to the liberties of a moral being—liberties to participate in social relations, to learn, think, discuss, decide, respond, act and accept responsibility'.[12]

Although I endorse many aspects of this secure claim—including the implication that it gives us a claim to have meaningful opportunities to contribute to other people's well-being—I take issue in Chapters 5 and 6 with the expansive, liberal view of freedom of association that Nickel invokes. I show that freedom of association is important, but slimmer than we tend to suppose. Freedom of association is also lexically secondary to our positive social claim rights which ensure that we have the social resources (i.e. social abilities, opportunities, and connections) we need to participate in the world of social relations.

3. *Degrading treatment.* We have a secure claim against severe pain, slavery, and rape among other things. 'Rape is degrading,' Nickel says, 'because it treats a person as a mere sexual resource to be used without consent, or because in many cultures it destroys [her] social standing as a virtuous and pure person.' This claim also 'requires individual and collective efforts to protect people against [such forms of mistreatment]. The severity of cruelty depends on how degrading it can reasonably be taken to be, the degree of malicious intent, and the amount of harm that it is likely to cause.'[13]

One of Nickel's insights here is that a person can be pilloried, and suffer a complete and sometimes life-threatening loss of social standing, once she has been grossly mistreated.

4. *Severely unfair treatment.* This secure claim concerns matters of ruinous injustice. We have a 'claim to freedom from such treatment and a claim to individual and collective efforts to protect [us] against it. For example, governments have a duty not to imprison innocent people, and therefore a duty to provide the accused with fair trials.'[14] I tackle the social dimensions of criminal justice, punishment, prison, and solitary confinement in the final chapter of this book.[15]

Below, I show why our core social needs sit among the non-contingent, fundamental conditions for a minimally good human life, and why, consequently, they are both *secure* and morally urgent. Before defending these ideas, let me acknowledge two worries that a reader might have about social needs.

1.1.3 Worries about Social Needs

1. *Is our sociality worth protecting?* The first worry is that, after young childhood, our sociality does not seem to be a morally urgent feature of who we are. Instead, it seems to be like our propensity to be violent, or our tendency to have status quo bias, framing bias, and loss aversion—traits that are sometimes useful, sometimes regrettable, and often objectionable. If sociality is like those things, then we shouldn't prize it and protect it. We should manage, constrain, and overcome it when we can.

In reply, undoubtedly, being social comes with high risks and assured costs. For one thing, our sociality makes us vulnerable to each other as potential victims. By having to rely on each other for survival and well-being, we are also at each other's mercy. Indeed, we are less safe within a community whose members are bent on destroying us than in a Hobbesian free-for-all state of nature, since belligerent communities are better organized, equipped, and able to harm us than belligerent individuals are.

For another thing, our sociality makes us vulnerable to being co-agents of wrongdoing. We are prone to group-think. We have no choice but to invest in the epistemic division of labour, relying on other people to know some things for us and to tell us about them. We also are generally aware of and receptive to the mood of the room. If we identify with a group, then we're more likely to conform to its prevailing attitudes and be party to any horrific acts the group perpetrates against people who are deemed to have offended it.

In the West, we have long admired fictional and historical loners, such as Robinson Crusoe, Thomas Stockmann,[16] Henry David Thoreau, and Richard Proenneke.[17] Possibly, we admire—or covet—their seemingly blissful, self-sufficient isolation because it suggests to us that we too could thrive on our own if we chose, free from the double-edged sword of interdependency.

But, despite the risks that inevitably come with being social, we should not regret, manage, or try to overcome our sociality. It has great value, as the rest of this chapter shows.

2. *Not all humans have such needs.* The second worry is that I overgeneralize when I say that we, human beings, have non-contingent, fundamental social needs. Undoubtedly, we all have these needs in babyhood, childhood,

and periods of incapacitation. But healthy adults lack the kinds of non-contingent, fundamental needs I describe, and the list of great loners is proof, so the objection goes.

In reply, other philosophers have argued powerfully against this individualistic image of human beings. Many feminists and care ethicists highlight both our fundamental interdependency and lifelong vulnerability.[18] Martha Nussbaum includes affiliation in her list of ten central capabilities, describing it as follows:

> Affiliation.
>
> (A) Being able to live with and toward others, to recognize and show concern for other human beings, to engage in various forms of social interaction; to be able to imagine the situation of another. (Protecting this capability means protecting institutions that constitute and nourish such forms of affiliation, and also protecting the freedom of assembly and political speech.)
>
> (B) Having the social bases of self-respect and non-humiliation; being able to be treated as a dignified being whose worth is equal to that of others. This entails provisions of non-discrimination on the basis of race, sex, sexual orientation, ethnicity, caste, religion, national origin.[19]

According to Nussbaum, the capability of affiliation, like that of practical reason, plays a distinctive role by organizing and pervading the other capabilities she identifies. Affiliation pervades the other central capabilities in being realized whenever they are realized; if the other capabilities are made available to a person, then the person is simultaneously respected as a social being.[20] She continues: 'Affiliation organizes the capabilities in that deliberation about public policy is a social matter in which relationships of many kinds (familial, friendly, group-based, political) all play a structuring role.'[21]

The kinds of goods that Nussbaum references in relation to *affiliation* are broadly similar to those we secure when we meet our *need to belong*, which I discuss below. However, the need to belong includes more than just our *abilities* to live with and toward other people in conditions of mutual care, concern, dignity, equality, and respect. The need to belong includes our positive exercise of those abilities, or our actual, effective realization of our capabilities, the importance of which Jonathan Wolff and Avner de-Shalit stress in their discussion of our interests in having secure functionings and not just capabilities.[22]

My own reply to this worry, that we are not fundamentally interdependent throughout our lives, will appeal both to empirical evidence (Section 1.2) and to the socialized ways we see the world (Section 1.3). For now, let me say that exceptional people are just that—exceptions. A person who can survive or thrive in isolation—particularly in long-term, unwanted isolation—is like the person who can survive prolonged, intense fasting or unwanted nutritional deprivation: a rare being. The stories about Japan's rent-a-family industry are counterexamples to the stories of the great loners. In his interview with Batuman, Yūichi Ishii reported that, since 2009, he has acted as the husband to over 100 women, with 60 of his roles being continuing ones. Early in his career, he was at one point in ten families at the same time—a workload he found unsustainable because 'you feel like you have someone's life on your shoulders'.

Our social needs are less age-specific or ability-specific than the second worry implies. We do have social needs throughout our lives.[23] First, we have the longest period of juvenile abject dependency from birth of any species.[24] To live well as children and to develop into well-functioning adults, we need highly intense, personalized care, nurturing, and support from a small, fixed, committed set of caregivers, as Mana's story with her stand-in father suggests.

Second, as we mature, we need close, reciprocal social connections that give us opportunities to become people on whom others may securely depend.

Third, when we are competent adults, we need social connections at least during critical periods of our lives that render us momentarily dependent, such as when we become ill, injured, impaired, or incapacitated; when we give birth, face the death of a loved one, or face our own death; when we endure a loss of social standing or employment; when we recover from life-redefining experiences such as imprisonment, torture, or abuse; and when we are unable to care for our own dependants.

Fourth, even when we are mature and healthy, we usually need to live harmoniously with other people to survive and flourish. Much of the value in our projects, goals, and decisions comes from our social connections which allow us to witness each other's efforts, share in each other's successes, and empathize with each other when we fail. (Admittedly, we can meet some of our companionship needs through close connections with non-human animals, but not all.)

Fifth, we need social connections as we return to a state of dependency in old age, if we are lucky enough to live to an old age.

Finally, less individualistically, our families, clans, tribes, friendships, communities, teams, parties, unions, assemblies, creeds, and faiths cannot exist and have the distinctive intersubjective value they usually have unless our social and material needs are met.

1.1.4 Social-Access Needs and Social-Contribution Needs

We have two types of core social needs. The first are our *social-access needs* to the social connections necessary for our personal security and meaningful prospects for well-being. The social connections most likely to fulfil our access needs are, of course, close, persistent, caring ones marked by frequent direct contact and mutual investment. And familial connections are a paradigm case. But they are not the only ones necessary for, and able to support, our personal security and well-being. In Chapter 4, I explore how our decent, non-associative interactions with strangers and acquaintances form a key component of our web of social connections.

The second type of social needs that we have are, more interestingly, *social-contribution needs*—to be able to contribute to specific other people's survival and well-being. Sustaining other people goes as much to the heart of what it means to be human as social access does. Being human means, first, having a deep interest in offering our care and company to others, usually to members of our own species, and notably to the people with whom we are already connected (if such people exist). Second, it means having a deep interest in others accepting our offer at least some of the time. As we mature, we develop a fundamental need to be needed, not just a wish to be wanted. In Chapter 3, I show that we need to be dependable, and indeed to be depended upon to contribute to specific others' survival and well-being according to our abilities.

Admittedly, I make a hefty generalization here. But my saying we have these deep social contribution needs is similar to saying that we have five fingers on each hand. Not all human beings do have five fingers, and it's possible that, at a given moment in history, the majority of people might have fewer or more than five fingers on each hand. Even so, it is true of human beings that we have five fingers on each hand. Similarly, it is true of us that we have social contribution needs even though a few of us might not have these interests, and our felt *desire* to contribute to specific people's well-being can wax and wane, and can be stifled or perverted. But, if it is stifled or perverted, we still *need* to contribute, in the same way that if we cease to desire to eat, we still need food. Our need to contribute is more than a contingent, psychological need that causes us distress when we're unable to support the people we treasure. It's a fundamental need grounded in (1) our narrow self-interest, (2) our interest in specific others' well-being, and (3) broader self-and-group-interests (Chapter 3).

1.1.5 The Need to Belong

Our two types of core social needs—our social-access needs and our social-contribution needs—can be understood through the lens of our need to belong. The *need to belong* is a well-established idea in psychology, understood as a 'need to form and maintain at least a minimum quantity of interpersonal relationships' marked by frequent interactions within a stable, enduring context of care and concern.[25] But the idea is little discussed in philosophy, and requires a proper conceptual specification. Here is a brief effort to specify the concept of *belonging*.

The *Oxford English Dictionary* defines *belonging* as being connected with something or someone in various relations; forming a part or appendage of something, such as being a member of a family, society, or nation; being an adherent of, or dependant of, something; fitting a certain environment, such as being a native or inhabitant of a place; or being one of a generation or time.[26] *Belonging* has connotations of *fitting, suiting, complementing, accepting, integrating,* and *being in harmony with*.[27]

In some domains, *belonging* also has connotations of reciprocity. We speak of things or people belonging *together*. *Belonging* in this sense is a joint property or symmetrical relation. To say that A belongs with B implies that B also belongs with A. Some idioms and catchphrases that describe *belonging with* in this sense are: 'We go together like a wink and a smile', 'apple pie and ice cream', 'apple pie and motherhood', 'love and marriage', and 'bacon and eggs'. Iconic couples that capture this image of belonging are Romeo and Juliet, and Abelard and Héloïse.[28]

This symmetrical notion of *belonging with* contrasts with an asymmetrical, proprietary notion of *belonging to,* which conjures up traditional images of fathers owning children and husbands owning wives. Children *belonged to* fathers. Wives *belonged to* husbands. Fathers and husbands did not belong to children or wives.

More contemporary images of *belonging to* are less hierarchical. Between partners, they are implicitly symmetrical, but nonetheless proprietary, allowing for the possibility that men might belong to women. The well-known country song 'You Belong to Me' (1952), by Chilton Price, captures the worried heartache of the left-at-home wife or girlfriend who cautions her beau while he is away at war: 'Just remember when a dream appears. You belong to me.' Modern images of relationships also allow that parents might belong to children. In many contemporary families, children take centre stage, receive the best things a family can offer, and learn to ask a thousand questions when previously they were expected to be seen and not heard. English professor Marlene Goldman has suggested that, in some ways, children consume their parents.[29]

Despite the distrustful possessiveness of some of these images, the idea of *belonging to* someone can have positive connotations. In Lucy Maud Montgomery's novel *Anne of Green Gables*, 12-year-old orphan Anne Shirley tells Matthew Cuthbert, when he collects her from the train station to take her home to live with him and his sister Marilla, how delighted she is at the prospect of having a family:

> Oh, it seems so wonderful that I'm going to live with you and *belong to you*. I've never belonged to anybody—not really. But the asylum was the worst. I've only been in it four months, but that was enough. I don't suppose you ever were an orphan in an asylum, so you can't possibly understand what it is like. It's worse than anything you could imagine.[30]

In her joy at coming to live with Matthew and Marilla, Anne also conveys her relief. She will *belong to* someone. She will be safe, protected, and valued. She will be able to depend on people to care for her.

Moreover, *belonging to* is less proprietary, though more hierarchical, when we speak of belonging to a larger group such as a family, tribe, clan, or society. Although the idea of *belonging to* a larger group carries the connotation that deference is expected, that connotation is less loaded than in the one-to-one case where one person *belongs to* another person.

A third notion of *belonging* that sits outside this contrast between non-hierarchical *belonging with* and hierarchical *belonging to* is *belonging in*, such as belonging in this family, in this school, in this town, or in this country. This notion of *belonging* best captures the kind of psychological ease we tend to feel when we have a clear temporal and physical sense that we fit, that we belong *here* and *now* in this house, community, state, and nation, with these people.[31] One reason that time-travel stories captivate us is that they make the familiar foreign often by putting a person in her home place in a different time.

All three of these variants of *belonging* help us to make sense of who we are. When we belong somewhere with, to, or in a set of people, then we have a place and usually we know our place. This means we know what is expected of us, often because we hold a well-defined, interpersonal role within the unit, such as mother, father, sibling, spouse, aunt, uncle, cousin, grandparent, or friend. These paradigms pervade most societies, and when we hold one or more of these roles, we usually have a satisfying sense of personal identity. Without them, we can feel lost and look lost, such as in the case of Mana, who was bullied at school for having a single mother.

Of course, we form life-defining bonds that imitate the dominant paradigms, as the rent-a-family stories show. And, we can also form life-defining bonds that depart from the dominant paradigms. For example, a young woman and an older woman who are not kin to each other might form a lasting loving bond: in Poland, the older woman is known as a 'sewn in' grandmother.[32] For another example, two young girls who are not kin might form a lifelong non-romantic bond, backed up by a legal contract.[33] Or a divorced parent of a young child might opt to invest in that connection rather than find a new partner, despite the raised eyebrows that decision will draw. Or a woman, her husband, and her boyfriend might all live together and raise a child together, leading a loving family life without the blueprint of the two-parent set-up.[34] The potential range of our identity-shaping associations is really only constrained by the limits of our imaginations. The associations we are inclined to imagine and realize for ourselves depend on our community's cultural norms, which can be enforced rigorously, and which make it all the more impressive when people form loving connections that deviate from the norms. Within different cultures, different types of association become dominant, and those types shift as cultural norms shift.[35] Consider marriage. In addition to the Western stereotype of the legal, consensual, church-blessed, self-selected, monogamous, heterosexual, adult marriage, there are many other possible models, including same-sex marriage, non-gendered marriage, arranged marriage, civil partnership, non-monogamous marriage, polygamous marriage, walking marriage (in which the spouses do not live in the same household), forced marriage, and informal partnership, all of which confer social identities on us, and all of which can to different degrees fulfil our need to belong. The moral merit of these models depends partly, but only partly, on cultural and environmental conditions.

I will return to belonging in Section 1.2 to outline some psychological research on what is called the *belongingness hypothesis*, and in Section 1.3 I will comment further on the self-understanding that we get from belonging.

For now, let me specify three concrete needs that flow from our core social-access needs and social-contribution needs.

1.1.6 Social Resources

Our core social needs give us concrete needs for three types of social resources:

1. *social abilities* to cultivate social opportunities and to offer, accept, and participate in social connections;
2. *social opportunities* to form and sustain social connections;
3. *social connections*, which are valuable in themselves, but also help us to form other connections.

Let me say a bit about each.

1. *Social abilities* are a complex set of skills, thoughts, attitudes, emotions, perceptions, and behaviours that enable us to lead socially integrated lives. They include:

1. preconditions for sociability, such as consciousness, subjective awareness, sentience of pain, minimally good health, cognition, and basic physical competence;
2. perceptual acuity, including the abilities to discern emotions and read body language;
3. abilities to attend and comprehend;
4. communicative abilities to express, understand, and respond;
5. richer abilities to feel trust, love, care, empathy, kindness, forgiveness, and compassion;
6. abilities (in caregivers) for maturity, responsibility, competence, nurturing, and dependability.

Of course. we vary in our social abilities. And possibly no one person could ever realize the full set of social abilities.

2. *Social opportunities* are the opportunities we need to meet and re-meet each other, to interact with each other, and to form and sustain supportive connections together. Meaningful social opportunities include opportunities:

1. to show decency, respect, courtesy, concern, and care for other people;
2. to engage in shared activities and joint narratives with others, and thereby to further others' enjoyment of the activities;

3. to share relevant knowledge and thereby to further others' understanding;
4. to show that we are trustworthy;
5. to give others the benefit of earning and receiving our trust in return;
6. to offer intimacy and understanding to others;
7. to be that mirror to other people which Aristotle says is why we are truly important to each other in the best sense—that is, to offer those corrections that enable a friend to cultivate the virtues.[36]

The last of these opportunities—to serve as a moral mirror and have others serve as a moral mirror to us—is provided in a rather interesting service offered by Ishii's rent-a-family agency. People can rent a person to scold them for a mistake or wrong they did, to help them to atone.

3. *Social connections* include a range of social links which, as noted above, sit along a spectrum of intimacy, from the trivial to the life-defining, from the momentary to the lifelong: including familial, creedal, professional, political, recreational, expressive, athletic, contractual, and fraternal associations as well as decent incidental interactions with strangers; all meeting a minimal standard of decency. The *kinds* and *number* of social connections that we fundamentally need depend partly on our stage of life and temperament. That said, the *belongingness hypothesis*, which I explore below, suggests that what we all need most is to be part of persistent, caring, direct relations with a small number of people who may, but need not, be our family members. We do not need, and are ill-served by, vast quantities of superficial connections.

Let's consider the relations between these three kinds of social resources. Our social abilities are conceptually, chronologically, and justificatorily prior to our social opportunities and social connections. Conceptually, without the notion of *social abilities*, we cannot make sense of either *social opportunities* or *social connections*, since *social abilities* capture what it is to be a social creature and, thereby, specify the features of sociability to be found in social opportunities and connections. Chronologically, without possessing social abilities, we cannot make use of social opportunities to form and sustain social connections. Justificatorily, we have little reason to protect each other's social opportunities or connections if we fail to ensure that, to the best extent possible, each of us develops adequate social abilities in childhood and can maintain those abilities as well as possible in adulthood.

That said, a chicken-and-egg problem presents itself here since, chronologically, we cannot cultivate the social abilities we need to use social opportunities and form social connections unless someone gives us close, nurturing support throughout our protracted childhood. In other words, having close social *connections* is a prerequisite for developing social *abilities*. So, chronologically at least, social connections precede social abilities (but, of course, they won't be social *connections* unless the depended-upon parties within them have adequate social abilities).

Moreover, conceptually, *social abilities* seem to make sense only once we have a clear understanding of what *social connections* are, since they tell us what abilities are needed to form and sustain them.

The chicken-and-egg problem does not extend to the justificatory ranking. Social abilities are the most fundamental resource of the three. They are the resource we cannot do without. If our social connections break down, we can try to establish new ones (unless we are thwarted), and the evidence I discuss below suggests that we can do this quickly even in adverse conditions. Similarly, if our current social opportunities give us no lasting connections, we can look for others (unless we are thwarted). By contrast, if we fail to develop adequate social abilities in childhood, then we will be permanently impaired in our capacity to lead socially integrated lives. And, if we are rendered unable to maintain our social abilities as adults, then we will be unable to continue to lead socially integrated lives.[37]

With the conceptual terrain of our core social needs on the table, let us turn to the three families of arguments for their moral urgency.

1.2 Empirical Arguments

1.2.1 Children

Indisputably, we have vital social needs as babies, children, and young adults. Both our present welfare as children and our future development depend critically on receiving personalized nurturing, modelling, and protection, if not love, from a small, consistent set of caregivers.[38] If our caregivers fail us, we are harmed not only in childhood but throughout our lives, as we're denied a broadly 'open future', to use Joel Feinberg's phrase.[39] Let's unpack these claims.

First, as Anca Gheaus argues, childhood is a distinctively, intrinsically valuable stage in our lives in which we can enjoy fully kinds of value that are different, for most people, from those that we can enjoy fully as adults. During childhood, we have privileged access to certain goods (unless we train ourselves to realize these goods as adults), such as open-mindedness, scientific drive, philosophical curiosity, interest in the world, fantasy, pretend play, artistic ability, physical agility, and flexibility.[40] For us as children to experience these rich goods fully, we need to feel safe, secure, supported, and connected. If we are denied adequate care, intimacy, and socialization as babies and young children, we will be unable to access these unique goods of childhood.

Second, without adequate, care, intimacy, and socialization as babies and children, we can experience severe developmental difficulties, the effects of which will dog us in later life, thereby both harming us in the moment and rendering us less able later to participate in reciprocal social connections.[41] Many children who grow up in appalling conditions *can* offer care, love, and companionship to others both as children and as adults. But many of them are unable to be caregivers in the practical sense of *taking care of* another being. Many are unable to take care of themselves. And, many are unable to take the initiative to sustain the social connections they have. Consider the children who grew up in Romanian orphanages under the Ceaușescu dictatorship, who endured chronic neglect and abuse that did lasting damage to their social abilities.

Matthew Liao argues that, to lead minimally good lives, children need not only adequately supportive care, but love, where *love* is defined as seeking 'a highly intense interaction with the child, where one values the child for the child's sake, seeks to bring about and maintain physical and psychological proximity with the child, seeks to promote the child's well-being for the child's sake, and desires that the child reciprocate, or at least, respond to one's love'.[42] Love also includes overall strong emotions of warmth and affection, while granting that these emotions can shift and take a multitude of forms. If a child is unloved, then her psychological, social, and physical development is threatened and potentially undermined. Liao observes:

> Studies of children in institutions found, for example, that children who did not receive love but only adequate care became ill more frequently; their learning capacities deteriorated significantly; they became decreasingly interested in their environment; they failed to thrive physically by failing to gain weight or height or both; they suffered insomnia; they were constantly depressed; and they eventually developed severe learning disabilities.[43]

Critics of Liao question whether the actual emotion of *love* is necessary to secure children the developmental goods that he cites and, hence, be the object of a right as he argues.[44] Although I put aside this particular debate about love, I note that Liao's definition of *love* is potentially broad enough to accommodate a variety of emotional responses, though undoubtedly some responses are, by nature, inconsistent with overall warm-hearted affection and valuing a child for her own sake.

Suffice it to say, we have undeniably deep social needs as children, the precise nature of which is best specified not only by philosophers, but also by biologists, paediatricians, psychologists, early childhood development specialists, and caring parents.

1.2.2 Belonging

The empirical evidence from psychology and neuroscience supports the claim that we have deep social needs *throughout our lives*. In general, we need to live in close proximity and relationship with other people to survive and flourish.[45] Reportedly, we spend approximately 80% of our waking hours with other people, generally preferring that time to the time we spend alone.[46] Also, reportedly, we tend to form social bonds quickly and easily even in adverse conditions (though, we might do this only when our previous bonds have dissolved and are unrecoverable).[47]

Psychologists Roy F. Baumeister and Mark R. Leary take an accepted point in psychological theory and speculation—that we need to belong—and formulate it as a primary human motivation to have both frequent interactions with, and persistent care from, a small set of people.[48] According to this *belongingness hypothesis*,

> human beings have a pervasive drive to form and maintain at least a minimum quantity of lasting, positive, and significant interpersonal relationships. Satisfying this drive involves two criteria: First, there is a need for frequent, affectively pleasant interactions with a few other people, and, second, these interactions must take place in the context of a temporally stable and enduring framework of affective concern for each other's welfare.[49]

Drawing on a wealth of psychological data, Baumeister and Leary hold that this primary interpersonal motivation to belong is universal among human beings, the cause of a great deal of human behaviour, emotion, and thought, and the driver behind many other motivations we have for power, achievement, approval, intimacy, and affiliation.

It is worth underlining that Baumeister and Leary stress the importance of *frequent* direct social contact with a *specific* set of people:

> Interactions with a constantly changing sequence of partners will be less satisfactory than repeated interactions with the same person(s), and relatedness without frequent contact will also be unsatisfactory.[50]

Through frequent contact with the same set of people, we build up intimacy, a history of shared experiences, and a joint narrative, which heighten the sense that we belong. (In Chapters 2, 3, and 4, I return to this insight that we need more than merely decent social contact from *someone*: we need frequent, repeated, supportive interactions with the *same* small set of people. I argue for this claim in Chapters 2 and 3, but then defend the value of non-associative interactions in Chapter 4.)

Many studies indicate that the *quality* of our relationships, not the quantity, is what matters. The ongoing, longitudinal Harvard Grant Study of over 700 men holds that the men who were most satisfied with their relationships at age 50 were the healthiest at age 80. Those men who were in securely attached relationships as they aged also retained sharper memories longer than those who were in insecure or hostile relationships.[51]

Interestingly, Baumeister and Leary argue that, while the *quality* of our social bonds matters more than the quantity, good quality does not require that we have our closest bonds with *particular* people like our biological mothers.[52] In principle, they claim, the need to belong could be directed toward and met in different ways by almost any human being:

> For example, one might imagine a young fellow without any family or intimate relationships who is nonetheless satisfied by being heavily involved in an ideologically radical political movement. There are undoubtedly strong emotional mechanisms associated with belongingness…but these could be understood as mediating mechanisms rather than as essential properties.[53]

In the same vein, Baumeister and Leary suggest that relationships are somewhat fungible: 'the loss of relationship with one person can to some extent be replaced by any other. The main obstacle to such substitution is that formation of new relationships takes time.'[54] Just as a pet-lover will get a new dog after mourning for the dog who has died, so too it seems that, if we are healthy enough, we will seek out, and usually secure, a new friend, partner, or ally when a previous connection ends. Our capacity for social relatedness is such that we can cultivate connections in different spheres to overcome the potential ill effects of being socially deprived in one particular sphere.[55]

Other psychology studies dispute these two claims. Studies on chronically lonely older people in nursing homes indicate that often they crave connections with their children and perhaps with their spouse, who may have passed away. Although surrounded by people, and possibly able to form new, supportive relationships, they do not form them and regard the ones they've lost as irreplaceable.[56] It may be only when *all* our pre-existing social bonds have irretrievably dissolved that we will accept otherwise unsatisfactory bonds as adequate.[57]

As the above points suggest, our need to belong is precise, rich, and demanding.[58] It aligns in many ways with Wolff and de-Shalit's treatment of affiliation in terms of secure functioning. That said, if our need to belong can actually be met in many ways by different people, then it is not as demanding as it may first appear. This bodes well for my aim in Chapter 2 to show that belonging is a non-contingent, fundamental, morally urgent need which appropriately animates the human right against social deprivation.

The *belongingness hypothesis* raises some big normative questions. First, what are our *moral* needs when it comes to belonging? Is membership in any kind of accepting group better than isolation? Does it matter if the social bonds that we can access to meet our need to belong are morally opprobrious?

Baumeister and Leary seem to say that our (psychological) need to belong could be met by a gang, the Mafia, a radical religious cult, the KKK, or a neo-Nazi group. The fact that such groups can thrive and command members' loyalty and sacrifice suggests that they do tap into our need to belong. But even if, in principle, a group with morally opprobrious ambitions can be loving and loyal to its members, it always poses the risk that its opprobrious ambitions will infect its internal dynamics. In practice, such groups probably fail to provide members with a 'stable, enduring context of concern and caring,'[59] and consequently do not really satisfy their need to belong. Even so, such groups are preferable to isolation, which is a highly detrimental experience, as I detail below. No one—let alone a child or vulnerable person—can really be expected to endure isolation when some form of social bond is on the table. An abandoned child may reasonably decide that joining a gang is much better than isolation, since it probably makes him safer from outside threats, gives him some sense of identity, and gets him a regular meal and a bed.

Second, could the belongingness hypothesis be falsified and, if so, what would that mean? Baumeister and Leary acknowledge that the hypothesis could be falsified either if many of us can live happily and healthily in social isolation or if many of us show no cognitive or emotional responses when faced with the prospect of significant changes to our belongingness status. But, as noted at the outset of this chapter, the evidence doesn't seem to falsify the hypothesis at least with respect to social isolation. We might like the idea of solitude in principle, but few of us seem to thrive in it.

Baumeister and Leary's own responses to this worry are first that:

> Falsification is only one relevant approach to evaluating a broad hypothesis about belongingness being a fundamental motivation...hypotheses about fundamental motivations must be evaluated in terms of their capacity to interpret and explain a wide range of phenomena...We therefore pay close attention to the potential range of implications of the belongingness hypothesis, in addition to examining how many falsification tests the hypothesis has managed to survive.[60]

Second, they review apparent counterexamples to the *belongingness hypothesis* where we seemingly put narrow self-interest ahead of collective-and-self-interest. Examples include refusals to help, which seems to be notoriously common when multiple bystanders are present and all fail to help in an emergency. Baumeister and Leary hold that the *bystander effect* appears to be robust amongst *strangers*, but in cohesive groups the opposite effect is observed; indeed, the mere prospect of future interaction seems to neutralize the bystander effect.

Another example is *social loafing*, whereby 'people reduce their efforts when submerged in the group, thereby gaining benefits of the group success without having to exert themselves maximally'.[61] Baumeister and Leary cite studies that suggest that our social attachments can override an inclination to loaf, especially if we feel we can make a uniquely valuable contribution. Similarly, in prisoner's dilemmas, we seem to shift away from a narrow self-interested strategy to a cooperative strategy when we have social attachments to the other parties. In Chapter 5, I consider an associational-freedom version of 'social loafing'.

A final example Baumeister and Leary give is the so-called *commons dilemma*, whereby we deplete renewable resources for short-term personal gain at the expense of long-term collective well-being. Evidence suggests that self-interested responses are reduced or overcome in conditions of social attachment where the group identity is highlighted. In Chapter 5, I explore an analogous phenomenon under the heading of an *each–we dilemma of sociability*.[62]

In sum, although some real-life Robinson Crusoes such as Richard Proenneke and perhaps Sara Maitland,[63] seem to defy the thesis that we need to live in close proximity with others throughout our lives in order to survive and flourish, such people are the exception, not the rule.

1.2.3 Fight or Flight

In the Prologue to his *Autobiography*, Bertrand Russell declares that he has sought love for many reasons and one of those reasons is 'because it relieves loneliness—that terrible loneliness in which one shivering consciousness looks over the rim of the world into the cold unfathomable lifeless abyss'.[64] Psychology and neuroscience evidence indicates that social isolation and rejection are highly detrimental to our health. Studies suggest that chronic loneliness, understood as perceived social isolation, and weak social connections generate the same threat response as pain, thirst, hunger, or fear in setting off a chain of anxiety-inducing physiological reactions known as the 'fight or flight' response. According to John Cacioppo and others, loneliness and unwanted social isolation are associated with lower levels of subjective well-being as well as with numerous adverse health outcomes and broad-based morbidity and mortality. First, loneliness can predict increases of systolic blood pressure over an extended period, and higher levels of loneliness are associated with greater increases in systolic blood pressure.[65] Second, loneliness is associated with increased depressive symptoms: loneliness and depressive symptoms influence each other reciprocally over time, suggesting that the two can have a synergistic effect of reducing well-being in older adults.[66] Third, chronic loneliness is also associated with obesity, the progression of Alzheimer's disease, increased vascular resistance, diminished immunity, reduced independent living, alcoholism, suicidal ideation and behaviour, over-expression of genes bearing pro-inflammatory responses, and mortality in older adults. It also can negatively affect our development in childhood.[67] Based on these and other findings, Cacioppo concludes that our social environment and how we perceive our social environment are fundamentally involved in sculpting, activating, and inhibiting basic structures and processes in our brains and bodies.

More strongly, Baumeister and Leary state that lack of *belonging*—rather than mere lack of social contact—constitutes a severe form of deprivation and causes a variety of ill effects:

Deprivation of stable, good relationships has been linked to a large array of aversive and pathological consequences. People who lack belongingness suffer higher levels of mental and physical illness and are relatively highly prone to a broad range of behavioral problems, ranging from traffic accidents to criminality to suicide. Some of these findings may be subject to alternative explanations, and for some the direction of causality has not been established; however, the weight of evidence suggests that lack of belongingness is a primary cause of multiple and diverse problems. It therefore seems appropriate to regard belongingness as a need rather than simply a want.[68]

Most vividly, in extreme cases, such as long-term solitary confinement or long-term quarantine, we face even greater psychological and physiological risks. First, in healthcare, patients held in long-term isolation reportedly can have six times the usual rates of hospital-associated complications such as pressure sores and falls.[69] Second, in criminal justice, studies indicate that prisoners held in long-term solitary confinement can suffer memory loss, hallucinations, panic attacks, self-mutilation, semi-catatonic states, and suicidal ideation and behaviour, and the effects can last long after their release and render them less able to reintegrate socially.[70]

The anecdotal evidence confirms this. People who have endured solitary confinement tend to report initially feeling depressed, lethargic, forgetful, and then mindless. They can sleep over twelve hours a day and lack the energy to read, eat, or move.[71] Journalist Shane Bauer reports that during his isolated detention as an Iranian political prisoner he needed human contact so badly that he woke up each morning hoping to be interrogated.[72] Similarly, a US military study of 140 naval aviators imprisoned in Vietnam reported that they found social isolation to be 'as torturous and agonizing as any physical abuse they suffered'.[73] Of course, even if we ultimately would prefer a hostile companion to no contact at all, that does not make a hostile companion a minimally adequate contributor to our social needs. People who endure brutal, hostile, degrading, or cruel social environments lack access to the social connections they need for a minimally good life.[74]

In many ways, coercive isolation adds insult to injury. It forces us into an environment that increases our motivation to connect socially, while categorically denying us the means to try to re-connect with other people.

In sum, the body of empirical evidence shows that social connections, particularly persistent relationships, are instrumentally necessary for us to develop and maintain basic cognitive abilities, physical abilities, and health. Being deprived in our access to these things is highly instrumentally disvaluable. That said, the empirical evidence alone does not show that social bonds are non-instrumentally valuable. To show that, we must turn to the phenomenological arguments and the respect-based arguments.

1.3 Phenomenological Arguments

Phenomenology involves the study of our subjective, first-person perspective on our experience, i.e. how we consciously experience the world and understand ourselves within it. Without delving too deeply into the complexities of either phenomenology or philosophy of mind, we can see that we experience the world largely in interpersonal terms: we make sense of who we are and what we value through our connections with other people. This is not surprising given the empirical evidence. Here are nine ways that our fundamental sociality manifests itself in how we experience the world.

First, we need intense socialization in childhood to have the kind of consciousness that enables us to have a first-person perspective on our experience. As noted above, children who are socially deprived in their early years fail to develop fully the cognitive, physical, emotional, and linguistic skills necessary to experience the world in the ways that typify our species and enable our perceptual and evaluative powers.[75]

Second, almost all the objects of our experiences are social. We understand most, if not all, objects of experience through social and cultural filters. Some objects are fundamentally social, such as human beings, our cultures, norms, practices, traditions, roles, and products, as well as other social species and their behaviours, responses, and products. Other objects are not explicitly social—such as mountains, trees, and non-social species—but the way they appear to us is shaped by our socialization.

Third, and related to this, empirical evidence indicates that our basic patterns of cognition show that we are fundamentally concerned with social connections. Much of our mental activity, conscious and unconscious, is oriented toward and shaped by our social connections.[76] We have a default neural network that is activated when our brains are at rest, and it focuses explicitly on social phenomena.[77] We also perceive people in terms of personal categories or attribute categories depending on our degree of connection with them; the people we know well we tend to perceive as distinct persons, and those we know less well we tend to perceive in terms of attributes such as traits, preferences, and duties.[78] We also recall and understand objects more or less well depending on whether they are linked to people with whom we are connected. Finally, we tend to have a mistaken impression that we, personally, are invulnerable to the mishaps that befall other people, and we tend to extend our mistaken impression to the people with whom we are closely connected. In our eyes, our loved ones are also less likely than the average person to suffer such mishaps.

Fourth, one of the key tools with which we make sense of our experiences—language—is both a social product and a socially dependent skill. Our built-in capacity for language is the result of millennia of evolutionary social development. But without adequate exposure to language in our early years, we are unable to use it competently. Indeed, without adequate exposure to a spoken language, we are unable to enunciate or discern its specific sounds.

Fifth, relatedly, the quality of our sensations—the very ways that we perceive the world, through seeing, hearing, smelling, tasting, and touching—are socially informed. As the example of language shows, our very ability to discern and distinguish sounds depends on our socialization. Native Japanese speakers who are not exposed to English in childhood have difficulty distinguishing and producing the two consonants /l/ and /r/, though this can be rectified somewhat with training.[79] Similarly, native English speakers who have not been exposed to Hindi in childhood cannot distinguish four distinct sounds akin to the English consonant /d/.

Sixth, when we are in close proximity with other people, as well as with many other animals, the way we experience the world is influenced by the way they experience the world and vice versa. Others' words give rise to thoughts and emotions in us. Others' behaviour causes changes in our own behaviour. Also, more interestingly, others' emotions can become our emotions through the firing of mirror neurons, which give us a brief direct experience of others' emotional states.[80]

Seventh, conversely, other people are a mirror to us in a less grand sense than the moral mirror noted above. They show us how we appear in the world. Their perceptions, judgments, and treatment of us shape the way we understand who we are within the world.

Eighth, the meaning that we give to our projects, activities, and hence our sense of ourselves, is informed by our social conditions. Much of the meaning in our lives comes from our roles and their responsibilities. As noted earlier, the most fundamental of these roles are deeply social, including mother, father, guardian, brother, sister, spouse, child, aunt, uncle, cousin, grandparent, friend, caregiver, colleague, partner, and team member. As part of her research for her article on Japan's rent-a-family industry, Batuman set aside her feelings of self-consciousness and hired a woman,

Airi, to play her mother for two hours, to try out the experience herself. During their afternoon together in Tokyo, they talked about Batuman's article and Airi said, 'I guess I'll just be a few lines', which prompted Batuman to feel suddenly guilty about her rented mother. Batuman then wrote that the worst moment came later, when Airi mentioned sadly that none of the daughters who had hired her had ever asked to see her again, implying that she'd failed as a 'mother'. And, of course, Batuman, who lives in the US, wouldn't be seeing her again either. This vignette highlights how much the rent-a-family roles step over the divide between professional life and intimate association, and tread through the minefield of fundamental personal roles that can define who we are. Of course, many more ordinary professions are also deeply social, and only make sense in terms of their service to other people, such as teacher, doctor, nurse, legislator, executive, soldier and comrade, journalist, police officer, judge, and counsellor, but their service is generally less intimate than that provided by rent-a-family actors. Other professions are social in more nuanced ways, such as architect, scientist, farmer, historian, writer, and pianist. Through these various roles, we shape our sense of who we are, what we can do, what we value, and what value we have.

Finally, our subjective experience—like that of most other animals—is defined by physical embodiment, mortality, and vulnerability. We share common elements with each other in our first-person experience of the world. To be human is to experience the world in ways very similar to other members of our own species, a trait which we intuitively recognize in each other and respond to as such.

As these nine points imply, we glean many benefits from our social nature. We know and can do much more than we could do were we a less social species. We also get to participate in the valuable practice of having identities, which we couldn't do otherwise. These phenomenological observations, like the empirical evidence outlined above, intertwine with respect-based arguments about our sociality to show how morally important our social needs are.

1.4 Respect-Based Arguments

1.4.1 Respect

We have duties to respect each other as persons. We have duties to care about each other's well-being. These duties necessarily include respecting and valuing each other as social beings whose first-person experience of the world is fundamentally intersubjective.

In more detail, we have a Kantian duty to treat each other as ends in ourselves where this entails respecting each other as reasoning and feeling beings with agency and personhood, whose identities and choices draw much of their significance from having meaningful opportunities for social inclusion.[81] Such respect requires that we honour those with whom we have social bonds; that we show fairness and decency to all others; that we have self-respect; and that we show empathy, compassion, and understanding to each other as vulnerable, interdependent beings. Indeed, we might go so far as to say that we have Kantian duties to take part in social intercourse and even to cultivate friendships, though not all those duties correlate with rights.[82]

Related to this, we have a respect-based duty to recognize the moral import of the empirical and phenomenological observations made above, such as the facts that (a) much of our sense of purpose is rooted in our social roles; (b) much of the value in our choices comes from our connections with people who share in our deliberations, witness our efforts, and are invested in the results; and (c) we suffer greatly when we are denied avenues to have connections, pursue joint projects, and hold meaningful social roles. Together these points confirm that any credible account of *autonomy* must fully acknowledge our fundamental sociability.

Adequate access to social inclusion is not just instrumentally valuable. It is also non-instrumentally valuable as a constitutive part of a minimally good human life. Direct, face-to-face social interactions and associations are necessary to, and constitutive of, many valuable endeavours, such as playing an instrument in an orchestra for a live audience, attending a live lecture, seeing a play in a theatre, singing in a choir, enjoying a friend's company, holding hands, ballroom dancing, playing football, wrestling, and so on. The *direct* contact is part of the good.[83] Such interactions and associations don't need to have any further purpose to them for us to justify having them.

The non-instrumental value of social inclusion has implications for different realms of activity. For instance, it means that we cannot dismiss as a regrettable side-effect the burdens borne by people who are coercively deprived of social contact for the sake of the common good. In the context of healthcare, for example, we should turn a critical eye on medical quarantine, both to question whether it is necessary when it is used, and to make concerted efforts to alleviate the harms it causes.[84] In the context of criminal justice, we should consider just how severe a punishment we impose on people when we segregate them from their families and, more acutely, when we isolate them in solitary confinement.

1.4.2 General Arguments

To the respect-based arguments adduced so far, we may add other normative arguments to support the claim that we are fundamentally social creatures with morally pressing social needs. Philosophers have explored the nature and normative significance of shared agency, the ethics of care, the distinctive goods and values of family life, the relational nature of autonomy, communitarianism, cosmopolitanism, solidarity, integration, and theories of vulnerability, embodiment, and intimacy, among others.[85] Some of these debates are referenced above, and many more will surface in what follows. For now, let's pick a few cherries.

Aristotle, for one, observes that 'without friends, no one would choose to live, though he had all other goods'.[86] True friendship (by which Aristotle seems to mean not just *friendship* in the narrow sense we use it now, but also our general sociability, that is to say, all of our stable, non-antagonistic connections with people) is necessary for a host of instrumental reasons. It gives meaning to our prosperity and power by giving us opportunities to be beneficent; it is the only refuge when we're impoverished; it helps us when we're young to correct our errors and when we're old to meet our needs; it stimulates us when we're adults to noble actions because, with friends, we are better able both to think and to act.[87] Friendship also seems to hold states together. Friendship within a state is something like unanimity, and it is both necessary for, and more important than, justice. '[W]hen men are friends they have no need of justice, while when they are just they need friendship as well, and the truest form of justice is thought to be a friendly quality.'[88]

Isaiah Berlin, paraphrasing Johann Gottfried von Herder, says that 'among elementary human needs—as basic as those for food, shelter, security, procreation, communication—is the need to belong to a particular group, united by some common links—especially language, collective memories, continuous life upon the same soil', as well as 'race, blood, religion, a sense of common mission, and the like'.[89] This is a potentially richer set of goods than those I am defending here, but it affirms that we are, by nature, deeply social creatures.

John Rawls, for his part, highlights what he calls the social bases of self-respect as one of five primary goods (along with basic rights and liberties, diverse opportunities, political influence, and income and wealth), without which we cannot pursue our life plans or cultivate the two moral powers (which are our capacity for a sense of justice and our capacity for a conception of the good). Rawls describes the social bases of self-respect as perhaps the most important primary good.[90] He also speaks more specifically of the difference that others' investment in our lives makes to our ability to pursue our life plans; he says that 'unless our endeavors are appreciated by our associates it is impossible for us to maintain the conviction that they are worthwhile'. He adds that associative ties also tend 'to reduce the likelihood of failure and...provide support against the sense of self-doubt when mishaps occur'.[91]

Non-Western philosophical traditions such as Buddhism emphasize not just the value of social connections among human beings, but also our connections with all living beings. Key Buddhist meditation practices focus on cultivating wholesome states such as loving kindness, compassion, appreciative joy at others' happiness, and equanimity, all of which aim at cultivating a sense of connection and intimacy with all living beings. In all of these lines of thought, and many others, philosophers recognize the universal, vital nature of our core social needs. However, they do not frame those accounts in the language of *social human rights*, which is one of the intended contributions of this book.

Before contrasting our social needs with our social desires, let me sum up what we have learned to this point. First, several important distinctions lurk within the concept of *needs*: (1) between non-contingent needs and contingent needs; (2) between *fundamental* needs and other needs; and (3) between morally urgent needs, trivial needs, and morally objectionable needs. Second, we have two types of non-contingent, fundamental social needs—our core social needs—which are our needs to access and to contribute to social connections. These give rise to more concrete needs for three kinds of social resources (abilities, opportunities, and connections). Third, at least three families of arguments—empirical, phenomenological, and respect-based—show collectively that having adequate access to social connections is both instrumentally and non-instrumentally valuable; and lacking access to social connections is highly disvaluable in denying us states of being that contribute to a minimally good human life. Together, these arguments confirm that our core social needs are genuinely morally urgent.

So far so good. But, when it comes to social needs, the devil is in the details. And, the details matter because they can make or break the claim that specific social needs ground human rights. For instance, what is the moral status of the need to be a parent or the need for sexual intimacy? Are these needs contingent? Are they morally important but not fundamental? Are they non-contingent, fundamental, and urgent? Are the desires with which they intersect under our control (we might desire sexual intimacy but wish we did not, just as we might crave certain foods, but wish we did not)?[92] To answer these questions, we must distinguish morally important social needs from social desires.

1.5 Social Needs versus Social Desires

Let's consider parenting. Many people desire to have children (usually their own biological children). But, equally, many people do not desire to have children, and some of those people describe themselves as being 'child free' rather than 'childless'. As an aside, we shouldn't speak of people as being either 'childless' or 'child free'. The first adjective is offensive to people who do not have children. The second is offensive to children. People who do not have children should be described simply as people who do not have children. I return to the topic of how we use language in Chapter 8.

Having a child seems to be what Frankfurt calls a *volitional need*, i.e. something that is needed because it is necessary to something else that the person desires. That is, the need to have a child derives from the person's wish to care for someone, for example, or to be in a parent–child bond, to pass on her genes, or even to collect childcare benefits.

But, if having children were simply a volitional need, that would not make it a morally unimportant need. In terms of both subjective and objective well-being, having children is very important to the people who do desire to have children, the full force of which they may not appreciate unless they struggle to have children. The moral force of the volitional need to have a child is, of course, insufficient to give a person a right to have a child, but it is sufficient to give her a right *to try* to have a child and a right to receive adequate, available medical assistance in that effort.

Having a child is, however, not just a volitional need. First, in any society where we must rely primarily on our family members rather than the state for support as we age, we have a non-volitional need to have a child (or children) in order to maximize our chances of surviving into old age. We have this need regardless of whether we desire to live to an old age.

Second, as a species, although we do not need every able person to have children (or to desire to have children), nonetheless we non-volitionally need enough people to have children if we are to persist as a species and meet our other needs.

Our needs for physical and sexual intimacy are trickier. The need for sexual intimacy seems to be a straightforward example of a volitional need. If someone did not desire sexual intimacy, she would not need it in any morally important sense and there would be no *pro tanto* case to provide it to her contrary to her wishes. Or, if there were a *pro tanto* case, it would be vastly outweighed by the wrongness of doing so. Moreover, typically, we do not view sexual intimacy as a necessary condition for a minimally good life: people can lead minimally good lives without sex. Sexual intimacy might be a condition for flourishing, but not for *minimal* goodness. And, indeed, it might not even be a condition for flourishing if we can lead flourishing lives without it, a question I leave for another day.

That said, the need for sexual intimacy is non-contingent in the sense that it is a need that, in certain stages of life, we typically cannot help but have as the kind of beings we are.[93] But, as noted at the beginning of this chapter, the fact that we cannot help but have a certain need does not make that need morally important or even morally acceptable (recall the case of a psychologically unwell person who has a non-contingent need (as the being he is) to engage in child abuse). Moreover, sexual intimacy is fundamentally morally important for the same instrumental reasons that parenting is morally important. It's a need that we need to have, or at least need enough of us to have, for us to persist as a species and meet all our other needs, social and otherwise. (That said, as we advance technologically, the instrumental necessity of sexual intimacy diminishes.)

In the cases of both sexual intimacy and parenting, our social needs intersect with our desires in complex ways. This intersection is noteworthy since it shows that, for some key connections at least, our needs are not just *volitional* needs grounded in our desires. If they were, then when we lack the desire for social inclusion we would have no independent need for the social inclusion we do not wish to have. For competent adults at least, our social needs would be purely contingent on our desires to lead certain sorts of lives with certain sorts of social arrangements.

The arguments in this chapter and the rest of this book show that our core social needs not only exist independently of our volitions, but are morally urgent. Moreover, even if some of them didn't exist independently of our volitions, that in itself would not cast doubt on their importance for a minimally good human life.

Conclusion

This chapter has unpacked and defended the claim that we are essentially interdependent, social beings who have non-contingent, fundamental social-access needs and social-contribution needs that generate morally urgent demands. This chapter argued that, regardless of whether we *desire* social connections, we have these two core social needs which are necessary for us to persist as the kind of beings we are. At many points in our lives, we are utterly dependent on others for our survival and well-being. And, even in our mature, healthy years, we generally need others—both as supports and as beneficiaries of our support—to survive and flourish. This chapter showed, through its brief description of Japan's rent-a-family industry, the lengths to which we will go to try to meet our core social needs including our need to be of value to other people. In the next chapter, we see how our core social needs ground key social human rights, including specifically a human right against social deprivation.

2
Social Deprivation

'...all the loneliness of age flashing upon her face, the loneliness of having outstayed one's welcome in the world, of being in it only on sufferance, the complete loneliness of the childless woman who has failed to make friends. It did seem that people could only be really happy in pairs—any sorts of pairs...'
  Elizabeth von Arnim, *The Enchanted April* (1922, 260)

Introduction

In Bernice Rubens's novel *The Waiting Game*, residents of the Hollyhocks senior citizens' facility play the 'game' of awaiting death. Many of them have no friends or family. Some of them bond with each other. But most do not. Although fictional, Hollyhocks depicts the life of many aging people today. Some receive visits from family. Others rely entirely on facility staff and other residents for social contact. Commenting on the 160,000 older people living in such facilities in Australia, John Watkins says that 'many [of those who are] not confined to their beds will spend their hours in oversized armchairs perhaps watching birds from the lounge window or silently waiting for mealtimes.'[1] In the UK, over 400,000 people over 65 lead similar lives in residential care facilities. The landmark 2016 BBC documentary *The Age of Loneliness* interviews a few such people, including a centenarian named Olive, who was widowed at 95 and has numerous children, grandchildren, and great grandchildren living near and far. With so many relations, she finds it a mystery that she lives on 'Lonely Street', and waits alone in her room for a visit from the residential care staff.[2] As an incidentally isolated person, Olive is an example of someone who endures *social deprivation*, understood as a persistent lack of minimally adequate access to decent human contact and social connection.[3]

In this chapter, Is how that we have a fundamental human right against social deprivation. This right is both a condition for and a constitutive part of a minimally good human life. Securing this right is also necessary for us to secure many less controversial human rights including our civil and political rights. Hence, when our right against social deprivation is violated, we suffer a grave social injustice.

In what follows, I specify the nature of *social deprivation* (Section 2.1), consider why it is neglected in theoretical and practical debates (Section 2.2), and outline what a right against it would look like (Section 2.3). Next, I argue that the empirical, phenomenological, and respect-based arguments from Chapter 1, along with two other families of arguments—reciprocity and desert arguments and instrumental arguments—show that the right against social deprivation is indeed a human right (Section 2.4). Then, I identify the duty-bearers and duties correlative with this right (Section 2.5), before, finally, responding to objections about the language of *rights*, burdensomeness, and feasibility (Section 2.6).

2.1 What Is Social Deprivation?

2.1.1 Forms of Social Deprivation

Social deprivation can take one of three forms: (1) coercive social isolation; (2) incidental social deprivation; and (3) persistently brutal or degrading social contact. When we endure one of these forms of social deprivation, our core social needs (i.e. our access needs and contribution needs) go unmet. Let's take each form of social deprivation in turn.

1. *Coercive social isolation* is compulsory, long-term, unwanted isolation. We endure it if we are placed in segregating institutions, such as solitary confinement in prison, long-term medical quarantine, isolated immigration detention, or exile to an uninhabited place. We can even endure it while living in a residential care facility, if other people compel us to spend a lot of time alone. We can also endure it outside of segregating institutions. If one person kidnaps another and holds her in isolated captivity, she endures coercive social isolation.[4]

When we endure coercive social isolation, we are rendered utterly dependent. We must wait impotently for someone to come to us. This might seem to be a necessary evil in some institutional settings, notably in cases of serious punishment or cases involving uncontrollably violent people. But, as I argue below and in Chapter 8, isolating people is usually not a necessary evil. It is usually just evil.

2. *Incidental social deprivation*, such as that endured by Olive, stems from neglect, not coercion. It comes in two varieties. The first is long-term, incidental, unwanted isolation that we cannot escape without help. An example would be a physically impaired, older widower whose spouse filled his social diary and who now lives alone and cannot get out of the house without help. A subtler example would be a young woman who suffers from severe epileptic seizures that have affected her brain development, has little family support, and is avoided by her peers.

The second variety of incidental social deprivation does not involve isolation. Instead, it involves fractured contact, such as when we receive decent, but infrequent or non-repeated visits from people. Anyone like Olive who relies on weekly healthcare visits for social connection and sees a different carer each week experiences incidental social deprivation. She is forever starting over socially. She shares no joint narrative or sense of mutual investment with anyone.

As this second variety of incidental social deprivation makes clear, *social deprivation* is not synonymous with *isolation*. We can be deprived of minimally adequate access to decent social contact even when we have adequate amounts of contact. Fractured or non-repeated contact ignores the real nature of our social needs, which include having access to some persistent connections.

Social deprivation is distinct from *isolation* for two further reasons. First, when social deprivation does involve isolation, it involves *unwanted* isolation. It is not solitude. People can reasonably embrace a period of solitude, as astronauts, explorers, nuns, monks, artists, and writers often do as part of their calling, without this raising the spectre of social deprivation. *Voluntary* self-isolation or solitude is comparable to fasting, which people can choose to do for a period without offending against the right to be free from hunger. Both the right to be free from hunger and the right against social deprivation which I defend here are, in the first instance, rights against persistent *unwanted* states.

That said, when people choose either solitude or fasting, both they and we must contend with the risks of their choice. Fasting can lead to ill-health, malnutrition, and early death. Solitude can lead to poor mental health and early death too. Atul Gawande reports that many long-distance solo sailors, who commit themselves to months at sea alone and face all manner of physical terrors including thrashing storms, fifty-foot waves, leaks, and illness, tend to report that the single most overwhelming difficulty they face is the 'soul-destroying loneliness'. Astronauts, Gawande notes, are screened for their ability to tolerate long stretches in confined isolation, and even so they come to depend on radio and video communications for social contact.[5] In other words, to be endurable, voluntary self-isolation takes training and a certain temperament. For both fasting and self-isolation, the decision to do it becomes a rights issue when it threatens a person's competence to decide whether to continue in that state.

Furthermore, following Brian Barry, we should view voluntary self-isolation, like voluntary self-denial, with some scepticism, since its 'voluntariness' depends on the range and value of available choices. If a person's available forms of social connection are hostile, degrading, or cruel, then she may well voluntarily withdraw from her social environment. But her decision won't differ much from a non-voluntary withdrawal.[6] Her withdrawal may well be due to adaptive preference formation or a sense of duress.

Social deprivation differs from *isolation* for a third reason: persistent social contact is socially privative when it is brutal or degrading. This is the third form of social deprivation.

3. *Persistently brutal or degrading social contact* denies us minimally adequate access to decent human contact and prevents us from leading a minimally good human life free from degradation and cruelty. In far too many prisons, people endure this kind of social deprivation, as they have access to social contact but not to *decent* contact, and they cannot escape their surroundings. The social world on display in the film *The Shawshank Redemption* (1994) captures this vividly. Although some of the men housed in Shawshank Prison manage to form decent, even loving ties with each other, their social world is horrific, being defined by violence, brutality, and sexual assault. And many ordinary, real-life prison settings are like this.[7]

We can also endure this form of social deprivation when we are not forcibly confined, but live in brutal conditions that compromise our ability to seek relief, which is the lot of many victims of domestic abuse. Just as we should look at someone's voluntary acceptance of isolation with scepticism, so too we should look at her acceptance of a brutal social environment with scepticism. We must look at the range and value of her options. If her options are either a brutal environment or isolation, she might choose a brutal environment, especially if she has experienced the soul-destroying effects of isolation. Many people who've endured long term solitary confinement report that they believed beforehand they would find it bearable, but found afterward that any companion, no matter how horrific, is better than no companion.[8] Of course, as noted in Chapter 1, that does not mean that a brutal companion, or even an indifferent companion, satisfies our core social needs.⁹

2.1.2 Related Experiences

Sometimes, we face the risk, but not the certainty that we will endure social deprivation. A competent person who is shunned by, or banished from, her hometown faces the risk, but not the certainty, that she will fail to find a new circle of people who will accept her.

Other times, we face neither the risk nor the certainty of social deprivation, but instead endure assaults on our closest social bonds that leave us otherwise socially connected. Such assaults often come from third-parties. Consider two inseparable, non-romantic, co-habiting friends who made the news in 2012. They were then 83-year-old Canadian Mildred Sanford, who suffered from a heart condition and dementia, and 73-year-old American Nancy Inferrera, who cared for her. The two had been in Canada for over three decades before their lives were turned upside down by the Canadian immigration authorities, who deported Inferrera for failing to have the correct immigration status. Following a public outcry, Inferrera received a three-year temporary visa on compassionate grounds.¹⁰ The Canadian government didn't detain Inferrera; they didn't deny her all access to social contact. Instead, they sought to rob her and Mildred Sanford of their closest social bond.

Assaults on our closest bonds can also come from within the bonds themselves. In Liane Moriarty's page-turner of a novel, *The Last Anniversary* (2006), a young girl, Grace, begs her mother, Laura, to speak to her. Laura ignores Grace for three solid weeks because Grace forgot a banana rotting in her school bag. Since Grace can access other social connections, Laura does not render her social deprived. But Laura nonetheless attacks Grace's deepest bond: her bond with *her*.

Although these related experiences do not fall neatly under the conceptual umbrella of *social deprivation*, they fall within the scope of this fundamental social human right that I will defend.

With the notion of *social deprivation* in hand, let's consider why the theoretical literature and international agreements tend to neglect the idea of a human right against social deprivation (Section 2.2). After that, I will flesh out the content of this putative right (Section 2.3), and outline the main arguments in its defence (Section 2.4).

2.2 The Neglect of the Right against Social Deprivation

Recently, philosophers of human rights have turned their collective attention to socio-economic rights and, specifically, to our economic-welfare rights to be free from poverty, to health, and to education. Philosophers continue, however, to view our social needs largely through the lens of economic-welfare needs. The need to be free from poverty is, of course, vitally important. But, we should not emphasize it while neglecting our distinct and equally important social needs.

Henry Shue argues correctly, for instance, that cognitive deficiencies caused by malnutrition 'can effectively prevent the exercise of any right requiring clear thought [such as civil and political rights]... And, obviously, any fatal deficiencies end all possibility of the enjoyment of rights as an arbitrary execution.'[11] But, he says nothing in his seminal work *Basic Rights* about the fact that cognitive deficiencies caused by social deprivation during critical stages of childhood development, such as a failure to acquire language or to learn to control bodily function, effectively prevent the exercise of rights requiring clear thought. He also says little about the fact that the deficiencies often caused by social deprivation during long-term, coercive isolation, such as depression, despondency, hallucination, self-harming, psychosis, or suicidal ideation and behaviour, can effectively prevent the exercise of rights requiring clear thought, social ability, and personal control; and that extreme deficiencies can result in early death.[12]

In a similar fashion, James Nickel observes correctly that human rights are not ideals of the good life. Rather, they aim to ensure the conditions of a minimally good life, as noted in Chapter 1. But, he is mistaken when he argues that:

> If we apply this idea [of a minimally good life] to economic and social rights, it suggests that these standards should not be much concerned with promoting the highest possible standards of living or with identifying the best or most just form of economic system. Rather they should attempt to address the worst problems and abuses in the *economic area*. Their focus should be on hunger, malnutrition, preventable disease, ignorance and exclusion from productive opportunities.[13]

Focusing on the worst problems and abuses in the *economic area* implies either that our interpersonal social needs are less weighty than our economic needs are or that our social needs are already met when we come to the human rights table, or that those needs are derivative of our economic needs and hence, if not already met, are addressed once our economic needs are addressed. But, none of these can be assumed. Economic resources only sometimes translate into minimally adequate opportunities for social connection. Indeed, although economic deprivation can correlate sometimes with social deprivation, good economic conditions can also correlate with social deprivation, as we saw at the outset of this chapter in the description of the many older people like Olive living socially deprived lives in residential care facilities. Families can only outsource the care of people like Olive to such facilities when they have adequate economic resources.

Adequate economic resources lack value in themselves. They are valuable only instrumentally for us to secure food, shelter, safety, health, education, employment, and so on. Equally, economic deprivation is not disvaluable in itself. It is disvaluable only instrumentally as a severe constraint on people's abilities to secure access to the services and goods necessary for a minimally good human life.

By contrast, as Chapter 1 showed, having access to decent social connections is valuable both instrumentally and non-instrumentally. To lead a minimally good human life, we need to have minimally adequate opportunities to access and contribute to social connections for their own sake. And social deprivation is disvaluable both instrumentally and non-instrumentally because it denies us states of being constitutive of a human life worth the name.

As noted in the Introduction to this book, philosophers who use idioms other than *human rights* have paid more attention to our core social needs than human rights theorists have—the most notable contribution perhaps being Martha Nussbaum's capability approach, according to which honouring our capability for affiliation is a key element of basic justice. Although *human rights* are not to the taste of all moral and political philosophers, they are a politically and legally potent conceptual tool, and they provide us with a concrete and well-specified reference point against which we can assess assertions of fundamental universal interest, basic need, and correlative duty. There is much to be gained conceptually and normatively by stressing that our core social needs have been largely omitted from the rapidly expanding human rights theory literature and in seeking to remedy that omission.

Unsurprisingly, the neglect of a right against social deprivation in human rights theory mirrors its neglect in international human rights treaties such as the *Universal Declaration of Human Rights* (UDHR), the *International*

Covenant on Civil and Political Rights (ICCPR), and the *International Covenant on Economic, Social, and Cultural Rights* (ICESCR). These agreements fail to mention our fundamental need to be protected from social deprivation, but include articles that seem to presume that we are adequately socially connected.

The UDHR comes closest to identifying a right against social deprivation in Articles 22 and 25. Article 22 enumerates a right to social security as well as a right to the realization, 'through national effort and international co-operation and in accordance with the organization and resources of each State, of the economic, social and cultural rights indispensable for [a person's] dignity and the free development of his personality'. Article 25 specifies a right to an adequate standard of living for a person and his family, and the right to security in the event of unemployment, sickness, disability, widowhood, old age, or other lack of livelihood in circumstances beyond his control. But these fail to capture the right against social deprivation.

First, 'social security' in Article 22 refers to social insurance, not our core social needs. Second, 'the social, cultural, and economic rights indispensable for dignity' it mentions would be those enumerated in the UDHR and other UN documents, which do not highlight fundamental needs for adequate access to social connections. Third, Article 25 skates over the fact that we need *opportunities* for social connection in order to secure a standard of living adequate for health and well-being.

Other articles in the UDHR touch upon rich social interests, such as the right to nationality (Article 15); the right to take part in the government of our country (Article 21.1); the right of equal access to public service in our country (Article 21.2); and the right freely to participate in the cultural life of the community, to enjoy the arts, and to share in scientific advancement and its benefits (Article 27). These articles presume we have minimally adequate access to social inclusion, and none of them captures it.

The ICCPR comes closest with rights against torture, cruel, inhuman, and degrading treatment or punishment (Article 7); the right to treatment with humanity if denied liberty (Article 10); children's rights to measures of protection required by their status as minors, on the part of their family, society, and the state (Article 24.1); and rights to have access, on general terms of equality, to public service in our own country (Article 25c). But these articles speak only to specific dimensions of our social needs.

Ironically, the ICESCR fares no better than the UDHR in identifying our core social needs. It presumes that our most basic social needs are secured, and focuses on loftier rights to have just and favourable conditions for work

(Article 7); to form trade unions (Article 8); and to marry voluntarily (Article 10); as well as the rights to be free from hunger (Article 11); to education (Article 13); and to enjoy the highest attainable standard of physical and mental health (Article 12). The ICESCR comes closest to social deprivation with the right to take part in cultural life (Article 15.1a). But, that right should be interpreted in relation to Articles 15.1b and c, which pertain to rights to enjoy the benefits of scientific progress, and rights to intellectual property.

A few international agreements do recognize specific rights against socially privative conditions, notably the UN *Convention on the Rights of Persons with Disabilities*. Article 19 enumerates rights related to living independently and being included in the community. The article highlights the rights of persons with disabilities to have opportunities to choose where and with whom they live on an equal basis with others; access to a range of in-home, residential, and community support services necessary to prevent isolation or segregation from the community and to support inclusion within the community; and equal access with others to community services and facilities that are responsive to people's needs.[14]

Article 28 enumerates rights to an adequate standard of living for persons with disabilities and their families (echoing Article 25 in the UDHR);[15] and rights to particular social protections, such as clean water, affordable services, assistive devices, retirement benefits and programmes without discrimination, as well as access for persons with disabilities to public housing programmes and, for those living in poverty, to assistance with disability-related expenses. Article 28 also singles out women and girls with disabilities and older persons with disabilities as having a right to ensured access to social protection programmes and poverty-reduction programmes.

While looking in the right direction, such rights are not human rights. They fail a synchronic universality test for human rights in the same way that children's rights and women's rights fail that synchronic universality test, since not everyone alive today can assert these rights. Not everyone has a disability or will have one during their lifetime. These rights are available to us if, and only if, we have a disability.

Another agreement that recognizes our interests against social deprivation is the *European Social Charter* (ESC). Article 30 states that 'everyone has the right to protection against poverty and social exclusion'. According to the *Explanatory Report* for the ESC (revised edition), 'social exclusion' refers to people 'who find themselves in extreme poverty due to accumulated disadvantages, who suffer from degrading situations or events or from exclusion, whose rights to benefit may have expired a long time ago or for reasons of concurring circumstances'.[16] The report continues:

> Social exclusion also strikes or risks to strike persons who without being poor are denied access to certain rights or services as a result of long periods of illness, the breakdown of their families, violence, release from prison or marginal behaviour as a result for example of alcoholism or drug addiction.

With this elaboration, the report authors gesture in the right direction, since they detach social exclusion from poverty. But they give an incomplete list of the experiences that can render someone excluded, and they ignore our general needs for access to decent human contact, opportunities for inclusion, opportunities to contribute socially, and protection of our existing connections from third-party interference.

A further example is Principle 7 of the UN *Basic Principles for the Treatment of Prisoners* (1990), which states that 'efforts addressed to the abolition of solitary confinement as a punishment, or to the restriction of its use, should be undertaken and encouraged', which fails to highlight a *right* against such treatment and shows how little attention human rights scholars paid, until recently, to our fundamental interest in avoiding social deprivation even when we are guilty of serious wrongdoing. The UN *Standard Minimum Rules for the Treatment of Prisoners* (1955), which largely overlooked the issue of solitary confinement, were revised and updated in 2015 and are now known as the Nelson Mandela Rules. They now take a strong, but by no means absolute, stance against solitary confinement (defined as 22 hours or more a day without meaningful human contact). Principle 43 states that restrictions and disciplinary sanctions may never amount to torture or to cruel, inhuman, and degrading treatment and, hence, this prohibits among other things the use of either indefinite solitary confinement or prolonged solitary confinement (exceeding 15 consecutive days). Principle 45 states that solitary confinement may not be imposed on persons with disabilities which would be exacerbated by it, may not be imposed as part of a person's sentence, and may otherwise only be used in exceptional circumstances as a last resort for the shortest possible time and with proper authorization.[17] The human rights case against solitary confinement tends to focus on the fact that it is torture. However, given the nature and importance of our core social needs, solitary confinement would be a human rights violation regardless of whether a given person found it torturous because it robs him of minimally adequate access to decent human contact. I return to this issue below and in Chapter 8.

Why have theorists of human rights, and to a lesser extent legal scholars, neglected such a foundational right such as a human right against social deprivation? One possible explanation is that we tend to ignore the basics. To date, scholars have largely ignored the idea of a human right to breathable air, even though breathable air is as paramount as it gets. However, the reason they have ignored a right to breathable air might not be because it is basic, since many other basic interests do garner attention, but instead because we tend to ignore those interests that are not currently under threat (or at least not currently under threat for those of us who tend to produce these analyses). Indeed, some thinkers, such as Shue and Nickel, make the presence of standard and recurrent threats—as opposed to merely conceivable threats or ineradicable threats—a necessary condition for human rights status. Nickel says:

> If we recognize specific rights at every point where an essential condition of a decent life is present, whether or not it is threatened at each of those points, we would have more claims and potential rights than we could remember, much less implement.[18]

Nickel also notes that human rights agreements tend to reference experienced dangers and injustices. For instance, the UDHR references the 'barbarous acts which have outraged the conscience of mankind', during the Holocaust and Second World War.

Since human rights are a potent rhetorical and political tool, we must attend to the kinds of threats we take seriously in human rights debates. However, Nickel and Shue move too quickly when they limit the focus to standard threats, and contrast those with merely conceivable threats, on the one hand, and ineradicable threats, on the other.

1. *Highly probably threats*. Between standard threats and merely conceivable threats, there are *highly probable threats*, which are sufficiently serious to trigger human rights talk. As we continue to wreak havoc on the environment, we face a growing chance that many of us will soon lack adequately clean air to breathe. So, although we might have no 'substantial and recurrent' threat to our interests in breathable air at the moment (and that moment is passing quickly for many people), we must have a human right to breathable air. Recognizing this fact might obviate a disaster before it gets too far underway.

2. *Human-made threats*. Between standard threats and ineradicable threats (acts of God), there human-made threats that were once eradicable but now no longer are. If the air quality in many places becomes permanently unbreathable, the credentials of our right against breathable air will still be in good order. People who live in extremely polluted areas will then have remedial rights to compensation, resource, mitigation, and relocation support, *in virtue of their right to breathable air*, which human activity compromised.

In sum, the best version of the *standard and recurrent threats* test is context-sensitive. It incorporates both highly probable threats and previously avoidable but now ineradicable threats.

All that aside, since many people's core social needs *are* currently under threat, we must look elsewhere to explain their neglect in human rights debates. A lamentable but likely explanation is that Western culture is individualistic—Western societies tend to see us as largely self-sufficient, independent beings who can choose to socialise or not as we see fit—and contemporary human rights norms are Western products. But even this explanation is not the whole story. Our neglect of social needs in human rights theory may stem more from the historical context of the two world wars, in which human rights norms developed as antidotes to political oppression, than from any general scepticism about our core social needs. Seeking a final explanation for the lack of attention to social needs in human rights debates is probably quixotic. So, let's put it aside and flesh out the core features of the human right against social deprivation before turning to its defence.

2.3 The Human Right against Social Deprivation

2.3.1 Negative and Positive Claims

Like most human rights, the right against social deprivation has negative and positive sides. It gives us negative claim-rights against coercive isolation and brutality. It also gives us positive claim-rights to the social support we need to have minimally adequate access to decent social contact, including support that guards against incidental deprivation. It protects us from having our capacities to lead a socially integrated life compromised: it protects both our abilities to benefit from others' care and our abilities to contribute to others' survival and well-being. (The social contribution dimensions of the right are distinctive; I explore specific violations of our social contribution rights in Chapter 3.)

In more detail, the right against social deprivation protects us against persistently inadequate or perverse social environments regardless of how we came to be in them. We might come to be socially deprived because other people harm us, or because we have behaved badly, or because we are simply forgotten. The right covers all such cases, in the same way that the right to be free from poverty covers all cases regardless of how we come to be impoverished.

In most cases, however, the right against social deprivation does not positively guarantee us a set of rich, loving relationships. Such relationships go far beyond the brute moral minimum that our human rights can secure. Instead, the right secures for us minimally adequate but meaningful *opportunities* to participate in social interactions that might lead to persistent connections. In short, the right protects us from *persistently* inadequate access to such contact. This important qualifier 'persistent' is undoubtedly vague. But it is no vaguer than the concepts that specify the parameters of other rights, such as 'fair', 'without delay', 'poverty', 'highest possible standard', or 'basic subsistence'. In practice, the parameters of 'persistent inadequacy' must take different shapes in different contexts. Most likely, though, protecting us from persistently inadequate social opportunities will require our governments to facilitate opportunities for us to connect, to incentivize us to connect and even, sometimes, to compel us to connect.[19] Since interacting with strangers is often a necessary precursor to establishing persistent connections, and since interacting also gives us chances to practise our social skills and learn about our abilities to attract friends and partners, our governments may need to set up specific forums and venues for ambient sociability, which is the cradle of companionate sociability.[20] (I discuss governments' duties further in Section 2.5.)

All that said, once we are in close loving relationships, our negative right against social deprivation can protect us from third-party interference because other people could not forcibly sever our closest relationships without assaulting us as social beings. Recall the case of Mildred and Nancy, whose relationship the Canadian government sought to sever without regard for its life-defining significance for them. Likewise, consider someone like Nelson Mandela, who, while in prison, was allowed contact with certain people only until he became attached to them and they to him. Mandela's guards often came to love him. And when that happened, third-parties severed their contact and brought in new guards. He had no right *ex ante* to be in contact with a particular set of guards or fellow inmates, but once he'd established bonds with them, forcibly severing their ties in order to stamp out those bonds amounted to an assault on him and them as social beings.

Similarly, we have no right *ex ante* to be given a child to raise: such positive provision goes far beyond the realm of human rights. At most, as adults, we have a right *to try* to have a child and to receive appropriate assistance in our efforts. That said, *ex post*, once we do have a child, both we and our child have a fundamental right to stay in a close bond together (if certain best-interest conditions are met). Likewise, we have no positive right to be provided with close friends. But, if we have close friends, we have a right against third-parties severing those friendships. We may also have positive rights against our *friends* severing those friendships. (I return to this contentious claim in Chapter 7.) In sum, when we are socially able, the right against social deprivation falls short of a positive claim to be given close bonds, even though we suffer greatly when we lack such bonds (Chapter 1), because human rights track the brute moral minimum. However, once we have such bonds, our negative rights protect those bonds from third-party interference which would assault us as social beings.[21]

During periods where we are highly dependent, however, we can claim more than this under the right against social deprivation. The most obvious periods of utter dependency in our lives are babyhood and childhood, where we have deep, rights-grounding needs for persistent, intimate care and support from a small set of caregivers (Chapter 1). Put simply, for the new-born baby or young child, it makes no sense to talk about associational or associative freedom. But it does make vital sense to talk about acute associative need. When we are babies and children, we have positive claim-rights to be provided with persistent, supportive care from a small set of associates. Indeed, we have positive claim-rights that, whenever possible, those associates include our parents, siblings, and other relatives. At other periods in our lives when we are not self-sufficient (and I've suggested that this is a lot of the time), we also have positive claim-rights to have persistent, supportive social bonds. When we are ill, injured, incapacitated, ageing, grieving, or otherwise dependent, we have positive claims to be in close association with specific other people. The normative force of these claims relative to competing claims to associational freedom will be explored in Chapters 4–7.

2.3.2 Civil and Political and Socio-economic Aspects

The right against social deprivation straddles the forced conceptual divide between *civil and political* rights and *socio-economic rights*, since it has both civil-political aspects and socio-economic aspects.

In the eyes of human rights law, a right against *coercive* social deprivation would not be a socio-economic human right, since socio-economic rights concern material conditions and economic resources. Rather, in the eyes of human rights law, a right against coercive social deprivation would be a civil and political human right that protects against cruel, inhuman, and degrading treatment. As such, if properly recognized, it would receive more expansive and privileged protection under human rights law (rightly or, in my view, wrongly) than socio-economic rights do.[22]

Additionally, when *incidental* social deprivation stems from wilful neglect, the right against it is a civil and political right. In other words, if we wilfully neglect someone who needs help to lead a socially integrated life, to the extent that we are cruel or inhumane toward her, then she can assert a civil and political human right against it.

Furthermore, the right against social deprivation is civil and political to the extent that it is interwoven with many other civil and political rights and, indeed, is a precondition for realizing those rights. For instance, our rights to practise a religion with others, to assemble peacefully, and to associate are all civil and political, interpersonal rights that require minimally adequate access to decent social contact. Likewise, our freedom of movement is partly interpersonal, since we need some freedom of movement to take the initiative to engage in the direct, frequent contact that triggers and sustains connections. Similarly, our freedom of expression is interpersonal, since we typically use expression to communicate. Likewise, as vehicles for recognition, acceptance, and participation within a community, our rights to due process, to vote, to stand for office, and to participate in governance are interpersonal in attenuated but nonetheless real senses. More basically, we cannot secure and sustain these rights without the close nurturing connections (at least in childhood) that make it possible for us to exercise rights requiring clear thought.

As this suggests, the right against social deprivation not only transcends but also potentially dissolves the division between civil and political rights and socio-economic rights. If it does, then it puts pressure on dominant accounts of human rights that trade on this distinction in order to grant civil and political rights greater legal and political protection. In the next section, I flesh out this implication of acknowledging that we have a human right against social deprivation.

2.3.3 Non-human Subjects

One worry about the concept of *human rights* is that it gives us a speciesist conceptual framework that endorses human supremacy. Will Kymlicka argues that accounts of our rights which appeal to some notion of *human dignity* regrettably accord us higher moral status than non-human animals. Other accounts of our rights which focus on our corporeal reality as embodied beings and our physical vulnerability (traits which we share with non-human animals) are preferable, as they avoid this kind of supremacism, and hence are not complicit in 'the ongoing moral catastrophe of our relations with non-human animals'. In his discussion of the wrongs of solitary confinement, Kymlicka maintains that my defence of the right against social deprivation wavers between these two accounts of human rights. He agrees with me that the human rights tradition has failed to attend properly to our rights as social creatures. But he maintains that I ignore the obvious explanation for this failure, which is that a dignitarian account of human rights necessarily grounds rights in something other than the needs we share with other 'social creatures'. He says that, rather than challenging this assumption, I broadly accept it and so limit the right against social deprivation to humans.[23]

It is true that, in both past writings and this book, I have limited my focus to human beings and I rely heavily on the implicitly exclusive conceptual framework of <u>human</u> rights to make my case for the normative force of our social needs. However, as the next section confirms, I do not rest my case for our right against social deprivation on human dignity. My claims in Chapter 1 that we suffer deeply when we are socially deprived, that we experience the world in fundamentally social ways, and that we must be respected as ends in ourselves are all compatible with the view that these same or similar facts are true of members of other species. Similarly, my claims in the next section—that reciprocity-based arguments and instrumental arguments bolster the case for the human right against social deprivation—also do not preclude the possibility that members of other social species can have comparable claims against social deprivation. In future work, I hope to show that much of what I say about sociality and non-contingent, fundamental social needs can be applied *mutatis mutandis* to other fundamentally social species. In short, although I defend the right against social deprivation as a *human* right, I doubt that it is only a human right. In my view, members of every social species have a comparable right against social deprivation.

Let's turn now to the main arguments for why the right against social deprivation is a human right.

2.4 Arguments for the Human Right against Social Deprivation

2.4.1 Five Arguments

The core argument for the human right against social deprivation has two premises:

1. We have a human right to the conditions necessary to realize a minimally good human life.
2. Having minimally adequate access to decent social contact and connections is both a necessary condition for a minimally good human life and a constitutive part of such a life.

I shall leave the first premise undefended, since others have argued eloquently for it.[24] I focus instead on the second premise. In Chapter 1, I presented three families of arguments that support the second premise: (1) *empirical arguments*, (2) *phenomenological arguments*, and (3) *respect-based arguments*. Briefly,

1. *The empirical arguments* indicate that, in general, living in close connection with specific other people is an ineliminable part of a good life. When deprived of the resources to form and sustain social connections, we suffer profound adverse effects.

2. *The phenomenological arguments* highlight the essentially social, and socialized, nature of our first-person perspective.

3. *The respect-based arguments* emphasize the social preconditions for treating each other respectfully as ends in ourselves.

These three families of arguments can be fortified by two further arguments about reciprocity and desert, on the one hand, and instrumentalism, on the other.

4. *Reciprocity and desert.* Sociability is paradigmatically reciprocal. Being social includes offering our social resources to others and seeking to receive

social resources from others according to our abilities. Typically, these acts of offering and seeking are one and the same thing (a point I discuss further in Chapter 5).

Social deprivation denies us the chance to do for other people what others have most likely done for us at least during our childhood, namely, make a massive investment in someone's well-being. If we are socially deprived, we lack the chance either to reciprocate this social care for our elders as they age or to offer this care to dependants, who might then reciprocate for us when we age.[25] Of course, some of us may not wish to reciprocate. Not all of us are able to reciprocate. And not all of us have duties to reciprocate. (When we accept a gift, we don't automatically incur a duty to reciprocate.) The point is that many of us desire to reciprocate, and all of us have a need to belong. Therefore, we shouldn't be denied the *chance* to reciprocate.[26]

Moreover, if we made a massive investment in someone else's well-being, we probably deserve to have someone invest in our well-being now, even if that person must labour more than reciprocity demands.

5. *Instrumental arguments.* The instrumental arguments for the right against social deprivation are analogous to instrumental arguments for some human rights already on the books, such as health and education.[27] Undeniably, the rights to health and education protect things that are valuable in themselves. *Becoming* fit, healthy, and educated are non-instrumentally valuable experiences; and *being* fit, healthy, and educated are non-instrumentally valuable states. Nevertheless, the central arguments given in international agreements for securing and enforcing the human rights to health and education are instrumental. (Admittedly, international agreements give us only one, less than philosophically pristine window into specific rights. But, they are instructive accounts of the instrumental value of certain rights.)

The defence of the right to basic education references its instrumental importance in achieving certain globally valuable ends. The UDHR states:

> Education shall be directed to the full development of the human personality and to the *strengthening of respect* for human rights and fundamental freedoms. It shall *promote* understanding, tolerance and friendship among all nations, racial or religious groups, and shall *further the activities of the United Nations* for the maintenance of peace.[28]

Similarly, the defence of the right to health highlights, first, the instrumental benefits of each person having the capacity to lead her life and to contribute to the human community without facing undue risks from others' unhealthiness, as well as, second, the benefits of protecting health in general within and across societies, and, third, through that, the benefits of promoting global ideals and values for the maintenance of peace, particularly when we cultivate safety and well-being with an emphasis on preventive medicine and decent care. A further, personal instrumental value in health, Joseph Raz notes, is that health increases our individual prospects of having a rewarding life: 'If not all, at least many forms of ill-health—involving as it does pain, suffering and disability—make fulfilling and satisfying life much harder to achieve, or even impossible.'[29]

The instrumental arguments for the right against social deprivation resemble those for the rights to education and health. At the personal level, positively socializing us as children and then protecting us from social deprivation are preconditions for the full development of the human personality with the prospects of having a rewarding life. Having meaningful access to social integration throughout life is also a condition for us to contribute to the human community. At the societal level, access to social connections is necessary for us to understand each other and thereby respect each other's rights and freedoms; and access to social connections is also necessary to promote understanding, tolerance, and friendship and to further the maintenance of peace.

2.4.2 Implications

Together, the five arguments for the human right against social deprivation explain why we need minimally adequate access to decent social contact and connection to secure the conditions for a minimally good human life. In more detail:

1. Social deprivation threatens our ability to develop and sustain basic cognitive and physical function. Thus, protection from social deprivation is necessary for us to exercise rights that require basic health, cognition, understanding, and physical aptitude.[30]
2. More specifically, social deprivation undermines our capacity to understand and exercise many civil and political rights. Thus, protection from social deprivation is necessary for us to exercise these human rights.
3. In addition, given its cognitive and physical effects, social deprivation puts at risk our brute survival interests in food, security, and shelter.

Thus, protection from social deprivation is necessary for us to secure economic-welfare rights of subsistence.
4. Coercive social deprivation is a cruel, inhuman, and degrading form of treatment. Moreover, both coercive and incidental social deprivation render us vulnerable to other types of cruel, inhuman, degrading, or severely unfair treatment because they harm us cognitively and physically, making us prone to depression, reduced immunity, and suicidal ideation, among other things, which make us less able to shield ourselves, assert ourselves, or seek redress for mistreatment. Thus, protection from social deprivation is necessary to reduce our vulnerability to gross mistreatment.[31]

To this list, we can add various things that go beyond a minimally good human life:

5. Social deprivation undermines in the present, and threatens in the future, the conditions for full autonomy.
6. Social deprivation conflicts with equality of opportunity to the extent that such equality depends on any of the elements outlined in points 1 to 4 above.
7. Social deprivation undermines our opportunities to engage with important domains of value such as meaningful employment, higher education, a sense of identity, self-respect, love, creativity, and achievement.

Since we can only enjoy various other rights when we are safe from social deprivation, it is tempting to say that the right against social deprivation is a *basic right* in Shue's sense, i.e. a right that must be fulfilled to fulfil *all* other rights, including other basic rights to physical security and basic subsistence. In new work that responds to my charge that he overlooks core social needs, Shue makes a noteworthy amendment to his account of basic rights to include our developmental social interests. He avoids the language of a right *against* social deprivation, because the 'against' downplays the positive duties that such a right generates. He also limits his focus to our social developmental interests in childhood. But, he does argue that the good of developing social abilities through social contact is as fundamental an interest as there can be. 'In effect, it is an interest in becoming human.' Protecting this developmental process, therefore, 'seems to be essential to the protection of all other distinctively human rights, making it a basic right.'[32]

I do not go so far as to claim that the right against social deprivation—or the right to be free from social deprivation—is a basic right. First, philosophers have subjected the idea of a *basic right* to sustained criticism that I lack the space to explore.[33] Second, undeniably, many human rights, like a right to breathable air, seem to stand independently of the right against social deprivation. Therefore, I shall shy away from saying that the right against social deprivation could be basic in any unqualified sense.[34]

I do say, however, that this right is *secure* in the sense that it's not conditional on good behaviour or good standing. If *many* human rights—including many civil and political rights, subsistence rights, education rights, healthcare rights, and, in extreme cases, all rights requiring clear thought—are indeed available to us only when our right against social deprivation is protected, then this right could not be conditional upon good behaviour unless our conduct could be so egregious that we somehow forfeit not only our right against social deprivation but also all of the rights that depend on its protection. Since the psychological and physical effects of long-term coercive social deprivation can be irreversible, our conduct would have to be egregious enough for us to forfeit *permanently*, not just temporarily, both our right against social deprivation and all the rights that depend on its protection.

Of course, the main reason that the right against social deprivation is *secure* is that minimally adequate access to decent social contact is too fundamental to deny to someone regardless of its relation to other rights. Could we justifiably pump dirty air into a person's prison cell, because prison should be burdensome? Surely not. Could we justifiably give him insufficient food so that he becomes malnourished, because prison should be burdensome? Surely not. Such needs are so fundamental that we can never justify depriving a person of them as a punishment. Our core social needs are similar: they are too fundamental to our lives as human lives. We cannot legitimately punish someone by denying him access to decent social contact.

2.5 Duty-Bearers

One challenge for the right against social deprivation is duty-bearers. According to Onora O'Neill, 'welfare' or socio-economic rights are unclaimable. Without an appropriate institutional scheme that specifies who bears the duties to secure these rights, we cannot know who, if anyone, bears such duties. In the case of our core social needs, her charge would be that, without an institutional scheme that specifies who bears the duties generated by our core social needs, those duties cannot be claimed and, therefore, cannot correlate with rights like a right against social deprivation.[35] Non-institutional duties to be inclusive may exist, but they do not correlate with rights. Talk of rights in this case is rhetorical, so the objection goes.

Here are three replies. First, as John Tasioulas notes, on an interest-based account of rights, the indeterminacy of the duties does not undermine the existence of the right. We can establish that a right exists without specifying the duties it generates, because a right exists when a person has an interest that is sufficiently strong to ground duties in other people. Specifying the precise duties and the identity of duty-bearers is a further step.[36]

Second, against the right against social deprivation, the O'Neillian objection misses its mark. This is because the right against social deprivation is more than a welfare right. As we saw above, the right against *coercive* social deprivation and social brutality is a civil and political 'liberty' right, since coercive deprivation and brutality constitute cruel, degrading, and inhuman treatment. Similarly, the right against *incidental* deprivation stemming from wilful neglect has civil and political aspects. And many overtly civil and political rights have interpersonal dimensions that cannot be secured without a right against social deprivation. Therefore, if civil and political rights are immune to the claimability challenge (though I doubt they are immune), then the right against social deprivation is immune to that challenge too.

Third, in terms of the duties they generate, civil and political rights are less distinct from socio-economic rights than thinkers like O'Neill imply. Tasioulas notes that the difference between what we can know about the primary duties associated with 'liberty' rights and those associated with 'welfare' rights is a difference in degree, not in kind. And O'Neill tends to minimize what we can know about the duties associated with 'welfare' rights before institutions allocate duties.[37]

We can specify the primary positive duties that correlate with the right against social deprivation as easily as we can for any other right. We can know, for instance, that governments are primary duty-bearers with fundamental duties to respect, protect, and fulfil our rights against social deprivation. In particular, first, governments have negative duties not to interfere unjustly with our existing connections, and not to thwart our social efforts to form connections. Second, governments have duties to review, and abandon wherever possible, all forms of isolated confinement in prisons, immigration facilities, and hospitals. I explore institutional segregation further in Chapter 8. Third, governments have positive duties to mitigate the effects of experiences that can thwart our social efforts, such spending time in prison, extended illness, friends' deaths, or forced migration. Fourth, they have duties to identify, and mitigate, the barriers that social deprivation can pose for democratic participation. Fifth, they have duties to attend to the social preconditions for equality of opportunity. Finally, they have duties to ensure that, when we are vulnerable, we have positive access to social connections commensurate with our needs.

We as individuals are also duty-bearers of human rights. First, we have duties to respect institutional schemes that protect us all from social deprivation. Second, we have duties to help set up such schemes if we can do so at little cost to ourselves. Third, we have duties not to deprive others of opportunities for decent social contact. Fourth, we have duties to attend to whether the people who are charged with guaranteeing for everyone minimally adequate access to decent social contact honour that responsibility. Finally, when certain conditions are met, we can have duties to interact and associate with *particular* people. This last category of duties is limited, but less limited than we might suppose. In Chapters 4, 5, and 6, I explore the impact that positive social claim-rights have on our interactional freedom, associational freedom, and personal morality.

2.6 Objections

This section addresses three families of objections to a human right against social deprivation. The first family contains four objections that pertain to my use of the language of *rights*. The second family contains two objections that pertain to undue burdensomeness and, specifically, illiberality and intolerability. The third family concerns charges of infeasibility.

2.6.1 The Language of Rights

A critic might object that the concept of *rights* is a poor choice to capture the moral force of our core social needs. This objection can take several forms:

1. Many of the social ills discussed above are *social bads* rather than *social injustices*, so the objection goes, and, therefore, I misdescribe them when I speak of rights violations.
2. Rights talk in general is at odds with certain ideals of sociability, specifically ideals of the family, which lie at the heart of any account of our social needs.

3. As argued by Laura Valentini, securing the right against social deprivation would often be demeaning to its beneficiaries.[38]
4. Whatever else its flaws, the right against social deprivation is conceptually redundant.

Let me answer these charges in turn.

1. *Social bads versus social injustices.* Let's put some meat on the bones of this first objection. *Justice* normally operates in the space of opportunities, rather than outcomes, the objection would go. Consequently, if someone can access good health services, but opts out and then experiences health problems, this is bad for her, but not an injustice, so the argument goes. By the same reasoning, if a person opts for social isolation and becomes less socially competent as a result, this is bad—for her and for others—but not an injustice. Similarly, if someone is a belligerent person, in ways she could control with effort, who alienates the people she would otherwise have as companions, this is a bad—for her and for others—but not an injustice.[39]

In reply, I grant that often persons' poor social situations fall short of being a *political* injustice to them. The competent person who removes herself from society suffers no injustice unless she renders herself unable to exercise agency to decide whether to remain in solitude and we do nothing to assist her. The belligerent person who makes herself unattractive to others suffers no injustice unless she renders herself unable to alter her behaviour and reintegrate socially, and again, we do not assist her. There is a tipping point past which a person can no longer make use of formal opportunities to choose to live otherwise. Then it becomes a matter of justice.

The realm of justice—the realm of rights—is shaped by our non-contingent fundamental needs. Those needs include meaningful social opportunities including social contribution opportunities. As I discuss in the next chapter, we suffer an injustice when we are dismissed as social threats, social nonentities, or instruments for use, rather than seen as potential social contributors. So social injustices can follow on the heels of social bads.

I acknowledge that we have a responsibility to make ourselves inclusion-worthy when we can. But I deny that failing to do so affects our core social rights. Even when we're less inclusion-worthy, we have secure rights to have minimally adequate social access and to be viewed as *potential* social contributors. This is analogous to our right to health. We have a responsibility to take reasonable care of our health. But, even when we harm our bodies by smoking or taking part in extreme sports, we have secure rights to access adequate healthcare.

2. *Ideals of the family*. A critic might argue that, while the right against social deprivation has a degree of the importance I attribute to it, the right is objectionable as a putative human right, since it offends ideals of the family. First, it threatens to take primary responsibility for social connections away from the family. Second, it introduces the formal, self-serving language of *rights* into family relations. The critic might say: Asserting rights-claims is, first, unnecessary within families given the nature of the bonds and feelings among family members and, second, threatening to those bonds and feelings which distinguish families as inestimably valuable associations. In this vein, Michael Sandel argues that the only value that rights might have for intimate relations is in providing a remedy for corruption within those relations.[40]

In reply, although 'asserting' and 'demanding' our rights might seem to be perverse in well-functioning families, and although state-level intrusion into well-functioning families is undesirable, nevertheless we must appreciate the contribution that rights, and the voluntary non-assertion of our rights, make to concepts that are central to intimate relations. Rights help us to make sense of concepts such as *supererogation, generosity,* and *forgiveness*, all of which are vital to good family relations. John Tomasi argues compellingly that the language of rights is important for the exercise of loving virtue in intimate communities: 'You cannot most properly be generous with what you do not know is yours; you cannot truly forgive without first recognizing a debt.'[41]

Moreover, although we tend to thrive when we form small units of mutual dependency marked by willing, committed, and loving participation, nevertheless these are not the only social arrangements in which we can cultivate the conditions for minimally good lives. Nor are these the arrangements in which many of us find ourselves. As the stories about Japan's rent-a-family industry show, we can sometimes purchase the conditions in which to cultivate caring connections with others; we can come to love people who play a role of interdependency with us. If we lack the material resources to contrive such solutions, however, then the language of a *right* against social deprivation becomes our ally.

3. *Demeaning beneficiaries*. Laura Valentini argues that compelling someone to befriend an intolerable person can demean the intolerable person. Valentini says that her argument is analogous to Elizabeth Anderson's critique of luck-egalitarianism:

> On Anderson's view, compensating people for their bad brute luck would lead governments to intrusively inquire about people's (lack of) natural

endowments, in order to determine whether they are 'ugly', 'untalented', 'unintelligent', and therefore disadvantaged through no fault of their own.

Similarly, in order to force some of its citizens to befriend 'the grumpy', a government would have to intrude into people's private spheres to determine whose lack of social connections is caused by 'grumpiness' and not by a voluntary choice. But how could a government go about determining who, in the relevant society, is 'grumpy and obnoxious' without thereby demeaning and disrespecting some of its citizens? It would seem that a policy of 'forcing others to befriend the grumpy' would add an official stigma to the disadvantage the grumpy already suffer.[42]

In reply, I take issue with the terms 'befriending' and 'the grumpy'. The first term overstates the duties that the right against social deprivation generates. The second term understates a socially vulnerable person's circumstances. (I return to the challenge of the genuinely 'intolerable' person below.)

More importantly, I take issue with Valentini's charge that a policy of securing decent social contact and connection to a vulnerable person would add an official stigma to her disadvantage. As Peter Jones notes, one reason to accord socio-economic/welfare needs the status of rights is precisely to remove the stigma of charity that haunts welfare support.[43]

Gauging whether a person is socially deprived is, first, no more intrusive than investigating other domains of political and legal activity, such as whether a person meets the *mens rea* requirement in a criminal proceeding. Second, gauging a person's level of social deprivation need not be intrusive at all if we focus on broad categories of people who are vulnerable to social deprivation, such as children, older people, immigrants, people with disabilities, people who are unemployed, and people returning after incarceration, and we support them regardless of whether they individually suffer from social deprivation. (Admittedly, some people will slip through the cracks, such as members of a category that we fail to identify as vulnerable to social deprivation.)

4. *Conceptual redundancy*: Could the right against social deprivation be subsumed under other recognized human rights such as a right to education, a right to health, or a right to physical security? Could it fall under a right against torture, cruel and inhuman treatment, or some combination thereof and, therefore, be abandoned as redundant?

The answer is 'no'. Although each of these human rights touches on important dimensions of our social needs, none captures the content and value of the right against social deprivation. Let's take each candidate in turn.[44]

(a) *Education*. We cannot subsume our needs for decent social contact and connection under a right to education for two reasons. First, our childhood social developmental needs are akin to our subsistence needs. Just as we need adequate food to grow taller, healthier, and smarter, so too we need adequate nurturing care to acquire the physical, social, emotional, cognitive, and linguistic abilities necessary for a minimally good human life. And it is no more appropriate to say that socializing us during critical stages of development is part of 'basic education' than it is to say that feeding us is part of 'basic education'.

Second, subsuming our core social needs under our education or developmental needs would imply that, once we have developed into functioning adults, we no longer have social needs that ground human rights. But, as Chapter 1 showed, we need decent social contact irrespective of any developmental or educative purpose it may serve. We need it even when we are fully developed, educated adults. The social nature of human life is not a contingent reality. It's part of a minimally good human existence.

(b) *Health*. To have basic physical and mental health, we do need minimally adequate access to decent social contact and connection. But subsuming our core social needs under health needs could distract us from the distinctive, *interdependent* nature of social interaction. Social needs are not purely health-related. They are sources of meaning, agency, and respect irrespective of our physical and mental health.

More optimistically, focusing on the intersection between health and sociality could help us to recognize the distinctive interpersonal dimensions of our health needs. For example, if we appreciate the impact that our core social needs tend to have on our health, then we might review our use of quarantine. Even though quarantining contagious people may be necessary to contain the spread of a disease, we should not dismiss as a regrettable externality its negative impact on the people thus isolated.

(c) *Torture; cruel, inhuman, or degrading treatment*. We could not subsume the right against coercive social deprivation under the right against torture alone, as this would invite an overly narrow reading of the right against social deprivation, of the criminal justice contexts in which it is an issue, and of the suffering that social deprivation engenders. In other words, as I noted above, even if someone didn't find solitary confinement torturous, it would still be a human rights issue. The right against coercive social deprivation does seem, however, to derive from the right against cruel, inhuman, and degrading treatment. Social deprivation in prisons occurs not only through long-term solitary confinement—which may well be torturous—but also through ongoing exposure to brutal and degrading social conditions that are not isolating and not necessarily torturous. Forced social deprivation of both the solitary and non-solitary variety is cruel, inhuman, and degrading, and renders a person vulnerable to other forms of cruel, inhuman, and degrading treatment. Protection from social deprivation is necessary to reduce our risk of exposure to treatment that we have a secure claim not to suffer.[45]

One reason that the right against all forms of social deprivation cannot be subsumed under the rights against torture and cruel, inhuman, or degrading treatment is that the right against social deprivation also protects us from *incidental* deprivation. The relevant comparison here is to the right to be free from poverty. The right against social deprivation, like the right to be free from poverty, applies both to coercive deprivation and to incidental deprivation. Both rights are rights to be reasonably secure from the risk of falling below a basic level of sufficiency.

If I have considered all of the viable candidate 'cover-rights', then no other right captures the content of the right against social deprivation. It is a distinct human right that protects our core social needs.

2.6.2 Undue Burdens

The relation between undue burdens and unfeasible burdens is complex and unclear. Undue burdens are sometimes feasible to secure. Requiring you to devote your days off to some cause of mine would be unreasonable, but feasible if you don't have other commitments. Unfeasible burdens are difficult or impossible to secure, but could be reasonable. Asking you to get me to the hospital at little cost to yourself when I am gravely ill is reasonable, but unfeasible if you are unable to help me. Undue and unfeasible burdens intersect at the point where the resource-costs of an otherwise reasonable burden place excessive pressure on would-be duty-bearers or third-parties. For now, I focus on two dimensions of burdensomeness: illiberality and intolerability.

1. *Illiberality*. A critic might object that the right against social deprivation is illiberal since it imposes undue duties to be inclusive that go against standard liberal views about freedom of association. The right is intrusive not only for providers but also for receivers, as Valentini's point noted above about demeaning beneficiaries is meant to highlight. In other words, the right against social deprivation disregards the associational freedoms of the

people it tasks with being more inclusive, as well as the associational freedoms of the people it forces into greater socialization. The critic might bolster this illiberality objection by highlighting that what matters to us is the *quality* of our connections. We crave personalized recognition. We want a name that identifies us as a social being (not a number, serial code, or tattoo). We want a regular place in someone's calendar and mind. We want a meaningful chance to be important to *someone*.

I will answer these charges of illiberality only briefly here, as I devote several of the subsequent chapters to analysing our interactional freedom and our associational freedom, arguing that these freedoms are lexically secondary to our positive social rights claims.

Briefly, then, the right against social deprivation, like a right to basic subsistence, implies both a context-sensitive approach and a division of labour. We don't have a duty to associate with *every* socially deprived person, or even with a *given* socially deprived person (unless certain conditions are met). But, as noted, we do have a duty to care that the people responsible for providing everyone with adequate social access honour that responsibility. Put simply, as moral agents, we have strong moral reasons to attend to the conformity of action with moral reason.[46] Hence, we are all subject to the reason to ensure that a child is cared for, even though the reason to care for the child directly applies only to the small set of people upon whom that responsibility specifically falls. Likewise, with general social inclusiveness, we are all subject to the reason to ensure that all of us have minimally adequate opportunities for social contact and connection. But the reason to act to include any one person applies only to particular people. When the people to whom that reason applies fail to conform with it, the reason extends beyond that immediate circle to those of us who are well-placed to bring about conformity with reason.

The specific worry that we intrude indefensibly into a socially disengaged person's life is comparable to the worry that we would intrude indefensibly into a fasting person's life if we were to force-feed her. As noted before, however, people can reasonably choose to fast or to self-isolate; but the long-term negative effects of their decisions often mean that eventually we may or must intervene.

2. *Intolerability*. A critic might argue that some people are genuinely intolerable, such as people who are highly contagious or violent. The critic might claim that isolating such people is a necessary evil, i.e. an *infringement* of their social rights. If that is correct, then we have no overriding duty to be socially inclusive toward such people even if they are vulnerable.

Four replies present themselves, some of which bolster my replies to the illiberality objection.[47] The first reply is that some people who are deemed to be 'intolerable' are not actually intolerable. A contagious person poses a health risk only to people who are vulnerable to her disease. She poses no risk to anyone who is immune. Therefore, isolating her may not be in *everyone's* or even the majority's best interests. Moreover, sometimes the benefits of contact outweigh the risk of contagion. If a contagious two-year-old must endure long-term quarantine, his parents might reasonably choose for them to stay with him despite the risk. I return to this case in the next chapter.

Similarly, even if a person seeking asylum poses a security risk, she probably poses no *social* risk that would make her more of a social threat than a contributor. Consequently, there is no reason related to social risk to detain her in isolation.

Likewise, a violent person can pose a threat to anyone who has direct contact with her, but posing a threat is not always a decisive reason to isolate someone. Consider an analogy. Armed, 18-year-old soldiers strolling through a civilian mall are dangerous, but no one would suggest confining them. Moreover, holding a dangerous person in isolation may be likelier to exacerbate her condition than lessen it. And, even when she is dangerous, she may be able to make a meaningful social contribution, especially if she has knowledge, training, experience, or information from which others may benefit.

The second reply to the intolerability objection is concessive. In extreme cases, we may have to resort to mediated contact with a person in order to protect other people. In doing so, we can still recognize her social contributions as meaningful. In addition to mediated contact, we might resort to non-human animal contact or, indeed, virtual worlds as a (putative) partial substitute for direct, interpersonal human contact. Whether these are acceptable ways to meet someone's core social needs is a matter for debate.

One difficulty with mediated, virtual, or non-human contact is that, even though such contact might alleviate our psychological distress, it fails to honour our fundamental interest in human social connections. Virtual and non-human interactions are imperfect. The right against social deprivation rests partly on a Kantian respect for us as ends in ourselves who can contribute to *human* interactions, and therefore purely virtual or non-human interactions cannot honour our social rights, even if they satisfy our psychological needs. Moreover, any *virtual* interaction—if it is indeed an *interaction*—that relieves our psychological distress because it is falsely presented to us as genuine will fail to respect us as social beings.[48]

The third reply to the intolerability objection highlights the point above that governments are primary duty-bearers of human rights. Therefore, we as individuals do not have rights-based duties to engage directly with a genuinely intolerable person (unless specific conditions are met; for instance, the parents of the contagious two-year-old would be correct to decide that one of them should remain in contact with the child as his primary carer). Instead, governments must provide professional or voluntary opportunities for socialization through regulated forums that protect any would-be providers' rights.

Even so, designated professionals are still people. This forces me to offer a fourth reply that bites the bullet and acknowledges that it may be impossible to realize all social rights of this kind. People who are genuinely 'intolerable' may have to endure inescapable rights infringements when their intolerability would make it unduly burdensome for any person to offer them minimally adequate access to decent social contact.

2.6.3 Feasibility

Most moral and political philosophers think that, for human rights to play the practical roles we need them to play in policy-making, regulation, and accountability, they must be *feasible*.[49] Most theories of human rights do not demand absolute feasibility as an existence condition for human rights. Instead, they temper the feasibility constraint with some aspirational elements. For instance, Amartya Sen denies that human rights must be feasible in any straightforward sense. He advances a *social influenceability test* which requires that other people be able to make a material difference through taking an interest in what that right protects.[50] He asks: 'Why should complete feasibility be a condition of cogency of human rights when the objective is to work towards enhancing their actual realization, if necessary through expanding their feasibility?'[51] The fact that some rights are not presently fully feasible does not in itself entail that they are not rights at all. Rather, 'that understanding suggests the need to work towards changing the prevailing circumstances to make the unrealized rights realizable, and ultimately, realized.' Pablo Gilabert develops this idea with the notion of *dynamic duties*, which are duties to expand the range of what is feasible by changing prevailing conditions.[52]

Nickel endorses a stronger feasibility test. He holds that human rights must pass an *implementability test*, which is that the duties imposed by a specific right be ones that most countries can successfully implement today.[53]

Nevertheless, Nickel says that human rights can exist and be high-priority goals even when there are considerable barriers to their (legal) implementation. He notes that affirming a given human right 'does not imply that we must immediately implement that right at the cost of sacrificing things that are of higher priority'.[54] Nor does it follow from the fact that a claim cannot be immediately implemented as a legal right that it should not be respected as a moral right. Consider a right to assistance during disability or illness. Nickel argues that, even if this right cannot presently be implemented as a legal right, 'it can be implemented as a moral right in the sense that people recognize as part of their morality the legitimacy of calling upon government and other people to assist one during illness and disability'.[55] Acknowledging such a right even in the absence of legal implementation brings with it, Nickel says, duties for both government and citizens to promote the growth of opportunities that will make full implementation possible as well as duties of charity and benevolence.

One problem with an *implementability test* is it seems to leave open the loophole of wilful disablement. If securing a basic need is infeasible in a country because that country's government has wilfully disabled itself by spending its resources on statues or bad investments, its people's basic needs should not lose their human rights status. The government has breached its citizens' human rights by misallocating resources.

An alternative, less state-centred standard of feasibility would highlight the role that international governmental institutions must play in protecting human rights. This approach would calculate feasibility based on coordinating global resources. So, in relation to social needs, we could look beyond states' resources to international bodies, NGOs, and human rights champions like Amnesty International and the Red Cross when considering what is feasible.

This feeds into a second thought: 'feasibility' is not just about *legal* implementation, since human rights can be implemented and honoured in many official and unofficial ways other than through legal entrenchment. As Sen notes, these ways include non-binding declarations such as the UDHR, grass-roots activism and publicity, and governments checking themselves in policy and general practice.[56] As Tasioulas observes, it is not a necessary condition for a right to be a human right that there be always a *pro tanto* reason to enact it as a legally enforceable right. This 'legal right presumption' creates artificial distinctions, such as between public and private duties, deeming the former to be correlative with human rights and the latter not. Moreover, it is unduly restrictive in (for instance) ruling out the possibility that an anarchist could speak of human rights at all, and ruling out from the class of human rights things that commonsensically are human rights though there is probably no reason to entrench them in law, such as the right to resist a tyrannical government.[57]

Not all defences of the feasibility constraint are tempered by aspirations to expand what is feasible. In its strongest form, defended by Raymond Geuss, the feasibility constraint says that human rights, particularly socio-economic rights, are simply liberal ideals. They are expressions of moral belief about what we would like to see enforced, but they are things to which we can only aspire. They are not things to which we can appeal to regulate conduct.[58]

Moreover, even in the more tempered defences of the feasibility constraint, philosophers seem to assume that it is regrettable that there are aspirational elements to human rights practice, that somehow this feature shakes the foundations of what human rights are and what they can do.

In other work, I have argued that feasibility is largely irrelevant to human rights.[59] Human rights can retain their practical importance, action-guidingness, and accountability power without it. One reason is that human rights are, if nothing else, *sustainability ideals*. To protect them, duty-bearers must *sustain* indefinitely a particular attitude, disposition, mode of conduct, state of affairs, or combination of those things, which they probably cannot sustain. What makes a sustainability ideal an ideal is not its *content*, but its *maintenance* over time.

All that said, in the case of interpersonal, social rights there are feasibility questions that we must address. A critic might say that, while it's all well and good to show that fundamental social rights are human rights, it's little comfort to the people whose social rights are breached to learn that it was infeasible to secure them. Therefore, focusing on practice, let's answer some specific feasibility worries about social rights.

1. *Commanding emotions*. A critic might doubt that our deep interpersonal interests could ground rights, because rights correlate with duties, and positive social duties seem to be infeasible to the extent that they require genuine attachment from duty-bearers, since our emotions cannot be commanded.[60] In other words, if 'ought implies can', then it's not the case that we have duties to feel attachment for particular other people, since we cannot control our emotions.

In reply, for one thing, we make a mistake if we assume that, to qualify as rights, weighty interests must generate only feasible duties. We can have reasons to do things that we are presently unable to do, such as *learn* to do various things including learn to care about certain people.

For another thing, if we want to hold on to 'ought implies can' in relation to our emotions, we need to look at the empirical evidence to see if our emotions really are outside our control. Social neuroscience and contemplative neuroscience studies indicate that we have more control over our emotions than we might like to acknowledge.[61] Even if we cannot manufacture an emotion on command, we can conscientiously cultivate certain emotional states and wholesome attitudes toward other people that can, in time, produce affectionate commitments to them.

2. *Resource scarcity*. A critic might worry about the institutional infeasibility of securing social rights when those rights are considered in conjunction with other legitimate political and social aims. One concern is potential resource scarcity where, in combination with other projects, social rights impose infeasible burdens on creditable social institutions such as welfare structures, which inevitably have limited resources.

In reply, for one thing, undeniably, substantial resource costs flow from securing social human rights including the right against social human deprivation. But substantial costs come in securing any given human right, and, more importantly, substantial costs also come in *not* securing a human right. The likely costs of not securing core social rights are impressive given the kinds of psychological and physiological risks that correlate social deprivation, elaborated in Chapter 1. It is reasonable to suppose that the costs of not securing this right are at least comparable to, if not greater than, the costs of securing it, especially since so many other human rights and domains of value depend on protecting this right.

For another thing, the demands of social rights may be no greater or less than those of many other rights, especially if we recognize that many rights typically branded as civil and political rights are social rights. For a third thing, if indeed social rights prove to be infeasible to implement alongside other major commitments, social rights are not necessarily the thing that should be sacrificed.

3. *Criminal justice*. A further concern about social rights is their potential to conflict with the legitimate aims of institutions such as criminal justice. In most societies, social rights would impose substantial restrictions on criminal justice processes, which in nearly all jurisdictions use some form of social deprivation as a mode of punishment.

In reply, it is true that most theorists hold that it is legitimate to respond to culpable wrongdoing by suspending normal relations with the person who has offended.[62] Typically, this means withdrawing, to a proportionate degree and for a proportionate period, the respect and recognition that it would otherwise be appropriate to show to her so that she may assume the restorative responsibilities that are hers in light of her wrongdoing. In a serious case, theorists have tended to think that it is acceptable, if not obligatory, to ostracize, physically isolate, exile, or solitarily confine someone who culpably engages in egregious wrongdoing. One argument is that, in light of their offending, people who have offended must have fewer or lesser social rights, especially given the costs of satisfying those rights.

However, suspending ordinary relations with a person who has offended need not and should not include denying her minimally adequate opportunities for decent social contact by subjecting her to long-term solitary confinement or extremely brutal prison conditions. Ordinary relations can be legitimately suspended when those relations are reoriented to focus on the person's restorative responsibilities. This reorientation keeps a tight connection between the wrong done and the censure communicated through punishment. It makes clear to the person what conduct of hers has been condemned and why, as well as what is expected of her by way of reparation.

Undoubtedly, practical problems confront such a model for punishment, since the wrongdoer may not accept that the responsibilities are hers. Prompting her to make use of forums and opportunities to restore relations will then be unsuccessful in an important sense. Moreover, sometimes victims may have no wish to be in contact with the wrongdoer, in which case the responsibilities may be honoured only indirectly or metaphorically. These contingent practical issues do not undermine the fact that responsibility-focused responses communicate blame and censure more appropriately than do socially privative responses. They better respect the wrongdoer as a person who is responsive to reasons, and are far less likely to cause the physical and psychological harms that haunt socially privative punishments. I explore these issues more fully in Chapter 8.

Conclusion

This chapter has shown that we have a human right against social deprivation. The chapter detailed three kinds of social deprivation (coercive isolation, incidental deprivation, and social brutality). It highlighted five kinds of arguments for the right against social deprivation—empirical, phenomenological, respect-based, reciprocity and desert-based, and instrumental arguments—and answered several objections. The chapter showed that this right is a fundamentally important human right, on which many other human rights depend. Therefore, it is paramount that we bring it, and social rights in general, to the forefront of human rights debates. In Chapter 3, I take forward my account of social human rights by defending the most contentious right proposed in these pages, namely, the right to contribute to specific other persons' survival and well-being.

3
Sustaining Others

Introduction

In a memorable scene in the period film *Gosford Park* (2001), Lt Commander Anthony Meredith takes refuge downstairs in the maids' pantry to escape the claustrophobic air of the aristocratic dining room, where his life failures are on display. The maid Dorothy finds him there in his black-tie outfit, eating jam out of a jar. He asks her why it seems that for some people everything turns out right, and for others, not. Quietly but passionately, Dorothy replies:

> I believe in love. Not just getting it. Giving it. I think as long as you can love somebody, whether or not they love you, then it's worth it.

Unbeknownst to Commander Meredith, Dorothy described her own situation: she secretly loves the butler, Mr Jennings. Startled by her reply, Meredith says: 'That's a good answer.' She'd reminded him that, unlike most of the people in the dining room, he has a wife whom he loves and who loves him.

This small scene captures the core claims of this chapter. First, we have a fundamental need to contribute directly to specific other people's survival and well-being. This need can fall short of loving others, but includes many of the attitudes and behaviours that naturally go with love. For ease of expression, let's call it our *need to sustain* others.[1] Second, we have a human right to be protected in our efforts to sustain others. Third, when we are denied the means to sustain others, we are victims of a grave injustice, which I call *social contribution injustice*.

After specifying what it means to *sustain* other people (Section 3.1), I explore the worst forms of social contribution injustice, which render us unable to sustain other people because we are compromised in one or more of the core social resources outlined in Chapter 1, namely, our social abilities (Section 3.2), social opportunities (Section 3.3), or existing social connections

(Section 3.4). This chapter concludes with some cautionary thoughts about sustaining and loving when our beloved does not reciprocate (Section 3.5).²

3.1 The Need to Sustain

3.1.1 Contributing to Others' Survival or Well-Being

Our need to sustain specific other people is interwoven with our need to belong. It is also distinct from our psychological urges *to try* to contribute, *to appear* to contribute, and to *matter*.

Merely *trying* to contribute, when we do, often won't secure the goods that *actually* contributing can secure, which I detail below. *Appearing* to contribute might secure those goods for a time, but not stably. And *mattering* to other people doesn't mean we matter to them positively. Our urge to *matter* can include being a negative force—a dominating power—in people's lives. The leader of an enemy gang *matters* to the people whom he opposes. He is significant in their lives, but not in a way that underpins and secures any persistent, stable, morally urgent need of his or theirs.

Our need to sustain others is rooted in (1) our narrow self-interest, (2) our interest in specific other people's survival and well-being, and (3) our broader self-and-group-interest. Let's unpack those claims here.

1. *Narrow self-interest*. We have strong self-preservation and meaningful-life reasons to contribute to others' survival and well-being. Sustaining others is a key way to satisfy our need to belong. By contributing to specific others' survival and well-being, we can make ourselves valuable, if not indispensable, to them. Sustaining others is a form of insurance, or assurance, within a social group. It makes it more likely that we, and our dependants, will be personally secure and will get to share in the group's material and social resources.

Having forums in which to sustain specific other people is also a key way to fulfil our moral responsibilities, to make ourselves inclusion-worthy, to learn from others how to be inclusion-worthy, and to improve our abilities to sustain others. It is also a source of self-respect and meaning, since we understand who we are partly through how we treat others. As Aristotle observes, by giving us opportunities to be beneficent, our various stable, non-antagonistic social connections give meaning to our prosperity and power.³

More richly, having the means to sustain others could be an ineliminable part of an objective account of well-being—a thought I leave for another day.

2. *Interest in specific others' well-being.* We can be other-interested in the same ways that we can be self-interested. Psychologically and morally, we can legitimately care as much, or more, for the life, health, and well-being of our nearest and dearest as for ourselves. Indeed, we can be invested in their welfare so much so that we disregard everyone else's interests, and make their welfare our aim. By being interested in our nearest and dearest for their own sake, we also have reasons to sustain at least some of the people on whom our nearest and dearest rely more generally for resources. Contributing to the well-being of a community can advance the interests of our nearest and dearest.

Of course, sustaining others does not guarantee that we will be valued for what we do. Equally, failing to sustain others does not guarantee that we will be disvalued or shunned. Some people can convincingly appear to sustain others without doing so. And some people can threaten others effectively to obtain goods without contributing to others' well-being. Moreover, some people can contribute to *some* people's well-being while harming many other people, such as the famous comedian who makes a million people laugh but also sexually assaults five dozen women. His social standing may depend more on *whom* he serves than anything else.

Despite these realities, contributing interpersonally increases the *chance* that we will be valuable and valued by other people. When we do not, cannot, or are forbidden to contribute, we become less secure in our social group, as we either free-ride or can seem to free-ride.[4] We also risk that our loved ones will become less secure. I return to this issue in my discussion of punishment and prison in Chapter 8.

3. *Self-and-group interests.* We have strong reasons to ensure the well-being of a broader group for our own sake, for our dearests' sake, and for the group's sake. Our need to contribute is rooted partly in the practical necessity of having enough of us in the group engage in sustaining others. If too few of us contribute socially to others' survival and well-being, then we lead poorer lives both individually and collectively. In Chapter 5, I explore this thought in relation to what I call *each-we dilemmas of sociability*.

Now, do these three grounds for our need to sustain others collapse into a sophisticated form of egoism? No. In terms of our psychology, we routinely engage in altruistic behaviour, arguably as often or more often than we engage in egoistic behaviour, and it would be perverse to view all our altruism as cloaked egoism. The pleasure we take in sustaining other people can be merely a legitimate by-product of sustaining them for their own sake, rather than our underlying, primary objective.

3.1.2 Contributions

We can contribute to someone's *survival* in obvious ways. We can meet her needs for food, water, security, shelter, and society. We can help keep her safe, share material resources with her, and heal and treat her. We can also meet her core interpersonal needs for physical closeness, respect, and companionship, since 'survival' for human beings is not mere persistence, but a minimally good *human* life. We can do some of these things from a distance or through intermediaries, but we can do others only ourselves, such as being physically close to her.

We can contribute to someone's survival without contributing to her well-being, and vice versa. For instance, we would contribute to her survival but not her well-being if we prolong her life when she is leading a life not worth living.[5] And we would contribute to her well-being but not her survival if we bring joy into her life when she is terminally ill.

For the most part, only competent adults can contribute directly to someone else's *survival*. By contrast, almost all of us can contribute in some way to someone else's well-being, and, of course, heightened well-being tends to enhance chances of survival. That said, the ways we can contribute to someone's *well-being* are harder to specify. In general, we can engage in meaningful joint projects, spend quality time together, do good deeds for someone, give someone gifts, and speak to her with affection and kindness. In their details, what contributes to someone's well-being depends on who we are, who she is, and the context. In other words, contributions to well-being are agent-relative, recipient-relative, and context-sensitive.

Often, someone's perceptions about what we do determine whether she internalizes our efforts as supportive or hostile. She may benefit from a loving hug from her child or spouse, but not from a stranger who makes her feel unsafe even if they are well-meaning. Similarly, she may be happy when a child repeatedly brings out the same toy to show her, recognizing that he's trying to connect with her, but feel puzzled or mocked if an adult repeatedly brings out the toy unless he also tells a joke.

Although perceptions matter, they don't always matter. Sometimes, we can contribute to someone else's well-being even if they don't recognize our efforts as supportive. An older person might contribute to the well-being of someone with Asperger's by allowing him to be involved in providing physical care for her, to improve his skills in social connections. He might experience a benefit without realizing that she has contributed to his well-being. Similarly, Dorothy from *Gosford Park* contributes to the butler

Mr Jennings' well-being without his knowing it, by supporting him in many small ways.

Moreover, sometimes, we can contribute to someone's well-being without intending or even realizing that we do it. We can make an offhand remark that enables someone else to face a problem in her life. We can endure an illness with grace and, thereby, be a model to someone on how to handle struggles. We can smile at a stranger who was feeling low, and lift their heart with our friendliness.

Although these complexities are noteworthy, in the discussion below I bracket them in order to advance my core claim that we have genuine needs—and rights—to have the means to sustain specific other people.

3.1.3 Injustice versus Tragedy

As I noted in Chapter 1, our need to sustain specific other people differs from the psychological *impulse* that most of us have to sustain others. That impulse can be stifled or perverted, and when it is, we can think we have no such need. In addition, our actual need to sustain others can wax and wane over the course of our lives, and, it is often deeper for the more vulnerable among us than for the more independent. But, despite these variations, our need to sustain specific other people is universal and morally urgent, irrespective of whether we consciously feel it, in the same way that our need for education is both universal and morally urgent irrespective of whether we consciously desire education or recognize the absence of education as a loss. Likewise, our need to be free from poverty is both universal (even though some spiritual leaders seem able to lead blissful lives in material poverty) and morally urgent, irrespective of whether we are cognizant of that need. As in the case of poverty, when our need to sustain others goes unmet, we are often acutely vulnerable to threats to ourselves, our beloveds, and our group.

Now, not all aspects of our need to sustain other people are rights-protected matters of justice and injustice. Certain aspects of this need are 'mere' moral fortune or tragedy, such as the following.

In Elizabeth von Arnim's novel *Enchanted April* (1922), Rose Arbuthnot, one of four English women who rent a castle together in Italy for the month of April, is distressed to find that, once she is at the castle, she is restless and discontented. The peace and beauty of the surroundings force her to see the empty busy-ness of her 'good works' back home, which had distracted her from her unhappy marriage to an uninterested husband whom she loves but whose voyeuristic literary work she abhors. von Arnim describes her as follows:

> Rose clasped her hands tight round her knees. How passionately she longed to be important to somebody again—not important on platforms, not important as an asset in an organisation, but privately important, just to one other person, quite privately, nobody else to know or notice. It didn't seem much to ask in a world so crowded with people, just to have one of them, only one out of all the millions, to oneself. Somebody who needed one, who thought of one, who was eager to come to one—oh, *oh how dreadfully one wanted to be precious!*[6]

Rose's situation is tragic: no one needs her. But she suffers no injustice. Or, certainly, she suffers no *political* injustice that gives society duties to secure her better opportunities to sustain anyone.

Were Rose a child, then her developmental interests might hang in the balance, and society would have duties to remedy her situation as a matter of injustice. But she is not a child. Were she subjugated to someone else's will, thwarted in her efforts to connect with people, or unable to connect with people without help, then society would have duties of justice to assist her. But, she is neither thwarted nor subjugated nor incapable of making social overtures. She is a competent, socially able adult who can act on her own decisions. She might suffer a private injustice at the hand of her husband, if she has some claim to his regard which he unjustifiably denies her.[7] But, she has no right to be provided with what she craves: someone who persistently *needs* her.

Also, less charitably, Rose is blind to two insights. The first is that she could be precious to someone if she were less fastidious about who that someone is. With her in Italy is another lonely person, Mrs Fisher. But Rose does not befriend her. Ultimately, Lottie, one of the other women, befriends Mrs Fisher. If Rose's deep wish really were to have *someone* need her, rather than to have her husband need her, she could find one among the 'millions of people' in the world.

The second insight is the one that Dorothy articulates in *Gosford Park* with her declaration: 'as long as you can love somebody, whether or not they love you, then it's worth it.' It's the same insight that W. H. Auden voices in his poem 'The More Loving One':

> If equal affection cannot be,
> Let the more loving one be me.[8]

In craving to be precious, Rose misses the value in loving and sustaining someone regardless of whether that person returns her love or even knows of it. In craving to be precious, Rose wants not just to sustain her husband and be needed by him, but to have him *know* he needs her. Admittedly, Rose would be remarkable, and bizarre, if she loved her husband without wanting him to value her in return. The point, though, is that people, unlike Rose, who endure real social contribution injustice often lack even that: someone they can love and sustain unrequitedly.

Let's turn then to our most important social resource—our social abilities—protection of which is necessary for us to try to sustain anyone.

3.2 Social Abilities

3.2.1 Developing Social Abilities

In Alfred, Lord Tennyson's famous lines, we're told: "Tis better to have loved and lost than never to have loved at all."[9] Worse still, though, is never to have been able to love. As outlined in Chapters 1 and 2, the most radical wrong that we can suffer as social creatures is be denied the nurturing care we need as children to develop the abilities to lead socially integrated lives. If our caregivers abandon, neglect, abuse, confine, and otherwise grossly mistreat us as children, then we suffer not only a present-oriented injustice in being robbed of valuable interpersonal goods to which we have a right, but also a future-oriented injustice in being denied what we need to develop the cognitive, physical, emotional, linguistic, and social skills to lead to socially integrated lives as adults in which we can sustain others.[10] What matters for the purposes of this chapter is that being mistreated in childhood stains our life-story and renders us forever limited in our ability to offer care, love, and companionship to others.[11]

Undeniably, many children who grow up in appalling conditions can offer care, love, and companionship both as children and later as adults. But many of them are unable to be competent caregivers in the sense of *taking care of* another person. One example, noted in Chapter 1, is the children who grew up in orphanages in Romania under the Ceaușescu regime, who endured chronic neglect and abuse that did lasting damage to their social abilities.[12]

Wilful mistreatment of children reflects, among other things, an unjust prejudice about their potential to contribute significantly to others' well-being.

Within the family, children contribute significantly to intimacy and social richness, by playing with siblings, playing with parents, educating younger siblings, possibly educating parents, and assisting with household social activities such as meals. The material value of children's contributions is particularly vivid in lower-income families that lack the resources to outsource family care and household maintenance. Older children also often contribute to the family's social health by adding to its material security through unpaid work such as minding younger siblings, which supports their parents' paid work. They may also have their own paid work or formal study that improves the family's conditions. Such contributions can expand the family's social opportunities by enabling them to take leisure time and be hospitable to others.

This point about children's social contributions highlights a general truth about social contribution injustice, which is that its victims include not only the person whose social resources are compromised, but also all the people who have a right to benefit from that person's social contributions—a point I return to below.[13]

3.2.2 Maintaining Social Abilities

It is not only in childhood that our ability to sustain others can be unjustly compromised. We suffer a similar injustice when we are denied what we need to *maintain* our social abilities in adulthood. This can happen when others neglect us or forcibly sever our social ties.

Many of us need help to form and maintain connections. When we are deprived of support and deprived of minimally adequate access to decent social contact, we can become chronically acutely lonely, and in time can suffer the erosion of our social abilities, such that we become ill-equipped or unable to sustain others.[14]

Such neglect doesn't always, but often reflects a prejudice that neglected people do not need to be taken seriously as social contributors who could sustain others. (Neglect doesn't always reflect prejudice, because people can be wrongly denied resources for structural reasons that do not track a conscious stance about their potential to use those resources.[15]) Although society might not actively label a person as a social threat or *persona non grata*, nonetheless it often proceeds incorrectly as though certain persons are unable to contribute socially in ways that the society should seek to access.

If we, as a society, did view more people, or all people, as potentially valuable social contributors, we would make political and social efforts to ensure that we benefit from their social resources.[16]

Here are two underlying reasons why neglecting people who need help to sustain others is an injustice. First, it undermines their autonomy and potential to flourish. Since much of the meaning in our choices comes from our social connections with others, and since some of our most meaningful choices centre on our social contributions, compromising more dependent persons' maintenance of their social resources undermines both their autonomy and their potential to flourish.

Second, it hinders reciprocity, as discussed in Chapter 2. If we allow persons' social resources to erode, we deny them the chance to do for others what their guardians did for them during their childhood, namely, make a massive investment in their well-being such that they could develop the very social abilities that might now erode.[17]

Note as an aside that the kinds of impairments that can prevent someone from accessing social settings do not invariably come with diminished cognitive and emotional ability. Moreover, even when a person has physical, cognitive, and emotional impairments, she may still have the potential to sustain others. In allowing herself to be cared for physically, an impaired person provides someone else with opportunities to show kindness, to cultivate empathy, to learn how to care, and to be important to her well-being. These are substantial social contributions. To make them, a person needs some cognitive and emotional competence so that she and her caregiver can have a joint narrative, but she need not have as much competence as a critic might think.

The same arguments about autonomy, flourishing, and reciprocity give us reasons not to sever each other's social ties, which we often do when we incarcerate people at a distance from their families, deport people, or otherwise place impossible burdens on families to keep their connections alive. I explore this issue in Chapter 8.

So far, this chapter has focused on our core needs to develop and maintain our social abilities, and on the central role that having social contribution opportunities plays in those endeavours. Some readers might think that the realm of justice ends here, and that we have only a right to the basic *abilities* to sustain others as well as a right not to be thwarted in our efforts to try to sustain others. But this is not where the realm of justice ends.

3.3 Social Opportunities

3.3.1 Having Social Opportunities

Let's turn to cases in which a person is denied meaningful *opportunities* to sustain others but her maintenance of her social abilities is left intact.

Imagine that a person named Sophie is coercively confined by her society to an experience machine that removes all direct access to human contact. Once she is in the machine, she is unaware that she is isolated. She believes that she is leading a normal life populated by the usual kinds of people. Consequently, her cognitive and emotional capacities for social connection get a regular, simulated workout and do not diminish over time. Although her social abilities remain intact, Sophie is a victim of social contribution injustice in her False World, because she has no opportunities to contribute to anyone else's survival or well-being. This not only risks her social connection opportunities in the future, but also eliminates any present connection opportunities she would otherwise enjoy with people. Moreover, it shows that her society does not take her seriously as a social contributor. Of course, in failing to take her seriously as a social contributor, her society might not actively express contempt for her. It might simply have some grand social aim and thoughtlessly treat her as a cog in the wheel of that aim.[18] (Sophie's False World also severs any existing social *connections* she had, which is the focus of the next section.)

Consider another case. In the 1998 film *The Truman Show*, Jim Carrey plays Truman, the unsuspecting star of a reality TV show whose whole world is a TV set. Truman is an orphaned baby, adopted by a TV corporation and raised by actors who play the roles of 'father' and 'mother', and then later connected to actors who play his 'friend' and 'wife'. Superficially, Truman's social relations resemble some of the rent-a-family stories discussed in Chapter 1. But, in Truman's case, *all* of his connections are manufactured, and they lack the emotional warmth that the rent-a-family stories displayed. In addition, Truman's world is a prison. He cannot leave the set which until adulthood he was unaware is a set.

The Truman Show does multiple types of social wrong to Truman. First, he lacks associational control. He is surrounded by actors who nudge and bully him into 'relationships' that fit the script. There's nothing organic in his social world unless he initiates it by being unpredictable.

Second, Truman has no authenticity in his social connections. Throughout his life, he has been deceived by people about his social world.

He has a 'wife' who hates him, neighbours who recite their lines, and a best friend who spouts lies. When Truman begins to suspect that his world is fake, his 'best friend', Marlon, says reassuringly that 'The last thing I'd ever do is lie to you', parroting words fed to him by the TV show's director. Toward the end of the film, Truman tries to escape by taking a sailboat out into the show's man-made ocean. The director generates a storm to force him back to shore, showing how vulnerable Truman is, since the director, actors, and crew are willing to put him at risk to get him to behave and give people a good show.

Although Truman's and Sophie's first-persons experiences in their fake worlds might be similar, *The Truman Show* is distinct from Sophie's False World in several respects and, hence, the objections against them differ. First, unlike Sophie, Truman has the chance to positively affect other people's lives in small ways, since actors are not emotionally immune.[19] Second, Truman can productively benefit from his real, negative social experiences: through them, he can learn and then adjust how he treats the people around him. Sophie might learn within her False World, but she has no chance within her world to put what she learns into practice in real interactions with people.

That said, since all of his connections lack mutual trust, honesty, and concern, Truman is unable to offer the intimacy, understanding, and care that distinguish genuine friendships and loving relationships. Among other things, this reduces the impact that his social contributions might otherwise have on people. Truman is both unjustly undervalued and unjustly overvalued as a social contributor. He is treated as an object for use, but also overvalued as a source of social investment. One irony of *The Truman Show* is that millions of people are invested in his life as viewers of the show; they care about him (to some degree) and wish him well.

Now, there are significant differences between these two cases of compromised social *opportunities* and the cases of compromised social *abilities* discussed in the previous section. First, the *experiences* of the wronged persons are dissimilar. Unlike a mistreated child or a stimulus-deprived neglected person, both Truman and Sophie believe they are surrounded by ordinary people, and they are possibly as happy in their worlds as they would be were they surrounded by ordinary people. Indeed, possibly, they are happier, if their worlds expose them to nicer or wiser 'people' (or actors) than the people they'd otherwise encounter in their lives.

Second, both Truman and Sophie have all the benefits of believing that they are genuinely sustaining other people. Specifically, they get to feel the good feelings that go with showing kindness and care. Put more strongly, when they make 'contributions', they bring into being within themselves the objectively valuable mental states of generosity, kindness, compassion, and empathy. Of course, what is missing is the objective value of genuinely and meaningfully contributing to others' survival or well-being. Also, their situations are precarious, as there is the ever-present risk of technological malfunction and radical disillusionment. Provided, though, that nothing malfunctions, they have the potential to be *experientially* much better off than the people discussed in Section 3.2.

Third, unlike the abused child or stimulus-deprived adult, Truman's and Sophie's abilities to sustain others in future need not be compromised by their current situation. Indeed, if their environments are experientially *more* enriching than the social worlds they would otherwise inhabit, then they could grow deeply through their fake experiences and become more socially able than they otherwise would be. If that happened, then their future social-contribution potential would be greater because of their fake social worlds, since, once released, they would be better able to maximize social opportunities when they arise.

These distinguishing features of Sophie's and Truman's worlds do not alter the fact that they experience social injustices. Rather, these features of their worlds show that it's possible to wrong a person by compromising her social resources and failing to take her seriously as a social contributor without causing her psychological or physical distress.

3.3.2 Having Adequate Social Opportunities

Within the set of opportunity-compromising cases, there are cases that give a person social contribution opportunities but do not give her quantitatively and qualitatively adequate opportunities. Imagine, for example, that Terry is a political prisoner and her social environment is restricted to her worst enemies and the prison culture around her is marked by brutality and cruelty. She makes what social overtures she can, but is greeted with repulsion and abuse. In this setting, Terry is systematically denied conditions conducive to cultivating social connections including, notably, joint narratives, mutual investment, and trusting relations. She is also a victim of prejudice: her worst enemies probably view her as a threat rather than a potential social contributor.

That said, ironically, Terry may have a unique opportunity to cultivate other social resources necessary to sustain others. Being surrounded by enemies can be a productive classroom in which to cultivate compassion, friendliness, and kindness, through necessity. Of course, her conditions remain unjust because she lacks an adequate degree of associational control and misses out on most valuable aspects of social connections, but the environment is not as radically socially deficient as that of complete isolation.

Consider next someone who is forced to keep company with, and only with, one or two other people, day in and day out. An extreme example comes in Jean-Paul Sartre's play *No Exit*, in which three people who've died and gone to Hell spend eternity together making each other miserable. But this kind of reality is also the lot of most people in prison who are forced to keep company with the same one or two inmates for months or years at a time.

Such people have insufficient associational control and insufficient variety in their social connection opportunities. They endure injustice in being forced to be *continuously* in the company of other people, carrying out all their personal activities, private functions, and emotional struggles in view of other people whose goodwill they cannot assume. They also suffer greater social injustice in being forced to be continuously in company with one or two *particular* people not of their choosing, especially if those people are unable to offer minimally adequate opportunities for *decent* social contact. Even so, these injustices are of a lesser sort than coercive isolation.[20]

This undue positive socialization, which coerces people to associate with particular persons, contrasts with the equally intrusive, undue negative regulation of people's social worlds, which forbids them to associate with people. The latter only ceases to be an injustice when the restriction is necessary to respect others' fundamental rights. Consider, for example, someone who is forced into exile either as a punishment or to neutralize tensions between political factions (as was common practice in ancient Athens).[21] This cuts him off from his pre-existing social connections and denies him any associational control over the day-to-day maintenance of those connections.

We have an understandable distaste for exile as a punishment. Yet we should find exile easier to defend than solitary confinement, because exile leaves a person with the option of trying to find a community that will accept him.[22] The exiled person is not abjectly dependent on others for social contact in the way that the coercively isolated person is. If the exiled person is lucky, then the people in the place where he seeks refuge will accept him, and he may then be highly socially included. Also, unlike the person in coercive isolation, if he fails the first time round to find people who will accept him, he can keep searching.

A subtler form of exile is purely social, not physical. Consider the following case. Suppose that a person finds herself in a foreign country and the local people ignore her. No one will tell her where she is or help her find her way. Even the government ignores her. She can leave but is not kicked out. She has close ties back home and simply goes without social interaction in this foreign land.[23] Since she is an outsider, she has no claim of community membership. Since she knows no one, she has no claim of personal history. Moreover, since she has affiliates back home and is at liberty to leave, she faces no threats to her social resources such as those discussed above. So, in being denied the opportunity to sustain people in this society, is she a victim of social contribution injustice?

The answer is that she endures prejudice without enduring unjust treatment. Her social resources are uncompromised, but this society refuses to see her as a potential social contributor. A society's default position should be to recognize a person as a potential social contributor and give due weight to the contributions she makes to others' survival and well-being. A society that refuses to see a person as a potential social contributor deems her to be beyond the pale.

3.4 Social Connections

3.4.1 Maintaining Social Connections

The first set of cases above focused on social abilities and the opportunities needed to support them. The second set of cases focused purely on social contribution opportunities. There is a third set of cases that neither denies a person social contribution opportunities *in general* nor undermines her basic social abilities. Instead, these cases compromise her efforts to form and maintain persistent social *connections*. Consider a case of non-repeated contact. Suppose that a person, Mary, is unable to solicit society without help due to impairment or confinement, and is given access to decent, friendly social contact from a health visitor that is minimally adequate in the number of contact hours (whatever that is). But she receives that contact from a different person each day. She never sees the same person twice. There's no continuity in her social interactions.

Mary is forever starting over socially. Although she has opportunities to show decency, respect, care, concern, friendliness, and kindness to people, she cannot form and sustain relationships, give and receive trust, cultivate a joint narrative, or build intimacy. She is radically limited in her chances to teach, console, comfort, advice, guide, and share with the people she meets. Only she carries a memory of the history of her interactions with people. She cannot be a witness to anyone else's life or they a witness to hers.

By lacking social connections, she lacks the *particular* social contribution opportunities necessary to pursue deeper ties with others, and this may erode some of her social abilities, such as the ability to share intimacy with others. (If a baby were treated this way, she would fail to develop the range of social abilities necessary to lead a socially integrated life.[24]) Indeed, we might recognize in such treatment a perverse, but effective mode of punishment, which allows the person to hope that she can be socially valuable, but then robs her of the kinds of continuous social contribution opportunities that would enable her to manifest her value in persistent connections.

Consider some cases of severed contact. The first is the story of Nelson Mandela mentioned in Chapter 2. While in prison, Mandela had repeated, decent social contact with his guards, but only until he became attached to them and they to him. Once attached, that contact was severed and those guards were replaced by strangers. Apparently, his guards were changed repeatedly because they each came to love him. The second case of severed contact is crueller. In it, a confined or dependent person is allowed social contact, but not with the people he already loves such as his children or spouse. In Nelson Mandela's case, he spent 27 years in prison, and for much of that time was unable to be a father to his children.

As we saw in the last chapter, a state's first duty when it comes to human rights is to *respect* them. Forcibly severing Mandela's ties with his family attacked both him and his family as social beings, irrespective of whether they could form alternative social bonds with others. That said, since Mandela had some social contact in prison, his situation, while terrible, was not as unjust as that endured by people who suffer persistent, coercive social isolation (or indeed persistent incidental isolation). Sometimes the injustice in these cases comes from undervaluing the importance of people's bonds. But sometimes the injustice comes from fully recognizing the importance of those bonds and using them as a weapon against people.

A related way that a society can attack people's deepest bonds is by forbidding their connections with each other (such as a romantic tie between a Jewish person and a Gentile under the Nazi regime) and, consequently, denying them the space to grieve if they lost their partner, since grief would expose their connection. This in turn denies them the space to make sense of the loss they have suffered, to engage in the grieving rituals around death, and thereby to sustain other people who are also grieving for the same loss or to sustain people who are grieving for other losses. More generally, by denying them an outlet to honour a loved one, it puts at risk their social abilities to commit, care, and be vulnerable to the loss of a loved one. One important condition for a healthy ability to sustain social connections is that people be allowed to grieve.[25]

3.4.2 Protecting Connections

Of course, society can deny people in other ways the chance to form and sustain decent connections. Typically, these ways intersect with other kinds of misfortune, vulnerability, or disadvantage.

First, our social needs intersect with our material, bodily, and cultural needs. A child who grows up in poverty may receive a poor education, which can impact on her ability to care for others later. Or, as noted above, a poor family may be unable to offer much hospitality, which narrows its range of social contribution opportunities. On this point, Jonathan Wolff and Avner de-Shalit say:

> engaging in such expressive activities as *doing good for others*, and *being able to show gratitude*, and even being able *to follow the elementary norms of etiquette*, are important functionings, and...those who cannot afford to do good to others, who cannot show gratitude, and so on, because they lack the (financial or physical) means or the time to do so, are disadvantaged.[26]

Here's a related vignette from Lucy Maud Montgomery's *Anne of Green Gables*. After meeting Diana, who would become her 'bosom' friend, young Anne Shirley is delighted when Matthew returns home with a box of chocolates for her. Anne says to Marilla Cuthbert:

> I'll just eat one tonight, Marilla. And I can give Diana half of them, can't I? The other half will taste twice as sweet to me if I give some to her. It's delightful to think I have something to give her.

It sounds syrupy, but Anne's delight in having something to give to someone she loves—a new experience for her as an orphan who had nothing material before to offer anyone—reflects a powerful human drive to be useful to others.

Second, our social needs intersect with our temporal needs. As Julie Rose argues in her captivating book *Free Time*, in order to effectively exercise freedoms such as the freedom to associate with the people we care about (as well as the freedoms to vote, to practise a religion, and so on), we need not just material resources, but also temporal resources. In the case of associating, we need not only adequate amounts of free time, but also adequate amounts of commonly shared free time to spend with our associates and with potential future associates.[27]

Third, as this implies, our social needs intersect with our political and legal interests. Society can limit our social resources by encroaching upon our political freedoms. By denying us freedom of expression and access to communication channels, by restricting our movement, or by limiting our freedom to practise a religion among other things, society interrupts our efforts to seek companions, to engage with others, to participate in culture, and to affect our world.

3.5 Indirect Victims

Social contribution injustice has multiple victims. As the above discussion shows, a clear indicator that we are essentially social is that we can be harmed, and wronged, when the people whom we love are wronged as social beings.

First, social contribution injustice wrongs not only its direct victim, but also the people who have a right to benefit from that person's use of her social resources. When a person's social resources are compromised, her affiliates' social resources diminish too (though not as much as hers) because they are denied access to the social contributions she would otherwise make to them. Put vividly, society compromises a child's social resources when it puts her father in prolonged solitary confinement. Indeed, unless the child has other forms of family support, society compromises her social resources when it puts her father in an ordinary prison. Similarly, society compromises an ageing couple's social resources when it houses one spouse in a retirement facility that the other spouse cannot easily visit.

Second, more generally, social contribution injustice wrongs the wider community that would otherwise enjoy the ripple effects of a person's and her associates' social contributions to each other. This ripple effect is difficult to quantify, but easy to recognize. It includes things like the person and her associates sustaining each other in ways that model caring relations to the community, and their willingness to extend their care to non-associates because they themselves feel secure and valued.

Admittedly, there's no guarantee that a person will make good social contributions if her social resources are uncompromised.[28] She may do more social damage than good. Even so, the risk of such damage does not remove the social injustice of compromising her social resources. This is because, first, compromising her social resources denies her a chance *to try* to make good social contributions. Second, it denies her a chance to learn from others *how* to make good social contributions.

The fact that social injustice has multiple victims signals that it is more common than we might suppose. So, even if compromising a person's social resources somehow wouldn't *violate* her rights (but only *infringe* them), it could violate the rights of the people who have a legitimate claim to depend on her, who would otherwise benefit from her social contributions, and whose claims are not overridden by the reasons that make our act an infringement of her rights. Put bluntly, the child of the father who goes into solitary confinement, the children of the mother who gets a long jail sentence in a brutal prison, and the older parents of the son who endures long-term medical quarantine are all casualties of severed social bonds. The impact on them does not end once their loved one's social segregation ends. For all of them, the impact can last long after the person is socially reintegrated.

3.6 The Darker Side of Our Need to Sustain

Let me finish this chapter by returning to W. H. Auden's poem 'The More Loving One', which I quoted at the outset:

> If equal affection cannot be,
> Let the more loving one be me.

These lines gesture toward a darker side of sustaining someone else. Paradoxically, when equal affection or effort between us and the person we sustain cannot exist, we might fail to sustain that person precisely because we sustain them better than they sustain us. Put in a question: How must it feel to be loved by someone more than we love them? How must it feel to have another person sustain us more fully than we can sustain them? Some imbalance between people's efforts is fine. It can stem from an imbalance in resources and abilities. But sometimes that imbalance can cause resentment, stress, or distaste. If the imbalance is too great, the sustainer might become repulsive to the person whom she sustains.

Returning to Rose who craves to be precious, we see that, in wanting to be needed and to have her husband know he needs her, she may do little or nothing to advance his well-being. She might instead be a symbol of his inability to be a good husband.

Conclusion

This chapter has shown that we have deep needs both to be dependable and to be depended upon by other people. This need is rooted in our self-interest, other-interest, and group-interest. Denying us the social resources we need to be able to sustain other people threatens our self-interest in many ways, by denying us the protection we should have to meet our moral responsibilities to dependants and associates, to learn from others how to be inclusion-worthy, and to improve our skills as a social contributor. Wronging us as social contributors also wrongs our loved ones, since we are mutually invested. Denying us the means to sustain them robs both us and them of meaningful love-labour; it alienates us from our caring efforts and from the people we seek to sustain.

The nature and strength of our need to sustain others depends on our capacities. To meet this need, we must have the three social resources articulated in Chapter 1: social abilities, social opportunities, and social connections. We are victims of social contribution injustice if these three resources are unjustly compromised in ways that cut off our access to fundamentally important realms of value. We are also victims of unjust prejudice when (a) other people fail to recognize that the social contributions we make are genuine social contributions, or (b) others fail to recognize that we have the capacity, in principle, to be social contributors. We are more likely to be victims of the prejudicial form of social contribution injustice if we are members of particular social groups, including children, people who have committed offences, people with severe impairments, older people, and people who suffer from other forms of disadvantage such as poverty, homelessness, lack of education, bigotry, and ill-health.

This chapter has shown that any discussion of social rights must attend to the contributive dimension of our social needs. The next chapter explores the tension between our need for social connections and our need for interactional and associational control.

4
Interactional Freedom

> For oft, when on my couch I lie
> In vacant or in pensive mood,
> They flash upon that inward eye
> Which is the bliss of solitude...
>
> William Wordsworth, 'I Wandered Lonely as a Cloud' (1807)

Introduction

In E. M. Forster's novel *Howards End* (1910), Helen and Margaret Schlegel meet a young man, Leonard Bast, while attending a concert with friends. When Helen leaves the concert early, she inadvertently takes Leonard's umbrella with her. After the concert, Margaret invites him to walk with her to their home to retrieve his umbrella. That small exchange sows the seeds for a tangle of social connections that leads to an unwed pregnancy for Helen, the death of Leonard, and a charge of manslaughter for Margaret's stepson Charles Wilcox.

The interactions among the characters that lead up to these major events include Margaret and Helen advising Leonard to change employers, as a result of which he ends up unemployed; and Helen bringing an impoverished Leonard and his partner, Jacky, from London to Shropshire to show Margaret how destitute they are, with the result that Margaret's fiancé, Henry Wilcox, is exposed as having had an affair with Jacky ten years earlier when Jacky was working in prostitution in Cyprus. Margaret, who had planned to ask Henry to give Leonard work, forgives Henry for the affair, and then writes to Helen to say she cannot assist Leonard. E. M Forster describes Henry Wilcox's thoughts on Jacky after Margaret forgives him for the affair:

> He had made a clean breast, had been forgiven, and the great thing now was to forget his failure, and to send it the way of other unsuccessful

investments. [In his mind,] Jacky rejoined Howards End and Dude Street, and the vermillion motorcar, and the Argentine Hard Dollars, and all the things and people for whom he had never had much use and had less now.

Henry's view of Jacky as someone who, to his mind, has dropped out of his 'general sphere' of concern, will resurface in the discussion below on the scope and force of our interactional duties.

Often, we are thrown into contact with people through small encounters like those that drive *Howards End*. Sometimes, we can choose whether to expose ourselves to such encounters. Other times, we cannot choose. In each case, we need to have some control over whether we become people's associates through such encounters, with all the normative baggage that *association* implies. Such control is necessary for our self-respect, personal autonomy, and well-being. Our interests in self-respect, autonomy, and well-being are strong enough that they give us substantial rights to associational freedom.

For similar reasons, we need to have some *interactional* control over whether we interact at all with people who are not our associates. And we need some control over *how* we interact with the people with whom we do interact, be they our associates or not. We have interests in being able to choose whether to chat with the talkative person sitting next to us on a long flight and, if we do, for how long; whether to hear out the person who comes to the door to proselytize; whether to listen to the sales rep who phones at dinnertime; and whether to answer the stranger who asks us for the time or for money.[1] And, when the stakes are higher, we have even stronger interests in being able to decide, for example, whether to engage with the person convalescing in the hospital bed next to us for several weeks, or with the person with whom we are confined in prison, or even with the person to whom we are physically conjoined.[2]

We all need routine moments of silence and solitude as a balm for the soul. We need that *bliss* which Wordsworth describes so well. And society benefits when we enjoy such moments. Empirical evidence indicates that we tend to make great creative leaps when we labour alone rather than in face-to-face groups.[3] But, of course, solitude—and the creative leaps it can generate—is a socially embedded experience. As Hannah Arendt puts it,

> even if I shun all company or am completely isolated while forming an opinion, I am not simply together only with myself in the solitude of philosophical thought; I remain in this world of universal interdependence, where I can make myself the representative of everybody else.[4]

Even so, we tend to underrate the bliss, and value, of solitude in our hyper-connected, contemporary world which prizes group-work and seems to make a virtue out of being constantly available.

Once we are in associations, we often find interactional control hard to come by, as caregivers well know. The comedian Tina Fey commented on parenting young children that anyone who enters the bathroom and refuses to leave whilst you're in there is 'a high-level boss'.[5]

Of course, it goes both ways. Once we are in associations, our associates have less interactional control too, because we have the same normative powers and claims over them that they interact regularly with us.[6] One reason that we find interactional control hard to come by in our associations is that, to live well, we all need routine moments in which other people acknowledge us, interact kindly with us, and confirm that we are accepted. When we're vulnerable, dependent, or growing up, we need constant reassurance that we are safe and valued. And we get that reassurance primarily from the people with whom we enjoy persistent, supportive, life-shaping associations (assuming that we have such people in our lives).

Many people who lack close ties rely on momentary interactions with non-associates for their sense of social inclusion. And most of us benefit from such micro-moments of connection even if we are socially integrated. It is through such micro-moments that, paraphrasing H. W. Wright, we satisfy our deep wish to be liked and admired, perform small services to each other, share our knowledge and opinions, cooperate, express sympathy and accord, and offer many small signals of affection and approval with a smile, a brightening eye, and all the elusive tricks of gesture and posture.

> In these ways only is congeniality of mind and temperament established between human individuals. The fulfilment of these same interests…is a necessary factor in the normal growth of self-esteem. Nothing contributes so much to self-confidence in any human individual as his discovery that he can impress and persuade others by his talk, that he can do what is required to extricate himself and others from their practical difficulties, and that his emotional reactions are understood and sympathetically responded to by others.[7]

One might disagree with Wright about the *greatest* contributor to self-confidence while agreeing with him that our ordinary, mutually supportive interactions offer a powerful site in which we can affirm our sense of self-worth. Indeed, his observation aligns broadly with the position I defended in the previous chapter: that we have a deep interest in being able to be valuable to other people.

Micro-moments of connection are also important, if not indispensable, to our physical and psychological health. According to social psychologist Barbara Fredrickson, when we connect harmoniously with someone else for a moment, a beautifully choreographed biological dance unfolds as our smiles, gestures, and postures come to mirror each other, and our heart rhythms, biochemistries, and neuro-firings become synchronized, creating a momentary resonance of goodwill between us. Having such micro-moments of connection in our lives changes us physically and emotionally for the better, making the rhythms of our heart healthier. And, the causal arrow runs both ways, Fredrickson says: our heart's capacity for love obeys the biological law 'Use or lose it'.[8]

We have, in short, two powerful, competing interactional needs: a need for interactional control and a need for social inclusion. The tension between these two needs highlights that our ordinary interactional decisions are governed not just by etiquette and prudence, but also by morality. Nowadays, we tend to take a cavalier, chat-to-everyone approach to our interactions, with the consequence that, unless some social norm excuses us, we usually feel pressed to respond to someone's social overtures even if we already feel depleted from other interactions, and even if we know that frequent direct interactions with a non-associate will often solidify into an association (as discussed in Chapter 1) with claims, duties, powers, and immunities that we might have good reason to avoid.

A key moral question then is: Which of our two competing interactional needs should prevail when they conflict? Is it right that we should feel pressed to respond, and remiss if we rebuff people's overtures? Do we act wrongly, but within our rights if we rebuff people's overtures? To answer such questions, we must address three more specific issues:

1. *Content.* What kinds of choices, attitudes, and behaviours does our interactional freedom protect?
2. *Scope.* How expansive is this freedom? How much interactional freedom do our interests in well-being, self-respect, and autonomy secure for us in principle?
3. *Value.* What is the value of interactional freedom? How does that value compare with the value of securing each other's core social needs regardless of our interactional preferences?[9] Which set of needs has lexical priority?

Interactional freedom is one of two forms of what I shall call *interpersonal freedom*. Our other form of interpersonal freedom is associational freedom. The next three chapters explore similar questions about content, scope, and value in relation to associational freedom, to determine how expansive is our freedom to associate or not as we please with whom we please in the ways we please, as well as what rights-protected space we have to act *wrongly* when we form, maintain, dissolve, and avoid particular associations. Those chapters also compare the scope and value of associational freedom with that of our other personal freedoms such as freedom of expression or religion.

Confident defenders of interpersonal freedom will answer questions about scope with statements like: 'There is no question of the state's forcing us [as adults] to be in social relationships with any other human beings.'[10] Or, 'We have the right to choose the society most acceptable to us.'[11] Such grand statements about scope lead to a particular answer to questions about value, namely, that our interpersonal *freedom* is of primary importance, and guaranteeing other people social inclusion is secondary. But both this chapter and Chapters 5 and 6 show that, in general, positive social claims necessarily take priority over interpersonal freedom.

The present chapter focuses on interactional freedom because it is an important issue that has received too little attention in normative theory. This chapter aims to give interactional freedom its analytic due. Let's start by pinning down what happens when we interact with each other.

4.1 The Nature of Interactional Freedom

4.1.1 Interactions versus Associations

Interactions are reciprocal actions through which we mutually influence each other. Typically, an interaction is a direct encounter that begins with an *interactional bid*. One person makes an overture or bid for connection to another person, expecting some response. That response may, or may not, leave the door open to interact further. If the second person responds (at all) in a way that leaves the door open, then the first person can decide whether to continue to interact. If the second person doesn't respond at all, then the first person's interactional bid fails and no interaction occurs. As this suggests, interactions have success conditions. *Trying* to interact with someone is insufficient. The second person must respond.[12] (*Trying* to interact is also often unnecessary. If we accidentally bump someone while walking down the street, that usually triggers an interaction even though we made no interactional bid.) If the second person responds by slamming the interactional door—telling the first person to shut up, for example—then the first person must decide whether to accept the dismissal. And if they don't accept it, then the interaction may turn nasty.[13]

Interactions can be decent or not, in their form or their content. The *form* refers to the manner in which one person addresses another, be it kindly or aggressively. The *content* refers to the substance of what she says or does. The person who slams the interactional door by shouting 'Shut up!' at her addresser does not display decency in either the form or content of her response. But she might be justified in being aggressive, if the interactional bid that he made to her involved sexual harassment, for example. (Many, but by no means all, aggressive responses to interactional bids fall within the category of micro-aggressions. According to one conception, *microaggressions* are 'the everyday, minor, and apparently innocuous "degradations, and put-downs" experienced by *members of oppressed, systematically disadvantaged or marginalized groups*'.[14])

People can use decent forms of interaction without using decent content, and vice versa. Someone's interactional efforts are decent in content but not in form when, for instance, she angrily shouts something trivial at someone: 'The door is over there!' And her interactional efforts are decent in form but not in content when she says something vicious in a gentle, friendly voice: 'You are not worth the dust which the rude wind blows in your face.'

Another element salient to decency is *context*. Gently saying things that are kind might in fact be unkind to someone. If the person to whom we are kind and friendly is someone we have rejected romantically, we might give that person false hope and make it harder for them to move on.

Let's put aside these complexities of form, content, and context to focus on our ordinary, deliberate, *decent* interactions with each other, which offer us brief moments of micro-connection. We can interact directly face-to-face or via various media. We can interact in a moment or after a long pause: two people corresponding by snail mail are interacting despite the time-lag. (Two people 'corresponding' by message-in-a-bottle are not interacting.) We typically interact verbally in speech or writing, which makes it tempting to equate *interaction* with *dialogue*. But *dialogue* has connotations that *interaction* lacks. A dialogue is necessarily a propositional activity. By contrast, our interactions often take non-propositional forms that include music, dance, physical touch, facial expressions, and joint labour. Such activities are generally communicative, but they need not convey propositional content. Also, a dialogue is a normatively loaded activity in which we are roughly equal players—both speakers and listeners—who aim to achieve some mutual understanding through our encounter. Our non-dialogic interactions often lack such ambitions.

Our ordinary, non-associative interactions tend to be momentary, one-off, and goal-oriented exchanges marked by mutual disinterest, courtesy, and a context-specific acknowledgement of each other's wishes. We exchange greetings with shop clerks, thank the people who brings us our post, and help people to retrieve wayward coins, receiving a 'thank you' in return. Such moments usually have no lasting effect on us.

But, as noted above, these moments *can* have a lasting effect on us. First, for the lonely older person, the weekly chat with the grocery store clerk, the brief exchange with the postal worker, and the visit to the doctor are vitally important if they are her primary sources of social contact. She may give such 'mere' interactions the meaning that other people give to their intimate ties.[15] Indeed, in the UK, 76% of GPs report that one to five patients a day come to their clinic because they are lonely.[16]

If a person is slightly more socially embedded in a collective association such as a local charity or chapter of a political party, for example, then she may imbue that connection with the meaning that other people give to their intimate ties. One problem is that, even though our need to belong can be met in many ways, momentary, non-associative interactions and collective associations are ill-suited to satisfy this need by themselves because, for one thing, they are often insignificant to the other participants and, for another, they usually exist for reasons other than to secure our core social needs.[17]

Second, regardless of how well-connected we are, momentary, non-associative interactions can weave themselves into the tapestry of our self-image. The film adaptation of *Howards End* contains a small but memorable scene in which Margaret Schlegel and Ruth Wilcox are walking together to catch a train. As they walk, Margaret happily tells Mrs Wilcox of an experience she'd had once on another train. She says:

> It was so romantic. It was in Italy. Yes, and the two trains stopped on either side. I opened the window and this man handed a rose across. I don't know where he got it...

This lovely, fleeting encounter was not life-defining, but nonetheless stayed with Margaret to become an anecdote she could share with friends of a stranger's admiration for her. In a small way, it became part of her self-conception.

Third, sometimes momentary interactions *can* be life-defining. They can become the *one* moment we regret, the day we wish we could do over, the person we prefer we'd never met, or the moment for which we're forever grateful. A chance conversation with a stranger who shares a crucial bit of information can lead us to pursue a different life-path. A one-night stand that leads to pregnancy has life-defining consequences for, at least, the woman and the child who might be born as a result.

Given the impact that momentary, non-associative interactions can have on our lives, it's worth commenting further on the cavalier, chat-to-everyone approach that we tend to take to interactions today. This approach contrasts with the more stilted but possibly wiser approaches of earlier times. Among the British gentry for example, it was impolite—and possibly still is impolite—to address someone to whom you have not been introduced. In Jane Austen's novel *Pride and Prejudice*, Elizabeth Bennett becomes distressed when her cousin Mr Collins informs her at the Netherfield Park ball that he plans to introduce himself to Mr Darcy, who is the nephew of Mr Collins's patroness, Lady Catherine de Bourgh. Elizabeth tries to dissuade him, telling him:

> Mr Darcy would consider him addressing him without introduction as an impertinent freedom, rather than a compliment to his aunt; that it was not in the least necessary there should be any notice on either side, and that if it were, it must belong to Mr Darcy, as the superior in consequence, to begin the acquaintance.

Mr Collins dismisses Elizabeth's advice and proceeds 'to attack' Mr Darcy, who shows astonishment, distant civility, and then contempt at being addressed. Mr Darcy's display of distant civility highlights an important distinction between acknowledging someone's overture, which I argue below we often have a duty to do, and actively taking up whatever form of continued interaction the person proposes.

In describing Mr Collins's efforts as an *attack*, Jane Austen flags an important question about interactions: When we make an interactional bid do we burden or benefit our intended addressee? The answer is, of course, 'It depends.' It depends partly on the content of the bid. If we ask someone for the time, we burden him in the simple sense that we request information. But we might also fortify him by reminding him that he can be useful to other people. (Indeed, according to some psychology studies, one way to make someone like us a little more is to ask a favour of them. This is the so-called Ben Franklin Effect.) If, by contrast, we offer our intended addressee free flowers, we support him in a simple sense by giving him a gift, but we may also burden him if he doesn't want the flowers, thereby forcing him to refuse them or take them unwillingly. His perceptions matter. But they only matter so much. He might view our bid as burdensome, yet ultimately benefit from it. Or he might welcome our bid, yet ultimately be harmed by it. In the case of Mr Collins, he intends to benefit Mr Darcy, or at least not harm him while benefiting himself, but he merely offends him.

Whether we burden our addressee also depends on the way we present ourselves to them. With some overtures, we essentially say 'Recognize me as a fellow human being', but with other overtures we essentially say 'Recognize me as your superior'.[18] For example, when a cisgender person asks a transgender person personal questions about their sexual identity, or when a stranger places their hand on a pregnant woman's stomach, or when a man makes a sexually aggressive overture to a woman, they are each saying to their addressee deliberately or not: 'Recognise me as your superior in the sense that I am entitled to approach you and engage with you in this way'. It is not always clear which kind of overture a person is making to someone, but the context will usually be revealing. The second kind of overture reinforces unspoken hierarchies; it reaffirms that the addresser has a *de facto* entitlement not only to approach their addressee in this way, but to receive a response from them. In the case of a man making a sexually aggressive overture to a woman, the message is essentially: 'Recognize me as a man who has a right to your attention in this moment and a right to your conciliatory response. Or else.' I return to these ideas below.

Between the bookends of our non-associative interactions and our persistent associations, there is the antiquated grey area of our acquaintances. Consider Jane Bennett's description of Mr Bingley in *Pride and Prejudice*. After Bingley leaves for London and Miss Bingley persuades Jane that he does not care about her, Jane says to Elizabeth, 'He may live in my memory as the most amiable man of my acquaintance, but that is all.' Jane's declaration is striking, since she loves Bingley. But propriety makes it unfitting for her to think of him as a friend or romantic prospect without some sign that he will continue to pay addresses to her.

Acquaintanceship is the garden in which closer ties grow, though those ties can be sometimes more like weeds to us than flowers. As noted at the outset, if someone takes the initiative to interact with us, and we respond without hostility, then, after enough back-and-forth, we are liable to her normative power, and she to ours, to expect that these interactions will continue in a way that cements a persisting association. An example of this comes in another Jane Austen novel, *Sense and Sensibility*. After being forced to relocate from Norland Park to Barton Cottage following their father's death, Elinor and Marianne Dashwood are invited by their kinsman Sir John Middleton to meet his guests, Anne and Lucy Steele. After meeting them, Elinor departs with the view that

> [t]he vulgar freedom and folly of the eldest left her no recommendation, and as Elinor was not blinded by the beauty, or the shrewd look of the youngest [Lucy], to her want of real elegance and artlessness, she left the house without any wish of knowing them better.[19]

But, through Sir John's bonhomie, Elinor is pressed to know them better. So she endures repeated meetings that lead to Lucy burdening her with the secret that she is engaged to marry Edward Ferrars, the man whom Elinor admires—a confidence that later strains Elinor's relationship with her sister, Marianne, who is kept in the dark. To have avoided Lucy's confidences, Elinor would have had to do more to prevent Lucy from forming associative expectations. Yet Elinor would have struggled to do this without giving offence to her benefactor, Sir John.

Interactions are a constituent element of, prerequisite for, and almost inevitable generator of associations. People are a 'family' in name only if they never interact with each other.[20] People are a 'family' in little more than name if they interact only indirectly or hostilely. By contrast, people *are* a family, even if they don't call themselves that, if they live together and depend on each other, and their interactions are direct, frequent, and mutually caring.

These affective features of care and love are one of many differences between paradigmatic intimate associations with family and friends and collective associations such as unions and clubs, which I elaborate in the next chapters. Other differences are that intimate associations require no further expressive, cultural, aesthetic, or political purpose beyond associating to motivate their existence. They can exist for their own sake, and they are distinguished by their interactions, persistence, and comprehensiveness. By contrast, collective associations usually have some further purpose as outlets for people to express shared values and pursue shared goals, and their members' desire to be exclusive tends to dominate discussions of associational rights.[21] Even a 'friends club' will be animated by an overarching purpose that can clash with individual members' associational aims. Since, however, collective associations—like acquaintanceships—are often the sites in which intimate ties grow, we should think of our associations not in binary terms, but as lying along a spectrum of intimacy with the more impersonal and instrumental at one end and the more personal and non-instrumental at the other.

Other distinguishing features of our most intimate associations, such as their small size, selectivity, and seclusion, derive from their interactivity, comprehensiveness, and persistence. Given that we must invest time and energy to sustain such associations, we can have only a few of them. Our positive decision to associate closely with persons A to F entails that we cannot associate closely with persons G to Z. And since, typically, we wish to invest our energies well, we tend to be selective about the people with whom we form close ties. (But, of course, we cannot always be selective. We cannot select our biological relations even though those are often the closest ties we have.[22])

Let's sum up what we have established so far. First, non-associative interactions can leave lasting impressions in our lives. Second, even when they fail to leave lasting impressions, they are personally and morally important, since they signal, and reassure us, that we are generally accepted. As I argue below, acknowledging each other through basic, decent interactions is a key part of respecting each other's humanity. Third, decent, non-associative interactions are the Petri dish for acquaintances. And acquaintanceships, which we often skip over nowadays, are the garden in which closer ties bloom. We may conclude therefore that, for all these reasons, decent, non-associative interactions are central to our practice of living harmoniously with each other. Such interactions both grease the wheels of human harmony and are meaningful sites of social connection in their own right.[23] And our interests in having good interactions can clash with our interests in having control over whether, when, and how we interact with people. Before assessing the normative implications of that clash, let's pin down the conceptual contours of interactional *freedom*.

4.1.2 Positive and Negative Interactional Freedom

Both interactional freedom and associational freedom have two sides. The positive side captures whatever freedom we have to interact or associate with other people. The negative side captures whatever freedom we have to *refuse* to interact or associate with people.

The positive or pro-social side of our interactional freedom captures both our *general* freedom to interact and our *particular* freedoms to interact with particular people. The general freedom depends on the particular freedom. If we have no particular freedom to interact with particular people (who may or may not be our preferred company), then we have no meaningful general freedom of interaction. And, of course, the particular freedom depends on the general freedom. If we have no general freedom to interact at all, then we have no freedom to have particular interactions with particular people.

The negative or antisocial side captures both our *general* freedom not to interact and our *particular* freedoms not to interact with particular people. Again, if we lack the freedom to avoid or terminate particular interactions with particular people, then we have no meaningful general freedom here.

Next, the positive side captures the range of interactive means we are at liberty to use, including audial, visual, haptic, physical, verbal, linguistic, and emotional means. Typically, we interact differently on the football field than in the courtroom, in the surgery room, in the trenches, on the street, or in the opera house. The norms that govern these settings are not purely prudential, aesthetic, or social. They are also moral, as we will see in Section 4.2. (Similarly, in the case of persistent association, the positive side captures whatever freedom we have to engage in specific kinds of association-defining activities, such as romantic, sexual, parental, fraternal, professional, mercenary, competitive, sportive, or collegial activities. The norms that govern these settings are also deeply moral.)

Both the negative and positive sides of our freedom are necessary for us to have a complete freedom, which is different from having *unlimited* freedom. *Completeness* means having both the option to act and the option not to act in a situation. Unless we have both options, we have but half a freedom. We can put the point either in terms of what is *permissible* or in terms of what is *possible*. Regarding *permissibility*, when we are forbidden to address other people, we lack complete interactional freedom, as we have only the 'option' not to interact. For example, in many prisons, prisoners must be silent, or whisper to each other and fear the consequences. For another example, in interactions with the Queen of England, people may not speak to her until she addresses them; nor may they touch her or turn their backs to her. Once the Queen addresses someone, she alters their normative, interactional position by making it permissible for them to respond to her.

Regarding *possibility*, when we *cannot* address other people, we equally lack complete interactional freedom. For example, a person held in isolation in a soundproof cell *cannot* interact with anyone and so has only the 'option' to be alone. In the spirit of Joel Feinberg, to say that we have *freedom* not to interact in such cases is similar, grammatically, to saying that a woman has two children when in fact she has three. To say that she has two children is correct, but misleading, since we assume that it means she has *only* two children.[24]

Conversely, if we have no option but to interact with other people, then again we lack complete interactional freedom. Sometimes, we are *required* to respond to people. For instance, some legal jurisdictions reject the right to silence; and jurisdictions that recognize the right to silence tend to make exceptions in some criminal proceedings, thereby commanding the people involved to speak. In other contexts, we *cannot* be silent, such as when we are being tortured and there too we lack complete interactional freedom. (Our screams are interactional bids, if not parts of an interaction.)

Briefly, the same analysis applies to persistent associations. If we have no option, morally speaking, but to associate with someone, such as the young baby whom we are raising, then we lack complete associational freedom. Equally, if we have no option, practically speaking, but to associate with some people, such as the twin with whom we are conjoined or the fellow workers with whom we are trapped in a mine, then we lack complete associational freedom. We have half a freedom, since we have only the option (if it can be called an 'option') to associate.

The same is true when we have no option *to* associate. If we are forbidden to associate with anyone, like the prisoner who is held in long-term solitary confinement, or if we cannot associate with anyone, like the solitary older person who cannot leave the house without help and so cannot easily sustain her connections, then again we really have but half a freedom. To say that we have a freedom to associate when we're duty-bound or forced to associate (or not) is misleading, since we assume rightly that *freedom of association* includes both the options to associate and to dissociate.

Now, some people are unable exercise *any* interpersonal freedom at all, such as babies, very young children, and people with severe cognitive impairments. Specifically, they lack the competence to exercise control over their core social environment: they cannot extract themselves from families or caregivers; they cannot introduce themselves to new acquaintances. Hence, they cannot be the subjects of rights pertaining to interpersonal *freedom*. Indeed, such freedom sits outside the scope of their interests. But, as we have seen throughout this book, they do have acute positive interactional and associational needs.

Similarly, some people are *not permitted* to exercise much, if any, interpersonal freedom; this is the lot of prisoners, slaves, and kidnap victims. Prisoners may be able to exercise *some* control if they are allowed to choose whether to form alliances, join voluntary prison groups, meet people who come to visit them, and divorce a spouse while in prison. However, they cannot choose their cellmates or lack of cellmates or the amount of time they spend with those cellmates. I return to the associational plight of people in prison in Chapter 8.

With the positive and negative forms of interactional freedom on the table, our next question to ask is: What *kind* of freedom is interactional freedom? Answering this question takes us into the territory of *scope*, since different personal freedoms can garner differently sized spheres of protected action.

4.1.3 Expressive Freedom or Associational Freedom?

Are our interactional efforts best understood as expressive acts or proto-associative acts or some other thing? Put differently, does our interactional freedom fall under the umbrella of freedom of *expression* or freedom of *association* or some other freedom?

At one level, our interactional bids seem to be well-described as expressive acts because they involve approaches. Hence, interactional freedom seems to be a freedom to approach, to address, to seek to engage with another person, as well as a jointly held freedom of two interacting people to continue their interactional activity unimpeded. As a form of expressive freedom, interactional freedom is not a general right to be *heard*. Nor is it a right to be responded to. It's a right to make an overture and, only if that overture is accepted, to continue to interact.

But, as Onora O'Neill observes, our standard purpose when we express something is to *communicate*. We don't aim merely to make noise and be ignored. So, when our addressee does not respond to us, she influences our possibilities for self-expression. 'Doing nothing', O'Neill points out, 'may convey disapproval and hostility.' And in extreme cases, it can signal ostracism or rejection. It can convey the message that we are not fully human. 'More commonly, doing nothing signals that what [we seek] to convey will be viewed as *mere* expression and not as a communication.'[25]

When we make interactional bids, we actually intend to do more than communicate. We intend to connect, to influence, and to affect our addressee, and to have her signal in response that we have succeeded. We also usually intend to learn, to share information, and to gain and affirm our sense of self-worth. We wish not just to address and be addressed in a call-and-response, but to sustain a moment of reciprocal connection with someone. Hence, our interactional bids amount to something more than either barebones noise-making expression or expression in the O'Neillian communicative-effort sense. Interactional freedom might seem, therefore, to be better categorized as a freedom to make associative efforts, a freedom *to try* to forge associations with others.

But an *associative* conception of *interactional effort* only works when it works. As noted above, in our momentary interactions with non-associates, we often try to curtail people's expectations which could lead to persistent associations.

However, even in those exchanges, we do aim to participate in the world of social connections, and we know that that world contains many routes to association which we might ultimately walk down even if we weren't looking for them.

The take-home message is that interactional freedom sits somewhere between expressive freedom and associational freedom, which is why I locate it under the heading of *interpersonal freedom*. One reason to care about its exact location between the two poles of expression and association is its scope. Our protected sphere for free expression is larger than our protected sphere for free association and dissociation (a point I discuss further in the next chapters).[26] Consequently, if interaction sits closer to (mere) expression than to association, then we enjoy considerably more latitude in our interactional efforts and rebuffs than we do if interaction is proto-associative. If interaction sits closer to association than to expression (as I think it does), then our interactional behaviour, especially our rebuffing behaviour, is constrained by the impact it can have on other people.

To unpack this last thought, let's return to O'Neill's point that, in extreme cases, we deny someone's humanity when we ignore her. This fact bears not only on the scope but also on the value of interactional freedom.

4.2 The Value of Interactional Freedom

A person who ignores a stranger's interactional bid might do so defensibly if he's rushing to the hospital to see his spouse, for example, or if he doesn't hear the person bidding for his attention, or if he is alone in a strange city, or if he is rightly angry with the bidder for her recent appalling behaviour.

He might also defensibly ignore someone's bid if he is reasonably feeling depleted from other interactions,[27] or if the bidder addresses him from an unjustified position of superiority. But, in ordinary cases where these extenuating circumstances do not apply and her overture says 'Recognise me as a fellow human', his rebuff essentially says: 'I don't worry about what you think of me. I doubt that you can do sufficiently important things for me or sufficiently serious things *to* me that I should worry about how my rebuff makes you feel.' He communicates both that she is inferior to him and that what she offers him or asks of him lacks value. In the extreme case, as O'Neill says, he signals that, to him, she is not really human.

The horribleness of this message forces us to reconsider our knee-jerk liberal belief that, when we exercise our interactional freedom to ignore a stranger, we probably do something rude, but not something immoral. Or, if we do occasionally do something immoral, we act well within our rights. The liberal view would say that we're not morally required to acknowledge *every* person who bids for our attention. Indeed, in general, we're not morally required to acknowledge *any* person who is not our associate. We're permitted to ignore them. And we have good, commonsense reasons for ignoring some people, including some of our associates, particularly when they have offended some norm that we endorse.

I reject these claims about moral permissibility. The default liberal view ignores the fact that the lines between social niceties, etiquette, and morality are blurry at best because our practices of polite acknowledgement (including much of what we call *etiquette*) are signals of respect.[28] Holding the door open for someone; saying hello, please, thank you, and good-bye; answering politely when addressed politely; listening politely; taking our shoes off when we enter someone's house; arriving on time; setting the table nicely for guests; giving gifts and accepting gifts in return, and so on are all ways in which we show respect in Western societies. Equivalent signals pervade all other societies. They convey our willingness to recognize and respect each other's humanity.

Neither a society nor a person can say that they respect someone else's humanity if they persistently fail to interact with her in ordinary, decent ways along these lines. Just as not providing food to someone who desperately needs it signals that we don't respect her humanity, so too does persistently refusing to interact with her, because it disregards her essential need for decent social contact. The negative impact that we have on her will be muted when other people pick up the social slack, just as the negative impact we have on someone by denying her food will be muted when others provide it. But the disrespect remains.[29]

The felt experience of universal disrespect—or dismissal—is described by Gregory P. Smith, who, after a childhood marred by domestic violence and time in an orphanage and juvenile detention centre, lived as a homeless person, moving 'up and down the eastern seaboard of Australia for a quarter of a century'. He says, 'every homeless person has one thing in common: they know how it feels to be an outcast.' Smith states that, 'I felt so invisible that sometimes being bashed was a relief: at least the thugs were engaging with me...In a twisted way, I sometimes felt a bashing was preferable to being "blanked" by the general public.' And, 'For the most part, to be homeless is to be see-through.' 'In my experience, the vast majority of passersby pretend that the unfortunate soul on the park bench or huddled on the inner-city footpath in front of them simply isn't there.' After two decades, he couldn't stand it, and retreated into the bush: 'As a bush-dwelling hermit, I was finally spared the humiliation of being ignored by the population.'[30]

My general point here, following Leslie Green, is that it's not enough for respect that, when we think about something valuable—like a person—we think of her in ways consistent with her value. That would mean that, to avoid disrespect, all we need to do is *not* think about her at all, which would leave us in a morally safe position when we thoughtlessly pass by the homeless person begging on the street, and would leave Henry Wilcox in a morally safe position when he casts Jacky from his mind like the vermillion motor car and other failed investments for which he no longer has any use. Instead, to avoid disrespect, Green says, we must give thought to the people who fall within our general sphere and we must give them thought that is consistent with their value. Green observes that some people about whom we do not think, such as homeless people, find themselves in that position owing to forms of social isolation or invisibility that are the products and expressions of disrespect for them.[31]

Admittedly, Green leaves vague what it takes for someone to fall within our 'general sphere'. It's context-sensitive, he says. But 'in our societies it does not require anything like the sort of reasons we have to know our friends, neighbors, colleagues, or customers—the knowledge that helps make them parts of our lives...[W]e do have a general reason to think about people about whom we can significantly think, should we turn our minds to it, and...a failing here can be a failure to respect them as persons.'[32] Needless to say, if someone makes an interactional bid to us, then that person comes within our general sphere: through their bid they make themselves someone about whom we can significantly think.[33] That said, a stranger need not bid for our attention to fall within our general sphere. Bidding is sufficient, but not necessary, for someone to come within our general sphere. The homeless person who is sitting quietly on the street corner may well not make a bid because she has bid unsuccessfully so many times before. But she nonetheless falls within our general sphere when we pass by because she is someone about whom we can significantly think.[34]

As this suggests, our 'general sphere' is not set by our preferences and habits but by our moral capacity to think and act. As such, the idea of a *general sphere* helps to specify the scope of our interactional duties: they are shaped partly by the parameters of our general sphere. In light of these thoughts, we must conclude that we do do something *pro tanto* wrong when we ignore people who bid for our attention. The next question is: Do we act within our rights when we do this wrong?

Above, I flagged that the stilted patterns of interaction that defined Jane Austen's day have some merits, because they manage our expectations for closer connections. Undoubtedly, we lose some spontaneously created value when we adopt stilted, reticent patterns of interaction, but we also avoid doing some harms too. For this reason, and for the reasons relating to self-respect, autonomy, and well-being noted above, we do have rights to rebuff many people's bids for connection even though doing so is often wrong. Our right to rebuff people is defeated, however, when no one else can or will step forward to take up interactional duties that must be honoured—namely, when vulnerable people do not receive the decent social interactions they badly need or when they are coercively denied access to human contact.

As this implies, in such cases our interactional duties are collective duties that pose collective action problems, coordination problems, and free-riding problems. Typically, anyone can do the interactional job—it just needs to be done. In this way, interactions are akin to rescue situations. Think of a woman who is attacked in a town square within view of our neighbouring houses. None of us calls the police because we all assume someone else has done it. We don't *all* need to call the police. Indeed, it's better if we don't all do that. But at least one of us needs to do it. And, the rest of us have a duty to ensure that it is done. The woman's right to assistance cuts across the distinction between rights *in rem* and rights *in personam*. She has a right to be aided, but no right that any particular one of us should do the aiding. She has, at most, a right against all of us who are well placed to aid her that we coordinate to ensure that she is aided.[35]

Similarly, the non-associated, vulnerable person who badly needs decent interactions to lead a minimally good life as a social being has a right to be aided, but no right that any particular one of us should do the aiding. She has a right that all of us in whose general sphere she falls attend to whether she is being aided. And, when push comes to shove, her right to be aided takes priority over our rights not to interact.

In both cases, the needy person has a right not just that we coordinate to ensure she is aided, but that we coordinate to ensure she is aided *adequately well*. Rescuers vary in what they can offer. In the same way that a person who has rotten fruit to share shouldn't be the one tasked with meeting starving people's needs, so too a person whose interactional skills are particularly poor shouldn't be left by us to meet a vulnerable person's interactional needs.[36] Our third-party duties demand more from us.

The necessary aid that a socially vulnerable person requires often includes the resources to support others. As we saw in Chapter 3, we have a deep, rights-grounding interest in being able to sustain specific other people. Often, a person needing access to decent interactions doesn't need social *rescue* in any simple sense. Instead, often, she needs the material resources and social opportunities to be able to serve others and to reciprocate their kindnesses to her. Jonathan Wolff and Avner de-Shalit note that many people with severe disabilities are distressed by their inability to perform simple services that typically express respect and friendship for others, such as making a visitor a cup of tea. Wolff and de-Shalit point out: 'This lack [of ability] can cut deep into self-respect.' They also note that many people living in poverty report feeling shame that they are unable to reciprocate in the giving of gifts. This inability is a serious disadvantage: in some places, it generates a risk of social exclusion. And in all places, it generates for people a feeling of humiliation and a loss of honour that they lack the means to express respect, love, or gratitude to others.[37] Wolff and de-Shalit quote Deepa Narayan et al.'s interview with a poor person from Ghana who said that 'being poor is when you know "good" but you cannot do "good" because you don't have the means.'[38] Moreover, as Wolff and de-Shalit note, disadvantages like these are often corrosive. They compound each other. One compounding disadvantage of disability and of poverty is that these experiences continue to be stigmatizing. When we ignore or shun people who confront these disadvantages, we compound their experience of inability, humiliation, and isolation.

Now, a critic might accept some of the above points, but argue that our interactional rights are conditional at least on our good standing and good behaviour. Non-associative interactional rights are not secure claims like (some) associational rights because we may permissibly shun a non-associate who acts badly, so the argument goes. The case *par excellence* is Captain Charles Boycott. The term 'boycott' comes to us from Boycott's story as a prominent object of organized isolation during the Irish Land War of the late 1800s. Boycott was the unpopular land agent for an absent landlord in County Mayo, who charged high rents and evicted non-compliant tenants. The Irish Land League encouraged the local community not to use violence in protest, but instead to refuse to interact with Boycott. The local people not only withheld their labour in his fields and house, but also refused to supply him with food, deliver his post, do business with him, or acknowledge him.[39] In short, seemingly, he acted so badly that he forfeited whatever interactional rights he could have asserted.

In reply, although we can appreciate the local tenants' reasons for ostracizing Boycott, our basic interactional rights are not conditional on good standing and good behaviour. One reason, as I argued in Chapter 2, is that many other rights are meaningfully available only when our fundamental social rights are protected. Therefore, these rights cannot be conditional on good behaviour except when our conduct is so egregious that we forfeit not only our right against social deprivation but also all our rights that depend on that right, including civil and political rights, brute survival rights, education rights, healthcare rights, and, in extreme cases, all rights requiring the maintenance of clear thought. Consequently, despite his abysmal conduct, Boycott retained his basic rights to have access to decent interactions of some sort with some people.

That said, rights are defeasible. And, the local tenants could appeal to their own rights to defend their refusal to interact with him. (When a person's right is *defeated* rather than forfeited he is owed some apology or recompense.) The local tenants could also point to the fact that their ostracism did not render Boycott socially destitute. Boycott differed from wholly ostracized people like the solitarily confined prisoner or the person banished to a deserted island, because he was well connected. He recruited 50 Orangemen to harvest his landlord's fields when the locals stayed away, and he had a 1,000-strong guard escort the workers to and from the fields. Additionally, he had vocal supporters in England, who saw his ostracism as an attack on a representative of a peer of the realm. After the year of crisis in 1880, Boycott left Ireland to retire in England. All in all, the harm that the locals did to him was modest, since he could secure his basic interactional needs in other ways.

In sum, Boycott's mistreatment of the local people made their breach of his rights less morally objectionable than it otherwise would have been. Assuming that no less coercive protest strategies were meaningfully available to them, and that their conduct did not reduce his existence below that of a minimally good human life, their breach, while not morally stainless, was both rights-protected and defensible all things considered.

Conclusion

This chapter has examined the fact that we all have fundamental interests in having interactional control according to our abilities to exercise it, rooted in our deep interests in personal autonomy, self-respect, and well-being. This chapter has also investigated our competing fundamental interests in having access to adequate interactional opportunities and positive interactional support, particularly when we are vulnerable, rooted in our core social needs as well as our interests in autonomy, self-respect, and well-being. This chapter has challenged the knee-jerk liberal thought that we do no moral wrong when we rebuff non-associates' interactional bids. It has also challenged the thought that, if we do do wrong, we are invariably rights-protected when we rebuff people. This chapter shows that we have at most a conditional right to rebuff people provided that their basic interactional needs will be met. I will elaborate my defence of this claim in the next chapter, where I explore more closely the moral fallout of our interactional and associational decision-making.

5
Dilemmas of Sociability

Introduction

In C. S. Lewis's *Lion, the Witch, and the Wardrobe*, Peter, Susan, Edmund, and Lucy Pevensie are evacuated from London during the Blitz like hundreds of thousands of other children, mothers, and babies, who were sent between 1939 and 1945 to live with families in the English countryside. Many children, like the Pevensies, were separated from their parents, grandparents, and older siblings. Some returned home after a few weeks. Others were billeted throughout the war. Many of the billeting families were conscripted into housing the evacuees. Both the hosts and the evacuees saw their freedom to dissociate and be exclusive within their families trumped by the evacuees' survival needs.

Similarly, at the end of the Second World War, as Laura Valentini notes, 'many [people] fled the Russian-occupied eastern parts of Germany and moved to the territories occupied by the British and American armies. Families residing there were forced to house refugees in their homes, in some cases for protracted periods of time. Here, the host families' interest in associating with whomever they wanted was set back, but, it would seem, justifiably so.'[1]

Although these two examples pertain to emergencies, they are not exceptions to how we should rank associational rights.[2] This chapter and the next show that our fundamental positive social rights to persistent associations take priority over our freedom of dissociation when the two conflict. One ground for this conclusion surfaces when we ask the familiar Kantian question that is the focus of this chapter: 'What if everyone did that?' Answering this question forces us to recognize that, while associational freedom is important, it is secondary to the positive social claim-rights that protect our fundamental social needs and are preconditions for any associational control worth the name. Other grounds for this conclusion that positive social rights take priority will be explored in Chapter 6.

The 'What if everyone did that?' question essentially asks whether we could rationally will it to be the case that everyone acts on some maxim, or, as Derek Parfit notes, whether we could rationally will it that *everyone* acts on some maxim rather than that *no one* does. This question applies to what Parfit calls *each-we dilemmas*. Such dilemmas arise in cases where:

> if *each* rather than none of us does what would be in a certain way *better*, we would be doing what would be, in this same way, *worse*.[3]

Such each-we dilemmas occur often in the realm of human sociality. For instance, Chapter 1 referenced the *bystander effect*, the *commons dilemma*, and *social loafing*. And Chapter 4 briefly considered the bystander effect when we all ignore someone's basic interactional needs. These examples of non-cooperative behaviour can serve our narrow self-interest as individuals only when not everyone adopts these behaviours. Hearteningly, Roy Baumeister and Mark Leary, whose work was discussed in Chapter 1, argue that these non-cooperative, anti-social behaviours tend to disappear when we have social attachments to each other, and even sometimes when we have no attachment yet, but only the future prospect of continued interaction.

The kinds of each-we dilemmas that interest us here pertain to our associational (and interactional) choices that make our lives go better individually, but that also make our lives go worse when all others make the same choices. For instance, what if everyone chose not to associate with a given person? What if everyone said: 'I'm not raising that baby', or 'I'm not caring for that older person'? Alternatively, what if everyone chose *to* associate with a given person? What if everyone said: 'I'm raising *that* baby' or 'I'm going to be *that person's* friend'? Or what if everyone chose not to associate with anyone else? Our ordinary exercises of interactional and associational control in approaching and avoiding each other would be highly morally charged if everyone else made the same choices.

In this chapter, I begin by summarizing and briefly critiquing the standard liberal view on associational freedom, which prizes exclusivity and is somewhat dismissive of the tension I have just highlighted between associational freedom and positive social rights claims (Section 5.1). I then review the features of each-we dilemmas (Section 5.2) before exploring six specific each-we dilemmas of sociability generated by the conflict between associational freedom and positive social claim-rights. The first three are dilemmas of negative sociality (i.e. dilemmas of dissociation). They are: (1) the *rejected person dilemma*, (2) the *rejected people dilemma*, and (3) the *misanthrope's dilemma* (Section 5.3). The second three are dilemmas of positive sociality (i.e. dilemmas of association). They are: (4) the *popular person dilemma*,

(5) the *popular people dilemma*, and (6) the *social butterfly dilemma* (Section 5.4). I then show that, when it comes to our attitudes rather than our behaviours, each-we dilemmas arise only in relation to negative attitudes, not positive attitudes (Section 5.5). To resolve the various each-we dilemmas of sociability that I identify, we must prioritize either negative rights to dissociate or positive rights to social connection. I show that, in all cases, positive social rights claims generally take priority over dissociative freedom. The priority of positive social rights has implications both for personal morality and for politics, since regulating our access to social resources is partly a matter of public institutions, a topic that has received little attention in political philosophy.[4] I explore the implications of social needs for institutions in Chapters 6 and 8.

5.1 The Value of Associational Freedom: Exclusivity

Liberal thinking takes for granted that the right to be exclusive is central and legitimate to freedom of association.[5] International agreements such as the Universal Declaration of Human Rights (Article 20) describe associational freedom in strong, consent-driven terms that highlight the value of exclusivity: (1) Everyone has the right to freedom of peaceful assembly and association, and (2) No one may be compelled to belong to an association. (I return to this article in Chapter 6 to show that its two sections not only conflict with each other, but are both false as they stand.) In a similar vein, Amy Gutmann states that 'the freedom to associate necessarily entails the freedom to exclude'.[6] These full-throated endorsements of exclusivity are rooted most strongly in the liberalism of John Stuart Mill:

> We have a right...in various ways, to act upon our unfavourable opinion of any one, not to the oppression of his individuality, but in the exercise of ours. We are not bound, for example, to seek his society; we have a right to avoid it (though not to parade the avoidance), for we have a right to choose the society most acceptable to us. We have a right, and it may be our duty, to caution others against him, if we think his example or conversation likely to have a pernicious effect on those with whom he associates.[7]

We can interpret Mill in one of several ways. First, we could read him as endorsing something like a Hohfeldian *permission* to associate or not as we please, when he says that we are not *bound* to seek any person's society and have a right to choose the society most acceptable to us. In other words, we have no duty to associate with any person with whom we do not wish to associate and, conflictingly, we have no duty *not* to associate with any person whom we favour and whose society is most acceptable to us.

However, second, we could read Mill as rejecting the permission *to form* associations as we please, since he goes on to say that we may have a duty to caution others against associating with a person of whom we disapprove, 'if we think his example or conversation likely to have a pernicious effect on those with whom he associates', and, by implication, presumably we too have a duty not to associate with the unfavourable person for the same reason that he may have a pernicious effect on us. This duty not to associate clashes with the idea that we have a right to choose the society most acceptable to us, which would include the society of those who may have a pernicious effect on us.

Third, we could read Mill as endorsing a Hohfeldian *claim-right* against interference which allows us to choose the society most acceptable to us even if we act wrongly in doing so. This gives us an expansive and broadly content-insensitive freedom, like the freedoms of thought, expression, and religion, which protects us from third-party interference, notably government interference, with our associational decisions.[8]

This third reading of Mill is difficult to reconcile with his 'very simple' principle (the harm principle) which constrains associational freedom as a freedom of *action* (in contrast with freedoms of thought and expression). Mill's harm principle severely limits the scope of our claim-rights to act wrongly when we choose the society we want to keep:

> the principle requires liberty of tastes and pursuits; of framing the plan of our life to suit our own character; of doing as we like, subject to such consequences as may follow: without impediment from our fellow-creatures, so long as what we do does not harm them, even though they should think our conduct foolish, perverse, or wrong...[F]rom this liberty of each individual, follows the liberty, within the same limits, of combination among individuals; freedom to unite, *for any purpose not involving harm to others*: the persons combining being supposed to be of full age, and not forced or deceived.[9]

As we will see, our mutually consensual choices to associate with specific persons can do both direct and indirect harms to excluded others in ways that conflict with the harm principle.

These various liberal endorsements of exclusivity are applied, first, to collective associations, such as teams, unions, and clubs, which assert rights to be exclusive as part of their identity. Second, they are applied to intimate associations among family members and friends, where exclusivity is both less contentious politically and seemingly unavoidable for reasons of identity and practicality, since we can be genuinely intimate with only a small number of people.[10] Third, they are applied to states, which assert a right to exclude people, such as undesired immigrants, on the basis of legitimate, national self-determination.[11]

One argument for the right to be exclusive focuses on personal autonomy, self-respect, and well-being. These three things give us powerful interests against being forced into associations with other people, such as a forced marriage or a forced parenting relation.[12] Similarly, the US Supreme Court says that our individual associational freedom protects our choices to enter into and maintain certain intimate human relationships *as a fundamental element of our personal liberty*.[13]

A second family of arguments for the right to be exclusive focuses on the core functions of our associations, including any expressive purposes they have. One expression-related argument highlights the assault on those functions and purposes that forced inclusiveness would (potentially) entail. Most starkly, the argument says that a right to exclude is a necessary precondition for us to form associations with specific purposes at all, such as active sports clubs, committed religious groups, or indeed loving, close-knit families.[14] A second expression-related argument holds that permitting associations to be exclusive on expressive grounds is essential to creating genuine space for dissent within a democracy.[15] Non-state expressive associations can check the state's power by giving us alternative avenues through which to shape our world; they enable us to coordinate our efforts and, thereby, better resist wrongful exercises of coercive power of the state.[16]

A third, related argument looks at other values that are realized when associates are allowed to be exclusive, such as teamwork, competitive advantage, group self-determination, and cohesiveness.[17]

Some thinkers extend such arguments for our personal rights to be exclusive to states. According to Christopher Wellman, the state is analogous in relevant ways to individual citizens. In liberal states, we citizens are morally entitled to control our self-regarding affairs, since we have strong interests in self-determination. This is why we may choose our own marriage partners and our own religion. So too, Wellman argues, the state has analogous interests in self-determination. For this reason, *ceteris paribus* we should privilege states' rights to exclude over immigrants' competing claims to be admitted.[18]

Wellman ignores, however, that, as individuals, we cannot exercise self-determination over our closest familial relations during our childhood, even though these relations define us at our core. We cannot choose our genetic parents, our gestational mother, or our developmental parents. We cannot choose our siblings, grandparents, cousins, aunts, and uncles, or the lack of them. In other words, we cannot choose our own biology, our biological relations, or our familial surroundings during our protracted period of childhood development.[19] Moreover, as parents, we have only a limited ability and arguably no claim-right to choose our children in any detailed sense.[20] Furthermore, we cannot choose our associates or lack of associates when we are utterly dependent, incapacitated, injured, ill, or very old.

The limits on our capacity for individual self-determination are analogous to the limits on states' capacity for self-determination—limits posed by a state's history, geography, resources, and neighbours (unless it conquers those neighbours). Given the significance of these limits on our individual self-determination, our individual associational freedom does not offer a credible argument by analogy for state exclusivity as Wellman suggests it does. If anything, it offers a credible argument by analogy for a limited vision of states' associational rights. States' rights to be exclusive, if they have such rights, are highly qualified. They turn on considerations of local and general well-being such as resource scarcity, overpopulation, and environmental damage. States can do significant direct and indirect harms to third-parties. States' rights to be exclusive, if they have them, should not take priority *ceteris paribus* over third-parties' rights not to be harmed.

In reply to the three previous arguments for our freedom of association as individuals, the right to exclude is both qualified and defeasible. This chapter and the next chapter show that we have no general moral *permission* to exclude other people. And, we have at most a defeasible moral *claim-right* to exclude them.

First, the value of the putative goods of exclusivity cannot be assessed independently of an association's aims. A neo-Nazi student club might display teamwork, competitive success, cohesiveness, self-determination, and self-respect. But if these traits have any value independent of their content, that value is outweighed by the gross disvalue in the cause they advance and the risks that go with this group's successful exclusivity. We might say that, despite that, the neo-Nazi student club should be allowed to exist and be exclusive for the *external* reasons that our society has collective interests in toleration, diversity, experiments in living, and freedom of expression. (Of course, in tolerating such associations, we run the risk that we endorse their intolerance toward the people whom they exclude, which is an unavoidable tension within liberal societies.)

Second, we must attend to the impact that exclusivity has on third-parties who reasonably desire to be included. Suppose that no grocery store in a town will sell food to a Jewish person. Suppose that no Caucasian-owned restaurant in a city will serve a black person. Suppose that the main business club in the country, the international golf club, or the state orchestra won't admit women. Certain legal and social checks must rein in our rights to be exclusive in our collective associations to ensure that we do not improperly limit others' rights to equal respect, consideration, and fair opportunity.[21]

Third, we must attend to the impact that exclusivity has on third-parties *generally* even when third-parties have no desire or reason to be included since, as Sarah Fine argues, free associations can have harmful effects on third-parties simply when associations engage in the activities that define their association:

> When a private club in a residential area regularly arranges noisy late-night gatherings, the group's actions have spill-over effects for the local residents. In that way, while seemingly going about its own business, the private club has the potential to harm the interests of nonmembers.[22]

Fine says this calls into question 'the presumption in favor of the group members' freedom to do as they please'. More radically, a neo-Nazi club that is actively fomenting violence against Jews has no right to exist as it does, since it threatens the lives and basic interests of the people it excludes. In a related vein, Andres Moles argues that bigoted private or intimate associations can foster mental contamination among members that subsequently alters the 'public ecology' of the broader society in problematic ways by exacerbating distrust, aversive attitudes, and aversive behaviour.[23]

These various responses feed into the issue I examine below, which is that exclusivity confronts us with the '*What if everyone did that?*' *problem*, generating each-we dilemmas of sociability that show that we will all do less well individually and collectively if we all take up the option to be exclusive than if none of us (or at least not all of us) take up the option to be exclusive.

Let's then explore how exclusivity generates the 'What if everyone did that?' problem, and why we can only resolve it in favour of positive social rights claims.

5.2 What If Everyone Did That?

Let's review the features of each-we dilemmas. According to Kant's law of nature formula, it is wrong to act in some way unless we could rationally will it to be true that everyone, rather than no one, acts in this way when they can.[24] Kant's law of nature formula applies best, Derek Parfit says, to acts of which it is true that: (1) it would be possible for many people to act in this way, (2) the effects of each person's act will be similar irrespective of the number of people who act in this way, and (3) the effects will be roughly equally distributed among the people involved.[25]

One common type of each-we dilemma, Parfit notes, is the *self-benefiting dilemma* (often called the *prisoner's dilemma*) in which each of us is a member of a group of whom it is true that we could either benefit ourselves or give some greater benefit to others that would be equally distributed among the members of the group, and each of our actions would not have a significant effect on the others' actions. In the classic prisoner's dilemma, our options are (1) to defect (i.e. confess to the crime) while our partner stays silent, in which case we will go free and our partner will get a harsh punishment of ten years in jail, or (2) to remain silent and, provided our partner does the same, both get a modest punishment of six months in jail. If we remain silent and our partner defects, then we get ten years and our partner goes free. And if we both defect, then we each get six years in jail. In short, it is best for us individually if we defect and our partner does not, but it is worst for us both if we each defect than if neither of us defects.

Self-benefiting, prisoner-style dilemmas may seem like a loose usage of the term 'dilemma', since in moral philosophy 'dilemmas' are cases of moral conflict where we have two competing moral duties each of which we can perform, but not in combination. The prisoner-style dilemma is best seen as a conflict between *individual good* narrowly understood and *collective or aggregated good*, which includes individual good richly understood as intertwined with others' good. Some of the each-we dilemmas of sociability explored below are also best seen as conflicts of values rather than conflicts of duties. There is the value of our making autonomous decisions about our associative position, and there is the value of us each having our core social needs met, which if ignored can lead to detrimental results for all. As conflicts of values, these dilemmas are not wedded to Kantian thinking, but they find their inspiration there.

The prisoner-style dilemma is a non-distributive each-we dilemma since there is no limited, divisible good to be distributed among the members of the group. It contrasts with distributive each-we dilemmas, such as Parfit's *fisherman's dilemma*:

> If each fisherman uses larger nets, he will catch more fish, whatever the other fishermen do. But if all the fishermen use larger nets, the fish stocks will decline so that, before long, they will all catch fewer fish.[26]

To be a dilemma, the *fisherman's dilemma* relies on a few assumptions. First, it assumes that there are enough fishermen fishing that their fish-taking will deplete the stocks over time and affect each other's ability to catch a given amount of fish. But, of course, this need not be so. If there were only two fishermen in the sea, then neither the largest net that each could construct nor their decision to fish every moment of their waking lives would affect the other's fish-take. As this implies, in distributive cases, the number of people matters. If that number is small relative to the resources, then there is no self-benefiting dilemma.

Second, the fisherman's dilemma assumes that catching fewer fish is worse rather than neutral or better for each fisherman. But, again, this need not be so. If the number of fish that each fisherman can catch once every fisherman is using a larger net is still more than she could possibly need or want, then the fact that she can catch fewer than she could if no one (else) used a larger net does not make things *worse* for her. This point also holds in the absolute terms of 'good' and 'bad' and not just in the relative terms of 'better' and 'worse'. The fact that she can catch fewer fish than she could if others didn't use larger nets is not necessarily bad for her or anyone else. Everyone's using large nets and catching (slightly) fewer fish might still yield an absolutely good fish-take for each. Hence, in the fishermen's case, we must deploy a notion of *sufficiency* to determine whether a situation in which we all act in a certain way is genuinely worse or bad for each of us, than if none of us acted in that way.

In what follows, I focus on *distributive* each-we dilemmas of sociability. These dilemmas arise when we use our social resources (abilities, opportunities, and connections) negatively or positively in ways that, if everyone does the same, lead to indefensible allocations of social resources. (We use our social resources negatively when we withhold them from other people, for example, by dissociating. We use them positively when we provide them to other people and, indeed, when we seek to receive them from other people.) It is part of the nature of social connections that offering social resources and seeking to receive social resources are typically one and the same thing. Given this reciprocal feature of sociability, it might seem that positive uses of social resources cannot generate each-we dilemmas.[27] But, as we will see, they can.

5.3 Three Negative Dilemmas

In many US grocery stores and restaurants, you'll see signs declaring: 'We reserve the right to refuse service to anyone.' This declaration captures the first dilemma of negative sociability. (I am not specifically discussing businesses' rights to be exclusive. I use this declaration to isolate the kind of each-we dilemma that arises if we universalize a decision not to associate with someone.) Let's call this the *rejected person dilemma*:

> If Andy shuns Jo, then he will feel safe, contented, and well. But, if everyone decides to shun Jo, then the result is not only bad for Jo, but worse for everyone's safety, contentment, and well-being than if no one (or not everyone) shuns Jo.[28]

It's better for each 'Andy' individually to shun Jo if others do not, because he then avoids costs to himself, exercises control over how and with whom he associates, and still shares in avoiding the bad outcomes that would result from everyone shunning Jo. Moreover, it is better for each Andy who is part of a small clique to shun Jo if others outside the clique do not shun her, since shunning (i.e. exclusivity) can strengthen the bonds within a clique, help the members in competitions, and enhance their coordination with each other.

However, each Andy faces costs if everyone shuns Jo—costs that are arguably worse than if no one (or not everyone) shuns Jo. Some of these costs turn on the fact that Jo's persistent social rejection will have substantial negative effects on her that could include depression, despondency, reduced immunity, loss of social ability and personal control, violence, psychosis, suicidal ideation and behaviour, and early death (see Chapters 1 and 2).[29]

First, when everyone shuns Jo, each Andy loses out on the possibility of benefiting directly or indirectly from the social resources that Jo would otherwise have contributed to the collective pool. Indeed, everyone in the group isolating Jo loses out on Jo's social resources not only at the time she is shunned, but also *permanently* if the social resources that Jo could have contributed to the collective pool diminish absolutely through her persistent isolation. Second, not only does the collective pool of social resources diminish absolutely, but the number of social threats increases absolutely, since Jo now poses new, and potentially grave, social threats to the group through anti-social behaviour and illness. Third, related to this, although Jo loses her own social resources, she does not lose her need to receive social resources. She can take, but not give. And, in fact, she needs *more* social resources post-isolation than she did pre-isolation due to the debilitating effects of her isolation. Hence, given the threats Jo poses and the resources she needs, it is worse for everyone if everyone shuns Jo than if no one (or not everyone) shuns Jo.

Fourth, even if the three above points do not apply in a case because Jo is an older person, nevertheless there are more general costs for everyone in shunning Jo, which lie in the risks for each member that arise when group members become less decent, charitable, compassionate, and friendly through their increased willingness to let people confront without help the awful abyss of social isolation and other evils of life.

That said, the costs of everyone shunning Jo are not evenly distributed across the members of the group. This is because, first, provided we count Jo as a member of the group, Jo bears the greatest costs in being shunned. Second, the size of the group affects how much the costs will be felt by all other members. Whereas in a small group, everyone will register the costs just noted, in a large group many Andys might not. However, even in a larger group, everyone faces the *risks* that go with each Andy potentially being the target of Jo's antisocial behaviour and potentially losing out socially because Jo is unable to give. (When a group is so large that the effects do not register in the lives of most Andys, then either the dilemma arises only for a subset of that group, or that group does not qualify as a 'group' in the relevant sense.)

A variant of the *rejected person dilemma* is the *rejected people dilemma*:

> If Andy shuns all people like Jo, then he will feel safe and contented. But, if everyone in the society who is not like Jo shuns all people like Jo, then over time this will be worse for the safety and contentment of all, and it poses the risk that the pool of available social resources will be smaller than the pool of needed social resources. (This dilemma turns on the assumption that the people like Jo are unable to secure social connections from each other.)

Once again, it's better for each Andy to shun all people like Jo if others do not, since he then avoids the costs of associating with such people, exercises control over his associational decisions, and shares in the benefits that come with those people not being universally isolated. Moreover, if each Andy is in a small clique, then shunning people like Jo, provided others outside the clique do not, may advance his clique's competitiveness, internal bonding, and coordination.

But, once again, it's worse for each Andy, and for everyone collectively, if everyone in the group shuns people like Jo. First, the people like Jo will continue to need social resources even though they will have few or none to give. In fact, each person like Jo will need more social resources than she needed before because her persistent deprivation will render her less able to function independently, seek out social opportunities, and contribute to social connections. Second, even if the number of people like Jo is fewer than the number of people with social resources to give, there may be fewer social resources in the pool than needed due to the increase in the social needs and decrease in the social resources of the people like Jo.

Third, in shunning people like Jo, everyone faces the risk that the group's commitment to decency, charity, compassion, and friendliness will erode, making it more likely that each member will have to confront alone the threats of social and material deprivation. A critic might say that this need not happen: Jo's shunning could be the unintended consequence of lots of people pursuing their own prudential good.[30] In reply, 'shunning' is never an unintended consequence. Moreover, unless Jo's isolation is invisible, we *risk* at least becoming more callous and indifferent toward such suffering by allowing it to persist.

Again, the impact of these costs on everyone depends on the size of the group. It also depends on how many people in the group are like Jo. If it's a large group containing few people like Jo, most Andys might not register the costs just listed. Nevertheless, everyone faces the *risks* that come with each potentially being the target of antisocial behaviour and social loss. (Again, when a group is so large that the effects do not register in the lives of most Andys, then either the dilemma arises only for a subset of that group or that group is not a 'group' in the relevant sense.)

To avoid the above risks, everyone must prioritize each other's basic social needs at least during periods of dependency such as babyhood, childhood, acute incapacitation, severe impairment, and old age. As discussed in previous chapters, we all needed someone to privilege our associational needs when we were children, for our sake as children and for our sake developmentally, so that we could acquire the capacities for both associational control and social contribution later in life. Since protecting children's positive social rights is a prerequisite for future associational control, these rights trump other people's negative rights to refuse association. Also, as discussed in previous chapters, we all experience moments of utter dependency in our lives, such as giving birth, facing death, and grieving for the loss of a loved one. We can meet these great unknowns with more equanimity when we have the solace of decent company.[31] Moreover, in the case of giving birth, a second being's fate is at stake. We have strong interests to ensure that, when we are dependent, our claims to respect, meaning, reciprocity and desert,[32] and present social contribution ambitions will be privileged before (at least some) others' dissociative interests.

When we are not at risk of becoming utterly dependent, these *rejection dilemmas* are resolvable in subtler ways that ensure we have positive rights to minimally adequate *opportunities* to cultivate social connections, but not to positive provision of them. However, since chronic rejection can put us at risk of dependency, others' freedom to refuse association is checked by the requirement that our minimally adequate social opportunities be meaningful and not render us dependent.

Another variant of the *rejected person dilemma* is the *rejection of everyone dilemma* or the *misanthrope's dilemma*:

> If Andy shuns everyone, then he will feel safe and contented and won't incur the burdens of interpersonal duties whatever other people do. But, if everyone makes that same misanthropic decision, then the result will be socially worse for all.

The *rejection of everyone dilemma* dissolves if we make an optimistic but reasonable assumption that, given differences in people's situations and temperaments, not everyone will seek to do as the misanthrope does. Provided that enough people continue to seek others' company, then, even if everyone who leans toward misanthropy were to become a hermit, there would still be enough people who avoid that lifestyle to constitute a decent society.[33] That said, this optimistic assumption begins to look naïve if the group we are talking about is a prison population or a closed society whose members have suffered the hardships of social deprivation. When enough people lose their capacities to sustain decent social connections we cannot assume that we will be able to maintain a decent society.

This point flags the presence of a related problem, the *autonomy dilemma*, discussed briefly in Chapter 2. If we choose to deprive ourselves of social connections by becoming a misanthrope, then we exercise autonomy in a way that can undermine our ability to continue to exercise autonomy because, in time, our social deprivation can compromise our abilities to function. As we saw, self-isolation is akin to fasting to the point of starvation: both choices can erode our practical reasoning abilities necessary for continued autonomy.[34] And, by rendering ourselves less competent to reason, we render ourselves less able to choose from what would otherwise be an adequate range of valuable options.[35]

The *rejection of everyone dilemma* is resolvable as a variant of the *egoist's dilemma*, in which a person's options are between acting egoistically or living in a society of egoists. The dilemma is resolvable because the misanthrope, like the egoist, must recognize that she will achieve her aim of acting as she wishes less well when all others act that way too.[36] If she shuns everyone when everyone else does the same, then she will achieve her aim of solitude less well because collective misanthropy will cause social connections to break down. Social chaos, dependency, and intrusion will run rampant, since acquiring the necessities of life takes coordinated social interaction.

5.4 Three Positive Dilemmas

When we use our social resources positively, we can face each-we dilemmas if everyone in a group puts pressure on the same social resources. There are at least three such dilemmas, which mirror the three rejection dilemmas just discussed. The first is the *popular person dilemma*, which mirrors the *rejected person dilemma*:

> If Andy seeks out Jo's company, Andy will be content whatever everyone else does. But, if everyone seeks out Jo's company, this will be worse for all, since Jo cannot provide company to everyone.

It might not be immediately obvious that it will be worse for *all* if everyone seeks out Jo's company. At the very least, it seems not to be worse for Jo and the people whose company she favours.[37] But Jo faces the risk of social overload and exhaustion, and her favoured friends face risks from the jealous people whom Jo spurns, which threatens their happy fellowship.

In one respect, the *popular person dilemma* is like the *fisherman's dilemma* with Jo's social resources standing in for the fish. If too many people put pressure on Jo's company, then there just won't be enough 'fish' to go around. But the *popular person dilemma* can be distinguished from the *fisherman's dilemma* because the apparent scarcity of social resources is due not to an absolute lack of resources, but to people's decision to see the available resources as limited by seeing Jo's social resources as the only ones worth seeking. (It would be like the fishermen deciding that only sea bass is worth catching.) If everyone took a broader view of valuable social resources and distributed their social efforts more equitably, then this distributive each-we dilemma would not arise. In principle, social resources are as plentiful as there are people able to offer them. Each new person joining a group does not increase the pressure on the collective pool of social resources if she has social resources to offer, and others in the group are willing to accept her social resources. Unfortunately, we do not always take this view of people's proffered social resources—a fact that shows that society has good reasons to regulate social connections, perhaps by requiring people to contribute community service in the form of social inclusion service or by nudging people to be more sociable.

The second dilemma is the *popular people dilemma*, which mirrors the rejected people dilemma:

> If Andy seeks society from people like Jo, then he will be socially engaged and contented no matter what others do. But, if everyone seeks society from people like Jo, this will be worse for all, since people like Jo cannot provide society to everyone.

This scenario doesn't create a dilemma if there are a lot of people like Jo and few people unlike Jo. It does create a dilemma, though, if the number of people like Jo isn't large enough to meet the social needs of all the people seeking their society. But, like the *popular person dilemma*, this dilemma is a manufactured one that dissolves if people are less fussy about their social preferences. The manufactured nature of such dilemmas shouldn't lead us to dismiss them because, as noted above, we are clannish creatures who favour cliques, clubs, and tribes of us-versus-them. We shape our identity and sense of security around being exclusive.

The third dilemma is the *social butterfly dilemma*, which mirrors the rejection of everyone dilemma:

> If Andy seeks society from everyone in the group, then he will be socially engaged, secure, and happy no matter what others do. But, if everyone seeks society from everyone in the group, then there will be unmanageable

pressure on the collective pool of social resources, and this will be worse for all than if everyone directed their social energies more fastidiously.

This scenario does not generate a dilemma if all members of the group socialize together: they just have a party. But the scenario does generate a dilemma if the social connections everyone seeks and offers are two-person interactions—being happy in pairs. In that case, everyone will put unmanageable pressure on the collective pool of social resources.

That said, the *social butterfly dilemma* might be partially self-regulating. Although it is true that we only have so much time to give attention in two-person interactions, it is also true that we only have so much time to *receive* attention in those interactions. So we face a choice either to limit the number of people from whom we seek attention or to seek shallow, fleeting attention from a larger number of people.[38] It is when conflicts arise between our choices that this dilemma remains intact.

5.5 Social Attitudes

The above dilemmas involve social actions. Both negative and positive social *actions* generate distributive each-we dilemmas. By contrast, in cases that involve only attitudes, *negative* social attitudes generate each-we dilemmas, but positive social attitudes do not. Here is a negative social attitude version of the *rejected person dilemma*. Let's call it the *animosity dilemma*:

> If Andy palpably hates Jo, and everyone else palpably hates Jo, then, even if Jo is not shunned by everyone, she will experience many of the same detrimental effects that she would have endured had everyone shunned her, which will be worse for everyone than if no one hated Jo.

Once more, whether Jo's suffering is worse for everyone depends partly on the size of the group and the ways that individuals' experiences impact the group. In a large group, the dilemma may not arise. In a small group or subset of a large group, it certainly will.

Of course, most likely, Jo has no right not to be *hated* by a given person (thought she may have rights not to be hated universally and not to be hated unjustly). Also, it would be difficult, if not impossible, to subject people's negative attitudes about her to regulation. The point here is that things are worse for everyone if everyone hates Jo than if no one hates Jo.

By contrast, positive social attitudes such as love do not create distributive each-we dilemmas:

> If each of us offers love to everyone and seeks love from everyone, there will still be enough love to go around.

Love is different from fish. When we offer attitudes of love and seek attitudes of love, we do not deplete the stocks of love. Instead, love has a multiplicative effect. As social neuroscientist John T. Cacioppo and his collaborator William Patrick note, well-regulated, socially contented people send social signals that are more harmonious and more in sync with the rest of the environment than do poorly self-regulated, socially disconnected people. Not surprisingly, Cacioppo and Patrick say, the signals that socially contented people receive back are more harmonious and better synchronized as well. 'This rippling back and forth between the individual and others is the corollary to self-regulation that we call co-regulation.'[39] A similar thought lies in Buddhist psychology, which says that humans have a limitless potential to cultivate this kind of multiplicative, loving kindness and compassion.

That said, a richer notion of *love* requires more than just attitudes of loving kindness and compassion. It requires that we be willing to do all kinds of things for someone as the occasion arises. This kind of loving takes energy, and hence when we offer it and accept it, we do deplete the stocks. Love in this richer sense is like fish.[40]

The multiplicative quality of positive social attitudes is significant for both personal morality and social regulation. Concerning personal morality, we have good reason to cultivate attitudes of kindness, compassion, and warmth toward each person we encounter. Doing so enlarges, rather than depletes, the collective pool of social resources. Concerning regulation, when thinking about how to allocate social resources, we need not worry that there might be problems of non-divisibility or scarcity of positive attitudinal goods (even if other problems of *direct* distribution abound). Such goods are neither non-divisible nor unavoidably scarce.

Conclusion

Each-we dilemmas of sociability give us a powerful, Kantian reason to conclude that, contrary to the standard liberal view, we lack a *general* moral permission to associate as we please: we cannot will it to be the case that everyone follow a permissive liberal maxim about association or dissociation, since that would be worse for all of us than if none of us follows such a maxim. Dissociating *completely* is the most radical act of exclusivity. And the Kantian reason shows that, even if we extricate ourselves from our morally obligatory associations by patiently waiting for our existing connections to end and judiciously avoiding new ones, we cannot then claim that we may choose permissibly not to associate with anyone ever again. This is because we cannot will it to be the case that every able person discharges their pre-existing associative duties in this way in order to gain a general license not to associate at all. Fundamental, positive associational claim-rights—to have associates (not necessarily of our choosing) during periods of dependency and to have meaningful opportunities to form associations when we are not dependent—take priority over our dissociative ambitions.

We cannot escape the conclusions to which the Kantian reason leads by arguing that, generally, we can make self-benefiting associative calculations because we can reasonably rely on others making different calculations, i.e. preferring or avoiding different people, investing differently in their associations, and seeking or avoiding association to different degrees. We cannot argue in this way for two reasons. First, even if we could rely on other people to make different associational choices, we would act impermissibly by acting in a way that we cannot universalize, since we would be free-riding on other people not acting in a way that they cannot universalize. Second, as a matter of historical and psychological fact, we simply cannot rely on other people making different associational choices, particularly when it comes to dissociating. Outside our deepest attachments, we tend to be sheep-like in our dissociative decisions: we tend to shy away from the people who are deemed socially disvaluable; these people include not just the objectionable Charles Boycotts of the world, but also people who are grieving, ill, recovering from illness, physically or cognitively impaired, facing criminal charges, social stigmatized, visibly different, or even demonized like the Hester Prynnes and Anna Kareninas whom our group has branded as *personae non gratae*.[41]

We also cannot escape the above conclusion—that, for Kantian reasons, we lack a *general* moral permission to associate as we please—purely by setting up the right political institutions. I defend this claim in the next chapter.

In addition to this Kantian reason, other reasons show us why we have no general moral permission to associate as we please. (A separate issue from this is whether we have a claim-right to act *wrongly* without interference when we associate or not as we please. I tackle this issue in the next chapter.) As noted in Chapter 4, whatever general moral permission we have to associate or not depends on our particular permissions to associate with particular people, and those particular permissions are hostage to various constraints including consent, the type of association, its burdens, pre-existing commitments, improper exclusivity and discrimination, and collective responsibility. In the next chapter, I shall explore each of these constraints in detail.

6
Associational Freedom

Introduction

In 2010, 33 men became trapped 700 metres underground in a mine near Copiapó, Chile. All 33 were successfully rescued 69 days later. They managed to stretch their three days' worth of resources for close to two weeks, when they were finally discovered. The men adopted a one-man-one-vote democracy. Key members of the group had distinct leadership roles: the oldest member became the group's religious leader, the member with some medical training became their medic. The foreman, Luis Urzúa, displayed a level-headed, good-humoured, accepting approach that focused on collective survival, which kept morale high. This case is an example of unintended close association. The fact that, through inclusivity and mutual support, all the men survived endorses my conclusion in the last chapter on how to resolve each-we dilemmas of sociability: positive social rights take priority over negative dissociative rights when the two conflict. The analysis of each-we dilemmas forms one part of my argument for the view that associational freedom is not what we tend to think it is. Associational freedom is not a general moral permission to choose the society most acceptable to us. One reason, as we saw, is that we cannot will it to be universal that everyone take a cavalier approach to their associative decisions. Other, more specific reasons, which I will explore in this chapter, pertain to consent, necessity, and burdensomeness. Associational freedom is also not a content-insensitive claim-right against interference with our associative choices when we act wrongly, akin to the other personal freedoms with which it is usually listed such as freedom of expression and freedom of religion. Instead, associational freedom is at most:

1. a highly restricted moral permission to associate (Section 6.1),
2. a conditional moral permission not to associate provided that our associative contributions are not required (Section 6.1), and
3. a highly constrained, content-sensitive moral claim-right that protects from interference only those of our wrongful associations that

honour other legitimate concerns such as consent, need, harm, and respect (Section 6.2).

My arguments for these three claims here, combined with the last two chapters, defend a narrow view of our interpersonal freedoms of association and interaction. In Chapter 7, I refine my account to accommodate the fallout of morally messy associative decisions which we have already made.

Let's begin here with moral permissions, focusing on the impact our individual associative decisions have on the people we directly affect, rather than on the aggregative, normative impact of everyone's associative decisions taken together.

6.1 Moral Permissions

6.1.1 Consent, Harm, Burdens, and Commitments

One simple reason that we have no general moral permission to choose the society most acceptable to us is that our own society might not be most acceptable to the people whose society is most acceptable to us. Consent often matters. If Jo wishes to be Andy's associate, but Andy does not wish it, then usually Jo may not form or maintain an association with Andy. Andy's consent matters even when his society is most acceptable to Jo.[1]

But, luckily for Jo, as we saw in Chapter 5, not all our associations must have mutual consent to be morally permissible. Indeed, some associations that lack it are not just permissible but obligatory. Think of parents and young children. If Andy is a young child and Jo is his mother, she does nothing wrong in having an intimate, mother–child relationship with him even though he is unable to consent to it. Indeed, she has a moral duty, not just a permission, to maintain the association, since without parental care Andy will suffer and fail to develop. So, here Jo has no moral permission *not* to associate with him even if his society is not most acceptable to her.[2]

More interestingly, some associations are permissible, if not obligatory, even when neither party consents. Think again of the 33 men in the Copiapó mining accident. Since they needed to depend on each other for their individual and collective survival for 69 days, they had to form personal ties regardless of whether they favoured each other's company.[3]

These examples show that *necessity* can constrain our negative permission to dissociate from someone by making our association obligatory. But necessity does not always make non-consensual associations obligatory. For example, it is not obligatory (in any straightforward sense) for a girl, Lalit, to marry the man of her parents' choice, Ali, even when her tribe's survival depends on it. Suppose that unless Lalit marries Ali her tribe will die out, as there are no other people of childbearing age and no other accessible tribes that they can join. Even so, the type of association and its burdens matter, and an under-age, forced marriage is overly burdensome and, of course, a gross violation of Lalit's rights to physical security, movement, and marriage. By contrast, it might be morally obligatory for Lalit to be friendly to Ali when her tribe's survival depends on it, since a friendly relation is not usually overly burdensome (or certainly not nearly as burdensome as the risk to her tribe).

That said, when a non-consensual association lacks necessity, this does not always make the association optional for the non-consenting party (or impermissible for the consenting party). Think of a friendly little boy, Kevin, who follows his grumpy, retired neighbour, Mr Gustafson, around because his parents are always working. The relation is important, but not necessary to Kevin's health and survival, since he does have a family and could find other neighbours to follow. And yet Mr Gustafson has some moral duty to associate with Kevin given both Kevin's need for a parental figure and Mr Gustafson's proximity and awareness of Kevin's situation. Again, the reasons for the moral obligation turn on the type of relation and its burdensomeness. The relation is important to Kevin and not particularly burdensome for Mr Gustafson.

But, of course, even *severe* burdensomeness doesn't always remove the duty to associate. It may be very burdensome for Jo to continue her relationship with her son, Andy, if he's psychologically unstable or wanted by the police. However, that doesn't remove her duty to associate with him. The intimate bonds between parent and child generate special duties that override many other considerations, partly because the relation is so important for the child. Similarly, Mr Gustafson might still have a duty to associate with Kevin even if the relation becomes burdensome, given his ability to avert the harm to Kevin that would come from neglect.[4]

Now, although mutual consent is often a necessary condition for a morally permissible association, it's not a guarantee of moral permissibility. Some consensual associations are not morally permissible. The reasons relate once more to the type of association and its burdens.

The burdens of some consensual associations lie in the parties' positions relative to each other. For example, a boss has a moral duty not to have a sexual relation with an employee, and a teacher with a student, and a president with an intern because, even if the association is mutually voluntary, it has sharp hierarchical contours. The subordinate party is poorly placed to assess the relation, may be harmed by it, and is vulnerable to domination during it and afterward.[5] The dominant party does a serious moral wrong in forming such a connection.

The burdens of other types of associations lie in the parties' positions in relation to people outside the association. Think of Romeo and Juliet, whose association puts them both at risk because their families hate each other. Or think of Thomas More and the Duke of Norfolk in Robert Bolt's play *A Man for All Seasons*. Once More is under suspicion for treason, he ends the friendship 'for friends' sake' despite the duke's objections, because it would be impermissible for him to maintain an association that endangers his friend.

That said, the *duke* may permissibly maintain his association with More. Indeed, he may have a duty to do this despite More's objection, which shows that there can be an asymmetry in people's permission to associate with each other. (In Chapter 7, I explore this asymmetry. I also explore the asymmetry that can arise between people's moral claim-rights to associate with each other without interference.)

More's case also confirms what we saw in Chapter 5 about each-we dilemmas and social attitudes: there is a difference between an association and the underlying attitudes that tend to sustain an association. In ending their friendship 'for friends' sake', More and the duke keep their regard for each other. They alter only the practical expectations they can have of each other.

Finally, the burdens of associations often fall not only on the participants, but also on non-participants. The president's affair with an intern affects not only the intern, but also the president's spouse, children, allies, political party, and constituents. The president's moral duty not to form that association rests not only on its hierarchical contours, but also on duties to other associates. Similarly, Jo has a duty to her son, Andy, not to adopt too many other children, since she couldn't be a good mother to them all.

6.1.2 Objections

In response to my claim that we lack a general moral permission to associate or not as we wish, a staunch, liberal defender of freedom of association might make two objections. The first objection is that we still have a general moral permission to associate in the abstract sense that we're morally permitted *to have associations*.

This is correct, but it has little content since, as noted in Chapter 4, our general permission to have associations is meaningless without particular permissions to have associations with particular people. If a person's only possible associations are all impermissible ones, then she has no meaningful permission to associate.

The liberal critic might agree that we should attend to each person's access to social connections, but deny that this entails truncating people's permissible associational freedom along the lines I have suggested, because we can establish appropriate state institutions to meet people's basic social needs. In short, the critic's second objection would be that basic social needs are a matter of political theory and policy, not a matter of personal morality.

In reply, yes, appropriate state institutions can do a lot. The state has a crucial role to play in ensuring that our core social needs are respected, protected, and fulfilled. Among other things, the state is ideally suited to coordinate our enterprises, facilitate connections, and fill gaps when they occur. The state can and should intervene, for instance, when children are growing up in slums with few, if any, parental figures around.[6]

However, state institutions can never *fully* guarantee our core social needs. Institutions such as nursing, social care, and community events may give us access to decent social contact and interaction. But, they will struggle to secure us access to *sustained social connection* and persistent association. First, our associations do not just persist. They are also often comprehensive displays of mutual investment, which state-managed provisions tend not to be. This is due partly to the operational realities of state institutions, such as time pressures, budget cuts, and changes in priorities, which can abort our efforts to cultivate persistent, diachronic joint narratives with each other. So, even though paid employees and volunteers can offer emotional connection and caring support to people who need it, they often struggle to forge or sustain persistent, comprehensive, proximate ties with the people they serve because of operational realities. Second, state institutions can only function when people are willing to assume the relevant offices and perform their tasks. Consider as an analogy the abortion stalemate in the United States, where, at the time of writing, women have a legal right to reproductive control, but find that fewer and fewer doctors and hospitals seem to be willing to perform abortions. In the case of sociability, if too few people are willing to assume the necessary offices or, indeed, if no one will take on the specific job of interacting regularly with a particular person, then that person's social needs will go unmet despite the presence of appropriate institutions. And we saw in previous chapters the costs that can flow from such neglect.

This outcome may be no worse than the outcome in which we don't rely primarily on state institutions to secure our basic social needs and everyone still shuns a given person. What it shows, though, is that we should not complacently assume that someone's rights will be satisfied when we establish appropriate institutions. The ethics of sociability is, in the first instance, a matter of personal morality. As individuals, we have moral responsibilities to make our social resources available to the collective social pool, if required. We also have duties not to render ourselves socially dysfunctional so that either we destroy our potential to contribute socially or we unduly burden the collective pool of social resources. In addition, we have moral responsibilities to acknowledge the social claims that people can have on us both in virtue of special bonds and legitimate past expectations, and in virtue of our proximity to them, our awareness of their situation, and our easy ability to alleviate their social suffering. Furthermore, we have moral responsibilities to find out whether the people who are charged with meeting the basic social needs of utterly dependent persons are fulfilling their duty.

Of course, in its coordinating role, the state can make it easier or harder for us to give our care and company to each other. For instance, the state makes it easier when it sets up appropriate venues for ambient sociability, which give us chances to engage in our personal projects near to each other, such as in playgrounds, parks, gardens, public squares, museums, and even laundromats and post offices. Such ambient sociability is the cradle for companionate sociability which can grow as we mingle with each other.[7] Venues for ambient sociability offer one way to further integration among people from different walks of life, where *integration* means socially significant groups fully participating on terms of equality in all domains of life.[8] Other ways to further integration include spatial integration of neighbourhoods, housing, and schools.

The state also can do a lot to make it easier for us to *sustain* the social connections we already have, by attending to such mundane matters as where to build the local hospital, prison, and retirement home, the length of standard working hours, the guarantee of common rest periods,[9] the availability of good, affordable transportation services, and the level of maternity and paternity support. In such ways, the politics of recognizing our sociability intersects with personal morality.

Let's sum up what we have established. Many factors can make our associations morally permissible or impermissible. None of these factors—consent, harm, type of association, burdens, pre-existing commitments, and collective responsibility—is morally salient to all associations. And no one factor, when it is salient, invariably determines whether our associative decision is permissible. What these factors do give us are further reasons, in addition to the Kantian reason (Chapter 5), to conclude that we have no general moral permission to associate as we please. This does not mean we have a duty to associate with any and every person. But it does mean that if a person either has special claims on us or her fundamental social needs cannot be met by others, then we have a duty to associate with *her*. By contrast, we have no such duty if an able person who has no special associative claims on us simply wishes to associate with us rather than with someone else.

Consequently, at most, we have a conditional permission not to associate that depends on, first, other people satisfying each other's positive associational claim-rights and, second, our own dissociation neither rendering us abjectly dependent on others' associative contributions nor undermining our ability to contribute associatively in future. Moreover, even when other people don't need our specific associative contributions, we have persisting associative duties, first, to care about whether other people's associational needs are being met and, second, to make our associative resources available to the common pool as required, to ensure that others' associational needs are met.

Now, even though we have no general moral *permission* to associate as we please, we may have a moral *claim-right* against interference that protects us when we make impermissible associative decisions. Such a claim-right is intuitively compelling given our deep interest against forced association and forced dissociation, even if we do wrong to avoid one association, end another, and sustain a third. In Section 6.3, I will explore how well associational freedom fits the garment of a Hohfeldian claim-right. Before turning to that, however, let's examine the profiles of the different kinds of morally wrong associations which the above analysis of permissible associations illuminates. There are five distinct ways that our associations can be morally wrong: in their (1) content, (2) form, (3) form and content, (4) form and likely content, and (5) indirectly. (They can also be wrong in their consequences, i.e. their general impact on people, as we saw in Chapter 5.) Let's take each type in turn.

6.2 Morally Wrong Associations

1. *Content*. Examples of associations that are morally wrong in their content include a persistently neglectful parent–child relationship; an abusive but otherwise ordinary adult, heterosexual, consensual, church-blessed marriage; and an orchestra that is rife with harassment. In each case, the association is morally fine in *form*. There is nothing wrong with parent–child relationships, marriages (putting aside background issues of structural injustice), or orchestras. The wrongness lies in their *content*. The prevailing content of each of the associations in these examples should be different.

2. *Form*. Associations that are morally wrong in their *form* should not exist regardless of their content. Examples include a chaste child marriage; a loving parent–child relationship formed through a kidnapping; a loving parent–child relationship formed through a life-generating rape; and an apathetic, harmless neo-Nazi group. We might add to this list, as a peripheral case, the rent-a-family example of ten-year-old Mana discussed in Chapter 1, who was supplied a 'father' but who, nine years later, still does not know that he is a hired actor. Hers is a peripheral case, not a paradigm case, because its form, while not unproblematic, is not as troubling as the other examples just given. The content of such associations is innocuous (for the associates), but these associations should not exist for one or more form-related reasons: (a) they came about through an illegitimate process; (b) they have an indefensible structure; or (c) they are defined by intolerable commitments.

In more detail, a chaste child marriage is wrong in *form* since it necessarily lacks the informed consent of the child or children, which it must have as the kind of relationship it is. It also poses risks and harms to one or both parties; it sets the terms of the parties' life courses, especially if they have kids together later. In short, the association becomes part of their identity. But, such an association is not morally wrong in *content* if the two parties treat each other respectfully, caringly, and age-appropriately.

The seemingly ordinary parent–child relationship that arises because the would-be parent kidnaps the child is morally wrong in *form*: it should not exist. But if the kidnapping parent raises the child beautifully, then the association is not morally wrong in *content*. We would not object to the association if we didn't know the backstory.

The seemingly ordinary parent–child relationship that arises because the biological father committed a life-generating rape is also morally wrong in *form*. The man who perpetrated the rape has no right to be in an authoritative parent–child relationship with the child who comes into being as a result. Yet if he cares for that child lovingly and well, then the association is not morally wrong in *content*. Again, if we did not know the background, we would not object to the association.[10] (In Chapter 7 I return to these cases to explore what we should say about such associations once they already exist.)

The neo-Nazi group that is apathetic and harmless does nothing wrong as a group; its behaviour—its content—is unproblematic. But, nonetheless it shouldn't exist, given its underlying commitment to exterminating Jews.

Often, the line between *form* and *content* is blurry, especially when an association's identity as the kind of association it is (its form) is intertwined with the specific activities the associates engage in (its content). For instance, if a business club is all-white, then it is probably morally problematic in both form and content, at least when (1) the group makes a prejudicial judgment about the people it excludes, (2) the exclusion knowingly relates to factors other than business expertise, and (3) this informs the group's collective activities, such as their selection procedures if nothing else.

3. *Form and content*. Some associations are *clearly* morally wrong in both their *form* and their *content*, such as an abusive child marriage, as in the case where Lalit's family marries her off to an uncaring Ali; a well-organized and effective neo-Nazi group; and Rapunzel's relationship with the witch who kidnaps her (form) and then locks her in a tower and dominates her (content).

We cannot rank either all form-wrongs or all content-wrongs as morally worse than the other. It's not obviously worse to be in a forced but benign marriage than in a consensual, abusive marriage, or vice versa. We can probably rank associations that are wrong in both form and content as morally worse than other wrong associations, but there will be exceptions to this rule.

4. *Form and likely content*. Some associations that are morally wrong in form are not necessarily wrong but likely to be wrong in content as well, such as the association between a 12-year-old mother and her baby. The child and baby's association is wrong in form and shouldn't exist for many reasons, including, first, that she was raped; second, that she's bearing intense responsibilities as a child-parent and is probably both incompetent and

inadequately resourced to fulfil them; and third, that she could not make an informed choice to become a primary caregiver. Given her immaturity, vulnerability, and resource deprivation, she and her baby are probably in an association that is wrong in *content* too.

5. *Indirectly wrong.* Some associations are not directly wrong in either form or content, but instead are indirectly wrong. Suppose that a young woman is kidnapped and held captive for ten years. Prior to being kidnapped she was a mother of a very young child. After her disappearance, the child goes into foster care and then is adopted by his foster family. Let's assume that the association between the child and the adoptive parents is morally fine in content. Their association is also morally fine in *form*, since the foster family did the right thing by taking him in, as this was vital to his well-being. And yet, in some sense, this adoptive parent–child association should not exist. Once the mother escapes, she has a *pro tanto* right to raise her child. She has done nothing to forfeit or waive her right. Indeed, the child and the mother *both* have claim-rights to be together, but it is now no longer in the child's interests to be raised by his mother who has been traumatized for ten years. It's in the child's interests to remain with the adoptive family.[11]

Many morally wrong associations that we can say categorically *ex ante* should not exist are morally messy because *ex post*, once they exist, they defy a principled analysis of their moral character. Morally messy associations put us in an intuitive tight spot, because we will be hard pressed to say with confidence what the morally right or even acceptable solution is in these cases. Should morally messy associations be severed, slowly dissolved, or allowed to persist as they are? I explore morally messy associations in detail in Chapter 7.

As we saw above, other features that can make associative decisions wrong cut across the form/content distinction. First, some associative decisions are wrong because people make objectionable choices for their dependants, as in the case where parents put an unwanted child up for adoption. Second, some associations are wrong because the associates impose serious risks on each other. Think again of Romeo and Juliet, who risk each other's lives to be together. Romeo and Juliet contrast with Thomas More, who refuses to risk the Duke of Norfolk's life and so ends their friendship. Some associations are wrong when they pose risks for third-parties. Through their connection, Romeo and Juliet pose risks to their families and to each other's families. (That said, it is more accurate to state that Romeo and Juliet act in a way that increases the chance that their *families* will pose risks to each other.) Third, some associative decisions are wrong because they blur the lines between autonomy and heteronomy. Examples include the lonely widower who does not believe he needs or should belong to the social circle that he cannot form without help, as well as the intern who is flattered but also finds it hard to refuse the president's advances. Finally, although not all acts of exclusivity are *pro tanto* wrong, some associative decisions are wrong because they are (illegitimately) exclusive, such as the orchestra, the military, the Church, the business club, or the restaurant that excludes certain people on objectionable grounds. In the cases of the military, the established Church, and the state-funded orchestra, their exclusivity is wrong for a further reason, namely, that they are public institutions.

Doing wrong is, of course, not the end of the normative story. The key question is: Which wrongful associations and dissociations does associational freedom protect? What are the *limits* of our claim-rights to make morally wrong associative decisions free from interference?

6.3 Moral Claim-Rights

6.3.1 Personal Freedoms

In Chapter 5, I noted some iterations of the expansive liberal account of associational claim-rights including, first, the United States Supreme Court analysis in *Roberts v. United States Jaycees*, which holds that associational freedom must be secure against state intrusion as a fundamental element of personal liberty, and, second, Article 20 of the Universal Declaration of Human Rights (UDHR), which states that: (1) Everyone has the right to freedom of peaceful assembly and association, and (2) No one may be compelled to belong to an association.[12] Let's focus on the UDHR article for a moment.

What goes unnoticed is that the two sections of the article conflict with each other. If (2) is true, then (1) can be at most the freedom *to try* to form peaceful assemblies and associations. We can have no right to *succeed* in associating with others if no one may be compelled to associate with us. And, if (1) is true—that we have rights *actually* to associate (and not merely to *try* to associate)—then (2) is false, since (1) requires that it be permissible, in principle, to compel others sometimes to associate with us.

It turns out that both (1) and (2) are false as they stand. As we saw in the previous section, it is sometimes permissible to compel association, and therefore (2) is false. And, as we will see now, in a general, content-insensitive form, (1) is false. It is a mistake to align associational freedom with other claim-rights of conduct, such as freedom of expression and freedom of religion, which do provide a largely content-insensitive protection of our personal choices. Freedom of association does not provide a content-insensitive protection of our associative choices. Let me explain.

Freedom of expression gives us a defeasible protected sphere in which to express ourselves in unencumbered ways that may be morally problematic, specifically, to say, write, draw, film, and display things that may be objectionable. That protected sphere does not immunize us from criticism, however, when we exercise it to act wrongly. For instance, although our freedom of expression defeasibly protects us from interference when we make highly offensive racist jokes, it does not immunize us from criticism for making such jokes. Some argue that freedom of expression does not extend to defamation or hate speech, but a true-blue liberal like Mill holds that freedom of expression *is* content-insensitive (excepting incitement to violence), and is in good standing even when our expression is not just offensive, but harmful.

Similarly, freedom of religion gives us defeasible moral protection to engage in objectionable practices, though the scope of that freedom is not wholly content-insensitive. As John Rawls argues, religious protection does not extend to human sacrifice: 'If a religion is denied its full expression, it is presumably because it is in violation of the equal liberties of others.'[13] Nevertheless, the scope for religious freedom granted in many places is more expansive than the protection of everyone's equal liberties would allow. For instance, in many US states, religious parents are exempt from child abuse and child neglect laws when they deny their child standard medical care, and they are equally exempt from the requirement that their children receive public education or its equivalent.

Some libertarian thinkers not only toss associational freedom into the same pot as freedom of expression and freedom of religion, but view the latter freedoms as examples of the former, and indeed as examples that demonstrate the priority of the negative option to dissociate over the positive option to associate. Concerning expression, Loren Lomasky argues that the realization of free speech incorporates some form of semantic association, and that prior to a liberty to speak one's mind there must be 'a permission to desist from echoing the words that issue from the commanding heights of pulpit or palace'.

> That is, freedom of speech is no less fundamentally a freedom not to give utterance to objectionable phrases than it is to give declaration to one's own beliefs and attitudes. Speech rights are, then, associational and, in the first instance, negative.[14]

And, on religion, Lomasky argues that, insofar as freedom of religion is understood as:

> the struggle of individuals to secure adequate scope to practice their faith alongside others who espouse similar convictions, this is a mode of positive freedom of association. However, these confessional congregations cannot begin to get underway until there is acknowledged a negative freedom to dissociate from the established church... To follow a preferred path to salvation was to eschew incompatible routes. Thus, freedom of religion is, in the first instance, a negative entitlement [to dissociate].[15]

Lomasky is mistaken about the priority of negative freedoms of expression and religion over positive freedoms of expression and religion. For the negative option to dissociate from Religion A to exist, there must be a pre-existing positive option to be a member of Religion A. We cannot leave associations that we were never allowed to join. Similarly, for the negative option to stop parroting others' words to exist, there must first be the positive option to learn the language, concepts, and expressions that make both imitative and original expression possible. We cannot speak at all without first having access to the tools of speech. Hence, the positive protection of access is necessarily prior to whatever negative options we have to turn away from it.

This does imply that freedom of expression and freedom of religion have associational aspects, but it does not imply that they are *associational freedoms*. We'd be mistaken to list associational freedom in the same breath as freedom of expression and religion because, unlike the latter two freedoms, associational freedom does not give us a largely content-insensitive, defeasible protection to act in morally objectionable ways. We have claim-rights to form some morally impermissible associations, but not many. Let's focus first on cases that lack mutual consent and then on cases that have mutual consent.

6.3.2 Cases Lacking Consent

As we have seen, some of our intimate associations are mutually consensual. Some are not. And, the absence of consent doesn't always pose a moral problem, such as in the case of most parents and young children. But sometimes it does. The question, then, is whether associational freedom protects morally wrong associations that lack consent. The answer is that sometimes it does and sometimes it doesn't. Here are three examples where it does.

First, sometimes, associational freedom protects guardians in wrongfully severing or redrawing associations on their dependants' behalf without their consent. For instance, for health but not life-saving reasons, parents might decide to separate conjoined twins before the twins are old enough to give informed consent; the parents' decision is morally problematic, but it falls within their sphere of protected associative decision-making.

Analogously, one conjoined twin might seek to be separated from her sibling without the other's consent, thereby radically redefining her sibling's sense of identity as well as her associative position. Provided that the separation does not threaten the non-consenting twin's life, we might privilege the exclusivity claim of the twin seeking separation, despite its moral wrongness. We would do so, however, for the sake of both twins, not just the excluding twin, since the non-consenting twin's interests are probably ill-served by remaining conjoined to someone who wishes to be separated from her.

Second, associational freedom usually protects parents in changing their own association even when it radically changes their dependants' associations. When parents divorce, the family's associational arrangements change drastically, and possibly wrongly, but nonetheless the parents' associational freedom protects them in terminating their own intimate association with each other. That said, such decisions can be morally messy (i.e. defy a principled analysis), as we will see in Chapter 7.

Third, associational freedom protects guardians in *forming* some morally objectionable associations on their dependants' behalf without their consent. For example, a girl's parents might agree to an arranged marriage, which she will enter once she has matured. Since it is arranged before she is approaching maturity, she is unable to give informed consent to the arrangement, and therefore it is wrong given the kind of association it sets up. But let's assume that the daughter will embrace the idea of an arranged marriage when she matures, and that the parents have good reason to believe that she will embrace it. Thus, the arrangement will be acceptable to her at the time that she is expected to enter the marriage. Although the parents acted wrongly when they made the arrangement, nevertheless they were arguably protected in doing so given their credible beliefs about their daughter's future values. (Let us bracket the issue of adaptive preferences.)

By contrast, first, associational freedom does not protect parents in pursuing an arranged marriage to which their daughter doesn't consent once she reaches a mature age. If they force the marriage on her, then they act in a morally wrong way that associational freedom cannot protect. They have no right to force her into a marriage. Her own freedom of association protects her from this imposition.

Second, associational freedom also does not usually protect us in forming friendships with non-dependent people who have no wish to associate with us. As noted in the first case of Andy and Jo (where Andy and Jo are unrelated), Andy's consent usually matters when Jo wants to be his friend. Her associational claim-rights of conduct do not protect her in hounding him with the aim of being his friend. The same is true in the case of Lalit, who refuses to be Ali's friend even though it could save her tribe. She may well have a moral duty to be his friend, but Ali has no claim-right upon her that she be his friend. He has no right of conduct to force his company on her. The associative duties that Andy, Lalit, and we have correlative to everyone's positive associational claim-rights do not translate, absent special claims, into duties to associate with particular people.

Third, associational freedom cannot protect us in forming associations that are otherwise unduly burdensome on either our would-be associates or third-parties. For instance, our associational claim-rights fall short of protecting us in forming unequal and harmful associations such as an adult's sexual relation with a child or a father's sexual relation with his daughter or a spouse's relation with their partner in a forced marriage. Associational claim-rights *might* protect a professor in forming a sexual relation with her of-age student or the president with an intern, but not without a lot of explanation that will undoubtedly refer to consent. Consent matters not only for permissibility when it does make associations permissible, but also for the proper parameters of our claim-rights to act wrongly. Let's look at consent in more detail.

6.3.3 Cases with Consent

One thing to note about consent/voluntariness is that it comes in different varieties and degrees. Concerning varieties, there are at least four possibilities:

A: A person chooses her associative position and endorses it once chosen.
B: A person does not choose her associative position, but then endorses it once chosen.

C: A person chooses her associative position, but does not endorse it once chosen.

D: A person neither chooses her associative position nor endorses it once chosen.

For any two-person association, there are sixteen possible combinations of attitudes: AA, AB, AC, AD, BA, BB, BC, BD, CA, CB, CC, CD, DA, DB, DC, DD, which show that we oversimplify when we proceed as though associations are either (mutually) consensual or not.

Moreover, concerning degrees, a person might exercise partial choice, coerced choice, or least-worst-option choice in assuming a given associative position. And she might subsequently endorse some parts of an association, but not all parts of it. I will explore the moral implications of these different varieties and degrees of voluntariness in Chapter 7.

For now, speaking simply, the kinds of morally wrong associations that claim-rights are well designed to protect are consensual associations that are not unduly harmful to either party (or to third-parties). That said, although mutual consent often gives our associative decisions claim-rights protection, nevertheless sometimes it does not. Here are three examples where mutual consent can do the moral work, one example where it cannot, and two ambiguous cases.

First, consider again the intern who voluntarily enters a sexual relationship with a president. Consider also the of-age student who voluntarily enters a sexual relationship with a professor. As we saw, these associations are morally wrong because the subordinate party is poorly placed to judge the relationship and is vulnerable to mistreatment during it and afterward. Nevertheless, mutual consent can explain why such choices sometimes fall within our sphere of protected associational freedom to act wrongly.[16]

Second, consider again Romeo and Juliet, whose relationship poses risks to them both. They willingly assume those risks and their mutual consent (if they were of age) explains why their claim-rights protect their association.[17]

Third, if both the Duke of Norfolk and Thomas More wish to remain friends after More comes under suspicion for treason, their rights to associate protect their continued friendship even though More does a moral wrong by continuing the friendship. Given the morally uncomplicated, admirable nature of friendship, the interests we have in friendships, and the mutual commitment that More and the duke have to each other, associational rights of conduct are well designed to protect More if he wishes to continue the friendship. By contrast, consent cannot do the work to protect an association that would rob us of all future prospects for associative choice. In other words, we cannot legitimately consent to being a slave, as it eradicates all future possibility for associative control.

There are also some ambiguous cases. First, the risk to the duke is like the risk a highly contagious mother poses to her baby when she wants to continue to be his primary carer. Yet, in the mother's case, consent cannot do the moral work, since the baby is unable to consent to the harm in the way that the duke can. Consequently, we have conflicting intuitions about the mother's rights. On the one hand, we might think that, given the morally uncomplicated, admirable nature of mothering and the inestimable value of the baby being loved, the mother has an undefeated moral right to sustain the association despite the risks to her baby. Alternatively, we might think that, while she has a claim-right here, her right is overridden precisely because the baby cannot consent.

Second, equally morally ambiguous cases include our claim-rights to have associations that burden non-participants. Suppose the president's affair with someone is morally impermissible only because of its burdens for non-participants such as the president's spouse and children, whose home life is damaged by the association. Presumably, the president's claim-rights do protect the extramarital association. By contrast, suppose that More's friendship with the duke poses a threat not only to the duke's life, but also to the lives of the duke's children. In that case, More's (and the duke's) claim-rights fail to protect the association. Their rights to associate would probably still exist, but be overridden by the threat to the duke's dependants. The difference in the two cases lies in the severity of the burdens.

Together, these cases show that our claim-rights protect some wrongful associations, but not many, since the nature of our relations matter. Therefore, the positive claim-right to associate is much more limited than the other personal freedoms with which it is usually aligned.

Although it is sometimes unclear where lie the boundaries of the right to act wrongly in our associative decisions, nevertheless those boundaries are narrower than the boundaries of our right to act wrongly under our other personal freedoms. In Chapter 7, I will explore the challenges that confront my narrow account of freedom of association. These challenges arise when we unpack what it means for associations to be morally wrong.

6.3.4 The Claim-Right to Dissociate

The negative claim-right to dissociate has no such restrictions. It *is* like our freedoms of expression and religion in that it gives us broadly content-insensitive protection not to associate when we have a moral duty to associate. For example, it protects Jo in refusing to associate with her son, Andy, Mr Gustafson in refusing to associate with Kevin, and Lalit in refusing to be friendly with Ali. It also protects the duke in refusing to remain friends with More, and More in refusing to remain friends with the duke (though More's act would be more right than wrong, and hence doesn't need a claim-right against interference to protect it).

That said, such negative claim-rights are defeasible. They can be overridden by the duties with which they conflict. Given the fundamental importance of the associational claim-rights discussed above—to have associates when we are utterly dependent and to have opportunities to form associations when we are not utterly dependent—the negative claim-right to refuse association will be overridden when those competing positive claim-rights have special force or cannot reasonably be met through other means. And, as we saw above, state institutions are only ever imperfect mechanisms to secure our social needs.[18]

Conclusion

The last three chapters have shown that interpersonal connections are an unusual and fascinating normative domain, given the distinctive moral demands that our social claims generate. There never was nor could have been an unowned pool of social resources like the unowned land of material goods that existed before we appropriated parts of that natural world and asserted property rights over them. Social resources, by nature, rest with us as individual persons, and this complicates any effort to honour each other's positive social claim-rights and to regulate the distribution of social resources. Even so, these three chapters have shown that our positive interpersonal claim-rights put pressure on some of our most complacent liberal assumptions, such as the assumption that we have largely unencumbered moral rights to interact or not as we wish (Chapter 4), and to associate or not with whom we please when it pleases them too (Chapters 5 and 6). Our interactional and associational freedoms—our interpersonal freedoms—are much more constrained, content-sensitive, form-sensitive, and process-sensitive than standard liberal thinking recognizes. These freedoms are also not as fundamental as we presume them to be. They are secondary to positive interactional and associational claim-rights which both protect our fundamental social needs and are pre-conditions for any interactional and associational freedom worth the name.

7
Moral Messiness

Introduction: Three Stories

Story 1. In Caroline B. Cooney's young-adult novel, *The Face on the Milk Carton*, cult-damaged Hannah kidnaps three-year-old Jennie Spring and takes her home to her parents, Frank and Miranda, presenting the child to them as her own. When Hannah then returns to her cult, her parents lovingly raise Jennie, not knowing that she's not their granddaughter. To protect Jennie from Hannah's cult, they move to a new state, change their names, do not tell her about Hannah, and present themselves to her as her biological parents. Later, at the age of 15, Jennie Spring, now Janie Johnson, realises that she was kidnapped when she recognizes her own three-year-old face on the side of a milk carton listed as a 'Missing Child'. For a long time, she does not confront Frank and Miranda, as she does not want to be separated from them and returned to her biological family.

Story 2. A young woman, Michelle, is kidnapped by a man, Ariel, and held captive along with two other women for over ten years. Prior to being kidnapped, Michelle was raising her toddler, Joey. After she disappears, Joey is put into foster care and then adopted by his foster family, Sam and Sara Smith. After 10 years, Michelle finally escapes from her captor, and wishes to be reunited with Joey.[1,2]

Story 3. In Liane Moriarty's novel *The Hypnotist's Love Story*, Patrick, a widower with a toddler named Jack, falls in love with a woman, Saskia, who dearly loves both him and his son. For several years, Saskia is Jack's mother; she toilet-trains him, worries about his colds, makes his lunches, and is the one he calls for at night when he has nightmares. Then, suddenly, Patrick decides to end his relationship with her. Since Patrick and Saskia are not married and since Saskia has not adopted Jack, she has no legal right to continue either to be Jack's mother or to be in his life at all.[3]

These three stories will figure in the discussion here of morally messy associative choices. This chapter is written in the spirit of Philippa Foot, who said in a lecture once that she found that one productive way of working is to write a paper and then write another paper saying why the first paper was

Being Sure of Each Other: An Essay on Social Rights and Freedoms. Kimberley Brownlee, Oxford University Press (2020). © Kimberley Brownlee.
DOI: 10.1093/oso/9780198714064.001.0001

wrong. Since a monograph, unlike a series of papers, ideally reads like a single line of melody produced in one divinely inspired sitting, my aim in this chapter is not as grand as Foot's. My aim is simply to tackle an important issue that I left unaddressed in the last two chapters where I gave an *ex ante* analysis of our associative decisions. I showed in those chapters that associational freedom is a constrained, content-sensitive claim-right against interference, which only protects us in forming wrongful associations that honour fundamental concerns about consent, need, harm, and respect. The issue I left unaddressed is: What is the moral status of our associative and dissociative decisions *when an association already exists*? As the three above stories show, the existence of associations, including morally wrong associations, changes the moral ballgame. *Ex ante*, some associations simply should not exist; other associations should not have the prevailing content or structure that they have; and still others should neither exist nor, if they do, have their prevailing content or structure. In other words, we have no claim-rights to create such seriously morally wrong associations. But, *ex post*, we cannot simply say that all such associations should be dissolved.[4] This is because the people involved have become intertwined. They have developed a joint narrative. Often, they are mutually invested, deeply attached, and interdependent.[5]

Acknowledging that the existence of associations changes the moral ballgame necessarily prompts me to expand my narrow account of associational freedom to accommodate some morally messy associations. I use 'morally messy' as a technical term to refer to associations that defy a principled analysis and put us in an intuitive tight spot about how to respond them. We cannot judge them by *ex ante* standards, since they now exist and yet, in judging them by *ex post* standards, we confront various problems.[6] I show that these problems may be intractable, yielding the result that we must take a case-by-case approach to morally messy associations. What this approach shows, very interestingly, is, first, that we can acquire rights by doing serious wrongs and, second, that some associations that are too wrong for associational freedom to protect *ex ante* do get protected by it *ex post* because, ultimately, they secure important social needs.

In what follows, this chapter specifies the nature of *moral messiness* (Section 7.1) before distinguishing what I call the *parasite problem* from another problem in the rights theory literature known as the *piggybacking problem* (Section 7.2). The chapter then shows why moral messiness is a problem. First, it sets bad precedents. Second, in its parasitic form, it generates strange moral asymmetries between the associates. Third, it seems to entail that third-parties are both permitted and forbidden to interfere. Fourth, it raises general concerns about how much correct procedures matter even though they promise quality control, expectation-satisfaction, predictability, uniformity, coordination, and accountability (Section 7.3). Then, the chapter explores three possible solutions to *moral messiness* and the *parasite problem*, which appeal to defeasibility, conditionality, and group rights, none of which prove to be compelling (Section 7.4).

7.1 Moral Messiness

To make the claims of this chapter vivid, let me analyse the three above stories in terms of their moral messiness.

In Story 1, Frank and Miranda Johnson have no moral claim-right to be in an intimate, parent–child relationship with Janie. Their association with her is wrong in form: it should not exist no matter how good its content is.[7] This is because *ex ante* no one has a moral right to kidnap a child, or to raise a kidnapped child, even if one is a loving parent to her: the relationship came about through an illegitimate process.

But, *ex post*, now that their relationship has existed for over twelve years, the moral ballgame has changed. Since Frank and Miranda raised Janie innocently, lovingly, and well for over a decade before the kidnapping was detected, they have a moral claim-right against others now to continue to be her parents. That claim-right derives largely from Janie's best interests as well as her wishes to remain with them once the kidnapping becomes known. In other words, their rights derive largely from *her* rights to be in this relationship. Their rights also derive, secondarily, from their own legitimate expectations, which have gone unchallenged for a dozen years.

It would be a *pro tanto* wrong to Janie, and derivatively to Frank and Miranda, to sever their connection, even though Janie's biological family who were raising her before has both a prior claim and competing rights to be her primary family. Saying this does not deny that it is also *pro tanto* wrong to Janie's biological family not to restore their connection with their daughter. For this reason, Janie, Frank, and Miranda's association is morally messy and puts us in an intuitive tight spot. Who should get to raise Janie?[8]

In Story 2, Sam and Sara Smith's association with Joey is not directly wrong in form or content. In simple terms, it *should* exist because it is vital to Joey's wellbeing that foster parents take him in, and later adopt him, after his mother disappears.[9] Yet, at the same time, this adoptive parent–child association is *indirectly* wrong. In a nuanced sense, it should not exist. Circumstances should not be such that Joey's mother has been kidnapped and consequently is unavailable to be his primary caregiver.[10] Once Michelle escapes, she has a right to raise her child. Indeed, both Michelle and Joey have claim-rights in their own right to be together. However, Sam and Sara also have claim-rights to continue to be Joey's parents; some of their rights derive from his interests and wishes and some are their own rights to share in the specific relationship goods of this connection which they did no (direct) wrong in forming.[11] Once again, the association is morally messy. Who should get to raise Joey?

Story 3 is an example of messily dissociating from an association that already exists.[12] Since Patrick is no longer in love with Saskia, we might think that he is well within his moral rights to act badly by severing his relationship with her. Indeed, we might say that he acts less badly by severing it than he would do by remaining in it. But to say that he is within his rights and acts less badly than he might do, we have to ignore the fact that, in leaving Saskia, Patrick also severs Saskia's bond with Jack, whom she has been raising as her own child.[13]

As this case shows, the existence of an association can affect the moral quality of dissociating by turning an otherwise morally permissible or at least claim-right-protected dissociative act into a morally messy one. *Ex ante*, often we may choose rightly or wrongly not to associate; but *ex post*, once we have entered and sustained an association, we may not simply leave the association with moral impunity, and we may have only limited claim-rights to act wrongly by leaving it. Consider, for instance, another dissociation case. Suppose a woman is offered a prestigious job in a different country. Her husband moves with her as her dependant. The woman then finds a new romantic partner and ends her relationship with the husband.[14]

The reason that many morally messy associations defy a principled normative analysis often lies in what I call the *parasite problem*. (I should note that Leif Wenar observed in correspondence that, in my cases, the 'parasites' don't actually harm their hosts. Therefore, in ecological terms, my cases are more like instances of *mutualism*, a term that describes a form of symbiotic relationship in which two organisms benefit from each other. However, I have opted to keep the label the *parasite problem*, to highlight that some of the parties' rights in my cases are produced by serious wrongdoing. The etymology of the term 'parasite' comes via Latin from the Greek *parasitos*, which means 'eating at another person's table', an idea that fits well with the cases I am considering and involves an activity that need not harm the host.)

Briefly, the *parasite problem* is that a person who has no claim-right of conduct in her own right can acquire a claim-right of conduct which derives from a second person's claim-right of conduct. This happens when the content of the second person's right cannot be realized without the first person's participation. When the second person has a specific claim on the first person that she participate, then the first person gains a *duty-based* claim-right to participate which depends on the second person's undisputed claim-right. Put differently, if a right-holder has an undisputed right to do something *interpersonal*, then there must be another person with whom he has a protected entitlement to do that thing with, even if the latter person has no right in her own right to do the thing in question. Both Frank and Miranda and, to a lesser extent, Sam and Sara, are parasites. They get their parenting rights from their 'hosts' (the children in question) and, in having those parenting rights, they benefit their hosts. In principle, the *parasite problem* can arise in relation to any necessarily interpersonal right, such as communication rights, cultural-membership rights, and professional-service rights. In this chapter, I bracket these other contexts to focus on associational rights.

Other morally messy associations do not involve parasitism. For instance, in a loving, committed marriage between two adults that was formed when they were *both* children, neither party is a parasite on the other. Instead, a wrong was done *to them* by others. Their association—which they embrace now—is 'wrong' in that it should not have come into existence, but it is not wrong because of any wrongdoing on their part. Since they are now committed to it, it is morally messy in that it defies a simple assessment of its moral status.

For another instance, consider an IVF clinic that accidentally swaps the genetic material of two couples, implanting the embryo from couple A into woman B and the embryo from couple B into woman A. The women give birth to the babies and raise them for a year or so before the mistake is discovered. None of the parents committed a wrong (unless they did wrong by accepting the risks of IVF treatment), but their associations with their gestational and genetic children are morally messy. Who should raise which child? (In a real-life case in the Czech Republic, two couples were given the wrong baby to take home after birth. After a year, they switched the children back, privileging the genetic connection over the year-long developmental connection.[15])

Morally messy *dissociative* acts do not involve parasitism. Patrick's decision to leave Saskia is morally messy because it destroys her relationship with

Jack, and because neither she nor Jack has a (legal) immunity from Patrick's decision. No one feeds off a 'host'.

The moral messiness of certain associative and dissociative decisions arises, first, from the fact that associating is inescapably interpersonal: associations necessarily involve the interests of two or more people, and people's interests can tend in different directions. People's interests can also tend in the same direction, but go against moral restrictions on the processes through which associations come about, their structures, and their content.

Second, moral messiness arises from the fact that not all our associations can or should be mutually voluntary either when they are formed or once they exist. We are put into associations as babies and young children that we could not choose, including parent–child relationships (or not) and sibling relationships (or not). We are given cousins, aunts, uncles, grandparents (or not). Some of us are later put into marriages, to which, in time, we may become deeply committed (or not). Finally, many of us, when we mature (or sometimes before we mature), assume the responsibility of being a parent, and we may not permissibly abandon that responsibility at will. Many of these connections serve our best interests and, once they exist, radically constrain our associative options.

Associations that are morally wrong in *content* are not as morally messy as associations that are morally wrong in *form*. This is because associations that are wrong in content will encounter a tipping point when the more vulnerable parties' best interests tip in favour of third-party interventions to dissolve the association. For example, if two people have an abusive relationship that becomes increasingly violent over time, conditions will ultimately tip in favour of dissolution even if the parties are committed to each other and have adapted to fit the association.

That said, Roy Baumeister and Mark Leary highlight participants' unwillingness to leave such associations, which suggests that, from the first-person perspective, associations that are wrong in content may seem just as morally messy as associations that are wrong in form:

> In many cases, people seem reluctant to dissolve even bad or destructive relationships. The apparent unwillingness of many women to leave abusive, battering spouses or boyfriends has prompted several generations of speculative explanations, ranging from masochistic or self-destructive liking for abuse to calculations of economic self-interest that supposedly override considerations of physical harm. The belongingness hypothesis offers yet one more potential perspective: The unwillingness to leave an

abusive intimate partner is another manifestation of the strength of the need to belong and of the resulting reluctance to break social bonds. The fact that people resist breaking off an attachment that causes pain attests to how deeply rooted and powerful the need to belong is…[But]…the tendency for battered women to return to their abusive partners has been explained in many ways, and the hypothesized reluctance to break off a relationship is only one of them.[16]

That said, associations that are wrong only in *form* encounter no such tipping point where the parties' best interests tip in favour of dissolution. For these associations, such as Janie's association with Frank and Miranda, it is not obvious that dissolution is the morally best, or even acceptable, thing to do.

In what follows, I focus on form-wrong associations, not content-wrong associations, since form-wrongs are trickier for my narrow account of associational freedom. Since many such associations involve parasitism, let's tackle the *parasitism problem* head-on, and begin by distinguishing it from a problem with which it intersects, the *piggybacking problem*.

7.2 Piggybackers versus Parasites

The much-discussed phenomenon of so-called *piggybacking* is described in different terms by Joseph Raz, who refers to the *double harmony* between the right-holder's interests and others' interests in the right-holder having the right in question. For instance, a journalist's rights—to access sensitive material, enter dangerous places, protect her sources, be secure against action for libel or breach of privacy, and report freely—would not have the same weight and importance that they do have, Raz says, if protecting the journalist's interests did not also serve society's interests in a free press.[17] There is a double harmony between the journalist's interests in having these protections and society's interests in her having them.

However, it is not so much the *weight* as the very *existence* of the journalist's rights that depends on society's interests in her having these rights. Her rights as a journalist are *grounded* at least partly, if not solely, in her society's interests in her having these rights.[18] Similarly, a judge's rights to decide cases are grounded not so much in her interests as in society's interests in her having these rights. Raz makes comments that seem to acknowledge this fact:

> aspects of freedom of speech cannot be explained at all except as protecting collective goods, i.e., preserving the character of the community as an open society. The freedom of the press illustrates the point... The justification of the special rights and privileges of the press [is] in its service to the community at large.[19]

Leif Wenar, Frances Kamm, and others argue that if protecting other people's interests is the underlying reason for protecting the journalist's or the judge's role-related interests, then the journalist's and judge's individual interests are insufficient, if not irrelevant, to ground the rights in question.[20] In other words, in these cases there is no double harmony between the right-holder's interests and others' interests in her having these rights. The right-holder's individual interests play no part in grounding the rights in question. She piggybacks on her society's interests in her holding this official role.

Wenar argues: 'Role-bearers [as individuals] often do not have interests in their rights [that are] sufficient to justify their having those rights. When they do not, they cannot within Raz's own analysis have rights.'[21] In the reference to roles, however, Raz offers a potential route to a solution, Wenar says—which is to say that rights do not attach to individuals. Rather, they attach to roles.

The point to highlight for present purposes is that piggybackers such as the journalist and the judge undoubtedly have their role-related rights. They are legitimate occupants of their legitimate official roles and have the rights to perform the functions of those official roles. The dispute is simply whether the journalist's and judge's own interests contribute at all to grounding their rights.

By contrast, a parasite, while like a piggybacker in not having individual interests that are sufficiently strong or suitable to ground rights, is an *illegitimate* occupant of her legitimate role and hence does not indisputably have the role-related rights that go with it. As noted above, Frank and Miranda have no moral-claim right in their own right to be in a loving parent–child relationship with Janie. They are not role-occupiers in the legitimate sense that ordinary judges, journalists, police officers, parents, and spouses are legitimate occupiers of legitimate social roles. (In one sense, Frank and

Miranda are analogous to the person who grabs a judge's gown from the judge's chambers, sits up behind the bench, and then dispenses justice fairly for many years before being found out.)[22]

But equally, as indicated above, Frank and Miranda have strong parental moral duties to Janie both before and after the kidnapping is exposed. Those duties give them duty-based rights to care for her, which derive from her claim-right to be in this parent–child relationship with them. Given that their performance in the parenting role is exemplary, their continued occupancy in the role is necessary for Janie's best interests and required by her legitimate expectations, and Frank and Miranda's own expectations have become legitimate by going unchallenged, they gain parasitic associational rights to stay in this parent–child relationship. (I will bracket for now questions about the merit of Janie's claim-right to be in this relationship.)

Sam and Sara Smith are, in a simple sense, legitimate occupiers of their legitimate social role as Joey's adoptive parents. As noted above, their role-occupancy over time is rooted partly in their own interests and partly in Joey's interests. (So, they are not piggybackers.) At the same time, in a more nuanced sense, they are not legitimate occupiers of their parenting role, since Joey should not be available for them to foster and adopt as their own. So, indirectly, they are parasites, since it is Joey's need to have a family, and Joey's need alone, that gives them the title to foster and adopt him.

Another parenting example to consider is life-generating rape. A person who commits a life-generating rape against another person has no moral claim-right in his own right to be a parent to the child who comes into being as a result of that rape. And yet, if the person who committed the rape were to raise the child lovingly and well for a long time such that the child came to have legitimate expectations of him and interests in remaining with him, then *ex post* the person would acquire parasitic rights-claims to be the child's parent. Indeed, in some cases, it might be in the child's *best* interests to be raised by him rather than anyone else including, perhaps, the parent who was raped. (In many cases, the child may be unaware of the story behind her creation. Consider, for example, a case of marital rape where the victim forgives and remains with the person who committed the rape. The child of such a rape could grow up without any knowledge that her life originated in an attack on someone.) Drawing on Wenar's kind-desire account of rights,[23] the child has a right to remain in association with the parent who perpetrated the rape provided not only that a child in a parent–child relationship has the power to impose duties of care on her parent (or to have those duties be imposed on her behalf) but also that she desires (or has reason to desire) that those duties be performed by that parent.

A further example is a child–adult marriage. A child who is married to an adult has legitimate claim-rights against her spouse to protect and care for her, especially if she's unable to return to her family. The adult spouse, who has no right in his own right to be in this relationship, gains a parasitic right to remain in it when the child's best interests and legitimate expectations require that he do so (which means among other things that he treat the child in an age-appropriate way). The same goes for the relationship between a president and an intern, discussed in previous chapters. Once such a relationship exists, the dominant party, who may have no right in his own right to form this connection given its radically inegalitarian contours, high profile, and risks, has specific duties to the subordinate party, which might not include maintaining the relationship, but certainly include resolving it in a way that protects the other's interests.

To see vividly the normative position of these parasitic wrongdoers, consider them in contrast with a highly contagious mother who has a life-threatening illness. The highly contagious mother has a right in her own right to be her child's primary carer, and the child has a right to be cared for by his mother. But, both the mother's right and the child's right are overridden by the child's best interests, which are to be raised by a caring person other than the mother until the mother is no longer contagious. Once the mother is free of contagion, authorities have a duty to restore her child to her and, most likely, to apologize to her for removing her child from her care if they did so against her will. By contrast, none of the adults in the three previous cases have a claim-right in their own right to be the primary carers that they are. (Of course, if a long time passes before the mother is free from contagion, then the foster parent will come to have some competing moral claim-rights, premised upon the child's best interests (and possibly the child's wishes) which must be considered alongside those of the mother.)

7.3 Why Moral Messiness Is a Problem

A variety of problems arise from moral messiness in general and parasitism in particular. None of these problems applies to every morally messy associative decision.

1. *Setting bad precedents.* Briefly, concerning parasitism, if we accept that parasites do have rights to carry out the functions of the role they've assumed, then we must confront the problems of vigilantism and bad precedents. It sets a bad precedent to imply that all a person needs to do to come to have the rights of a parent, for example, is to kidnap a child or to engage in a

life-generating rape against someone, and then manage to participate in raising the child long enough and well enough that the child comes to have legitimate interests in that person continuing to raise her.

A context in which people tend to make effective, if not malicious, use of the parasitic value of longevity is in custody battles, where the parent who has a child in her primary care during a contested divorce and custody case has an interest in stalling as long as possible because the longer the child remains in her care, is settled in school, and is doing well, the stronger the argument for preserving the *status quo* in the child's best interests. Stall tactics were used effectively by the lawyer representing the biological father William Stern in the 1986 Baby M surrogacy case. The lawyer delayed the trial so that the baby stayed with the biological father and his wife for a long time before the trial began, so that the judge would be more likely to rule that it was in the baby's best interests to stay with the father. Such parents and lawyers use the passage of time not merely to change our intuitions about the child's best interests, but also *actually* to change the child's best interests.

Bad precedents can arise in non-parasitic cases too. If two children put into a marriage come to embrace the relationship when they are mature, then their families may feel vindicated and at liberty to take the same approach for their other children. Also, other families may see this marriage as a model and feel licensed to make similar arrangements for their own children.

Bad precedents can also arise by morally messy dissociations. Compare Paul Gauguin, who left his wife and children to become a renowned painter, with a fictional Paul Gauguin-2 who was inspired by this success and left his own family, but failed to gain recognition as a painter. Even if the impersonal value of Paul Gauguin's art vindicates his decision to abandon his family, he sets a bad precedent that other would-be artists such as Paul Gauguin-2 might follow.

2. *Moral asymmetries*. We saw in Chapter 6 that moral asymmetries can arise between associates. There, we focused on asymmetries in moral *permission* (not asymmetries in moral *claim-rights*). We saw that, whereas the Duke of Norfolk was morally permitted, if not obligated, to remain a friend to Thomas More, More was not permitted to remain connected to the duke in a way that would threaten the duke's life.

Here, we are concerned with asymmetries between associates' moral claim-rights against interference. In parasitic associations, one party has a right to be in the association and the other party lacks a right in his own right to be in it. For instance, the vulnerable parties in the kidnapping cases, the child marriage case, and the life-generating rape case each have a right to be in their respective morally wrong associations, but their wrongdoing-associates do not, at least not according to *ex ante* reasoning.[24]

This difference in moral status between the undisputed right-holder and the parasite is noteworthy, since we tend to assume that associational claim-rights apply to and protect both parties: either both parties have a protected sphere in which to associate with each other in a particular way or both parties do not.

3. *The permissible interference problem*. In both parasitic and non-parasitic cases, third-parties seem to be both permitted to interfere and prohibited from interfering with people's associative decisions. For example, on the one hand, third-parties seem to be permitted to interfere with the parent-child association of a man who commits a life-generating rape and a person who kidnaps a child, since *ex ante* these wrongdoers have no right to have access to, let alone be the primary carers for, the children they are raising. This conclusion seems unavoidable if only for the precedent-setting reasons just noted; it would be highly regressive to allow that all a person needed to do to become a parent is kidnap a child or rape someone such that it leads to pregnancy and birth, and then participate in child-rearing for a long-enough period to solidify a bond. On the other hand, if the child's associational rights are intact, then *ceteris paribus* third-parties are forbidden to interfere with the child's association with this willing, competent parent, especially if the relationship serves the child's best interests and the child endorses it.[25] Therefore, we seem to get the conclusion that third-parties are both permitted and forbidden to interfere.

Indeed, we seem to get the conclusion that third-parties are both *required* to interfere and forbidden to interfere. It seems not just that third-parties *may* prevent these wrongdoing parents from continuing in the associations they are in. Arguably, we are *required* to intervene to prevent them from continuing in those associations. Equally, we seem to be not only forbidden to interfere, but required to enforce the duties within those associations. If, indeed, the *de facto* parents in these cases (or the adult spouse of a child) have the responsibilities that both they and their dependants say they have, then third-parties, notably society and the state, have a duty to ensure that these parents (or the spouse) are protected in fulfilling those caring duties. They get duty-based rights to continue the relationship.

Similarly, in non-parasitic cases, third-parties seem also to be both permitted and forbidden to interfere. In the case of a under-age, forced marriage that the two spouses now embrace as adults, third-parties are permitted to interfere for bad-precedent reasons, but forbidden to interfere for autonomy-respecting reasons (assuming that the association is wrong only in *form*). Likewise, in an IVF mix-up case, third-parties arguably have duties to help the two couples reach an acceptable solution (if there can be one) that is in the children's best interests. But what are those best interests, especially when the parents' preferred solutions differ?

4. *How much do correct procedures matter?* As noted above, having correct procedures for legitimate social-role occupancy promises several goods including quality control, expectation-satisfaction, predictability, uniformity, coordination, and accountability. But moral messiness and parasitism suggest that, in some contexts at least, correct procedures matter less than we assume.[26] Or rather, moral messiness and parasitism suggest that the correct procedures are often not the ones we think they are. The above suggests, for instance, that a child's best interests should always prevail, which means that sometimes, through no fault of their own, people can lose their right to parent a child, and a person who has done serious wrong can secure the right to parent that child.

7.4 Possible Solutions

There are at least three possible strategies we might adopt to try to resolve the dilemmas created by both moral messiness and the *parasite problem*, none of which prove to be fully compelling. The strategies appeal to: (1) defeasibility, (2) conditionality, and (3) group rights.

7.4.1 Defeasibility

Rights have special normative force. They are called conversation-stoppers, argument-thresholds, and trumps. They are special, weighty reasons that tend to override competing considerations to pursue other social goals. They are a check on straightforward consequentialist reasoning. In virtue of these special properties, rights secure for persons a basic level of equal treatment, protection, and freedom. Such equal protections are only genuine if rights cannot be easily defeated. As Peter Jones puts it:

> If rights can be removed or overridden when they come up against competing considerations, that may seem to imperil their very character

as rights... [For example,] what sort of guarantees would we possess if the right to a fair trial or the right not to be tortured were not absolute [i.e. indefeasible]?[27]

But, of course, despite their normative force, rights are not absolute. As we saw in Chapters 4 and 5, rights are sometimes defeasible. First, some rights are more important than other rights. When more important rights conflict with less important rights, the more important rights should usually defeat the less important rights. For instance, we saw that positive social claims are generally more important than associational freedom. Second, sometimes a projected bad outcome is so horrific that it surmounts the argumentative threshold posed by competing rights, at least when the rights at stake are not fundamentally important.[28] In slightly stronger terms, Jones states: 'For virtually every right that one might assert it is possible to think of circumstances in which there is a plausible case for setting that right aside.'[29]

The defeasibility of rights offers a possible strategy to dissolve morally messy associative decisions, if such decisions are invariably defeated by competing considerations. To test this possibility, let's return to Story 1. Janie's claim-right to remain in her loving parent–child relationship with Frank and Miranda is defeasible (by hypothesis), and so too, in turn, are Frank and Miranda's parasitic rights which depend on Janie's right. If Janie's right is actually *defeated* by her biological family's prior claim and competing rights to be in a family relationship with her, then so too are Frank and Miranda's rights. If not, then her rights, and their rights, defeat her biological family's rights.

What factors are salient to determining which rights are defeated in this case? Does it matter that, in Janie's biological family, she has brothers and sisters whom she doesn't know and who don't know her as well as her biological mother, father, and grandparents? These people all have legitimate rights claims. Do they collectively defeat hers (and with hers, Frank and Miranda's)? Or, does it matter that whereas the members of this larger family all have each other, Frank and Miranda have only Janie, since their own daughter, Hannah, has vanished and they've no other family? Do Janie's legitimate expectations and wishes defeat the claims of whichever parents she does not wish to live with? Do Janie's best interests and no one else's trump all other considerations? These questions show how complex the project is of trying to untangle the competing claims to determine which rights are defeated and which stand firm. They can leave us with no confidence about any conclusion we draw on which rights should prevail.

Similarly, in Story 2, Joey's claim-right to stay with Sam and Sara, and his claim-right to be returned to Michelle, as well as Sam and Sara's claim-right to remain Joey's parents and Michelle's claim-right to be reinstated as his mother, are all defeasible (by hypothesis), giving rise to a similar set of messy questions about the relative importance of competing considerations.

In Story 3, Patrick's claim-right to terminate Jack's association with Saskia is defeasible (by hypothesis), and it bumps up against Jack's and Saskia's moral rights to remain in a relationship with each other. However, conventionally, we privilege the (official) parent's claims over others' claims in the name of general parent–child-relationship interests. We might think that Patrick's giving Saskia something like visitation rights would be the best solution, but this is at his discretion, and not the product of her rights trumping his.

The problem with the defeasibility solution is that a right is not much of a right if it is *always* defeated by competing considerations. And, to avoid parasitism, we would have to say that *all* the rights that generate parasitic rights are always defeated by competing considerations. If intersubjective rights are so very defeasible that they do not stand up to any counter-pressure, then they are not much of an argumentative threshold. They do not trump anything. They have no special normative force.

One way forward might be to unpack defeasibility in terms of a proportionality test: Is the interference with a given undisputed right proportionate and, hence, justified (i.e. an infringement, not a violation)? Such a proportionality test would have at least four conditions. First, the interference with the right serves a legitimate aim. Second, there is a rational connection between that aim and the interference with the right in question. Third, no less restrictive means will suffice to achieve the legitimate aim. In other words, the interference is necessary. Fourth, the legitimate aim is indeed more important: it is weightier than the right at stake.[30] This kind of approach would give us a set of tools to combat some of the questions that the above cases raise. However, this approach is unlikely to yield the result we would need to avoid all parasitic and non-parasitic cases of moral messiness. The result we would need is that all rights that would lead to parasitism are invariably defeated by competing considerations.

7.4.2 Conditionality

Whereas defeasibility and absoluteness pertain to the moral *weight* of rights, conditionality pertains to their *nature*. Most, if not all, rights are conditional in some respect. Consider, for example, contractual rights. If you hire me to paint your house for £500, my right to the £500 is conditional on my painting your house. Similarly, a medical professional's right to treat people suffering in a war-torn area is conditional at least on her having the requisite medical expertise. But is it conditional on anything else? Are her rights to practise and her patients' rights to receive her care conditional on her having a proper license to practise in that jurisdiction? Likewise, are children's rights to be raised by willing, competent parents conditional on those parents both coming to be parents through legitimate processes and not engaging in serious wrongdoing (that does not harm the child)?

Serious wrongdoing is a deal-breaker for many rights, but not for all. As we saw in Chapter 1, some rights are *secure*, which means that we have them independently of whether we meet certain standards of good behaviour and good standing. Secure claims cannot be forfeited through bad behaviour. I have followed James Nickel in holding that we have four such secure claims: (1) a secure claim to have a life; (2) a secure claim to lead a life; (3) a secure claim against excessively unfair treatment; and (4) a secure claim against degradation and cruelty.[31] In fleshing out the details of these secure claims, we have seen that they cover many cases that generate moral messiness and parasitism, notably intimate relations of dependency and care, emergencies, and core service provision. Consequently, the conditionality of rights will not enable us to avoid the parasitism problem.

Moreover, there is a difficulty in claiming that some right—such as a child's right to be raised by a willing, competent parent or cared for by her adult spouse—is constrained by a thick notion of *competence* that rules out coming to be a parent or spouse through indefensible means. The difficulty is that, empirically, persons who become parents or (chaste) spouses of a child through indefensible means may well be competent parents and spouses in all other respects.

7.4.3 Group Rights

A third possible solution is to say that interpersonal rights are group rights, not individual rights. On this reading, either the parties in question have a group right to act together or they do not. Hence, either a given adult and child have a group right to associate with each other in a parent–child way or they do not. Either two people have a group right to be spouses or they do not. Concerning parasitism, a group-rights analysis means that there is no conceptual space to say that one party has a right to act interpersonally with another party, but the other party has no right in her own right to act interpersonally with the first party. A group-rights analysis avoids such moral asymmetries in claim-rights. Either they both have a right or they both don't.

A group-rights analysis also avoids the problem of permissible interference. A given association either is or is not protected by a group claim-right. If the group has no right to act, then third-parties may permissibly interfere. If the group has a right to act, then third-parties may not permissibly interfere.

However, there are several problems with a group-rights analysis. First, it cannot avoid the *bad precedents problem* or the related *devaluing-of-correct-procedures problem*. Second, a group-rights analysis ignores that often one of the two parties in question is guilty of serious wrongdoing. Third, a group-rights analysis has difficulty explaining how interpersonal rights such as intimate associational claim-rights arise and dissolve. It is easier to explain such events with an individual-rights analysis. Fourth, the positive and negative sides of interpersonal rights, such as freedom of association, would then have different subjects. Whereas the negative right to dissociate and refuse to associate would be an individual right, the positive right to associate would be a group right.

Finally, a group-rights analysis has difficulty specifying the rights-claims that parties in question have on each other. The claims that spouses have on each other, for example, aren't group-right claims which they share. Rather, they are individual claims that each has upon the other, and these claims may differ from one another (e.g. a man doesn't have a claim on his wife that she support him in various ways during his pregnancy). For these reasons, a group-rights analysis will not enable us to evade the parasite problem.

If these are the best solutions available, then morally messy associations and parasitism are intractable problems that force us to take a case-by-case approach.

Conclusion

Our world of social connections is wonderfully diverse and morally messy because our associations necessarily involve two or more persons' interests. We cannot associate alone. And, when we opt to dissociate, we often do this at the expense of someone who would otherwise be our associate. Our choices about how, when, why, and with whom to associate are inescapably bound up with other people's associative interests.

From the analysis in this chapter, we can draw the following tentative conclusions. First, some, but not all, morally messy relationships are matters of bad luck, tragedy, or injustice done to the parties in the relationship. It is tragic and unjust for two children to be forced to marry; it is tragic and unjust for an adult and a child to be forced to marry. In other morally messy relationships, one of the parties to the association is guilty of the wrong that produces the connection. When that party's wrong leads to parasitism, we confront distinctive moral issues, such as the *moral asymmetry problem* and an acute version of the *permissible interference problem*. Second, when we favour dissolving an association, that dissolution should be achieved in a way that best serves the associates' interests. This might be a gentle transition in some cases and, less frequently, an abrupt termination in other cases. Third, some forms of conventional association should be given greater protection in law. For instance, former common law step-parents should have some legal rights, e.g. visitation rights.[32] The broader conclusion to draw is that, when the balance of reasons favours protecting a morally messy associative decision, the narrow account of associational freedom I have advanced must be expanded to accommodate it. Let us now turn back to more formal, social, and political institutions. In the next chapter, I examine the implications for institutions and policies in taking positive social rights seriously.

8
Segregation

Introduction

Segregating institutions such as prisons, hospitals, orphanages, and immigration centres can assault our social bonds. Sometimes, they undermine our very abilities to lead healthy social lives. They also often dehumanize us by disregarding that we remain deeply social beings even when we are contagious, undocumented, dangerous, or guilty of egregious behaviour.[1]

In this chapter, I home in on one particular institution—prison—as the site *par excellence* of the particular social injustices that have animated me in this book. These social injustices, while most vivid in prison settings, pervade Anglo-American criminal justice systems. First, we tend to doubt whether people who have offended are able to contribute meaningfully to others' survival and well-being.[2] Second, we are led by that doubt to concretely mistreat people who have offended.

In this chapter, I also highlight parallels between our criminal justice practices and our practices in other segregating institutions such as hospitals and immigration centres. I highlight both the ways we physically segregate people and the ways we use branding and markers to symbolically segregate people.

In Section 8.1, I explore how and why we continue to use classificatory terms in some domains that reduce people's lives to a single feature, such as an offence. In criminal justice, we use terms such as 'offender', 'criminal', 'crook', 'felon', 'convict', 'lawbreaker', 'outlaw', and 'delinquent', as well as a host of others that make it hard for a person who has offended to see themselves as anything other than the sum of their offences, let alone as a meaningful contributor to others' well-being. In parallel ways, we use reductive labels in immigration settings, such as 'refugee', 'immigrant', 'alien', 'outsider', 'stranger', 'non-native', and 'foreign national', and in healthcare, such as 'patient', 'invalid', 'sufferer', 'victim', and 'case'. These latter labels are less poisonous than their criminal justice equivalents, but nonetheless ignore the complexity of people's lives. I argue that we should abandon all such labels and revise the attitudes that they reflect.

Being Sure of Each Other: An Essay on Social Rights and Freedoms. Kimberley Brownlee, Oxford University Press (2020). © Kimberley Brownlee.
DOI: 10.1093/oso/9780198714064.001.0001

In Section 8.2, I unpack how our prejudicial attitudes feed into, and from, the concrete ways we treat the people whom we tend to segregate. In criminal justice, when we view people as the sum of their offences, unsurprisingly, we treat them in ways consonant with that identity and, consequently, do concrete social injustices to them. We do this most notably but not exclusively in our prisons, where we stretch people's social ties to breaking point, give them sentences they sometimes cannot spend, and deny them help to reintegrate socially after they have served a sentence, thereby compromising their social resources. Again, parallels exist between our practices in prison and other segregating institutions, especially in immigration centres and hospitals that divide families.

In Section 8.3, I pinpoint which social rights, if any, people forfeit when they are justifiably segregated, and which rights, if any, people retain but have infringed (i.e. justifiably overridden) for public-good reasons.

Finally, in Section 8.4, I address two objections. The first, pertaining specifically to offending, is that the corrective justice system is the place in which people who have offended make their social contributions. The second, pertaining to segregation across institutions, is that some people genuinely are social threats, not contributors. Both objections can be answered.

Before proceeding, let me bracket one important issue, which is whether criminal justice and punishment are *by nature* practices that perpetuate the kinds of interpersonal social injustice I have discussed in this book.[3] I shall not answer this question. Instead, I shall focus on the particular kinds of punishments that we tend to use in Anglo-American systems, notably long-term incarceration, temporary segregation in isolation, long-term solitary confinement (used in the US, Australia, UK,[4] and Canada,[5] for example), and indeed execution (in the US), as well as the kinds of attitudes that we tend to adopt in Anglo-American societies toward people who have been convicted of criminal wrongdoing.

8.1 The Language We Use

8.1.1 Essentialist Language

In many domains, we have learned to be attentive to the language we use to describe people, recognizing that our language reflects, and fuels, specific perceptions of people. Thankfully, we no longer refer to people as 'handicaps' or 'retards'. We no longer speak of 'the disabled', 'the poor', or the 'undeserving poor'. We no longer speak of married women as 'a man's better half' or 'the Missus'. Instead, we speak of 'people with cognitive impairments', 'people who are living in poverty', and 'married women'. If we're sufficiently attentive to our language, we do not even refer to people with disabilities as 'disabled people', but as 'people with disabilities'.

Essentialist language is often disrespectful since, first, it reduces a person's identity to a feature, trait, or act that ostensibly sums up the core of who he is; and second, it often highlights a feature that historically (and sometimes still) carries a stigma. The first part raises the spectre of inaccuracy and misunderstanding; the second part brings the whiff of prejudice. Both make it likely that we will act in ways that are patronizing, demeaning, and potentially harmful.[6]

Concerning inaccuracy, essentialist language can be innocuous or laudatory in itself. The terms 'wife' and 'mother' have positive connotations. But even that language can be problematic when it hides salient information and misleads us about who the person is and how she lives, such as when the person to whom the terms 'wife' and 'mother' refer is 11 years old.

Concerning prejudice, we now recognize that our tendency to use essentialist language in domains such as disability or poverty is evidence of our ignorance and disrespect, and sometimes downright bigotry. By contrast, as noted above, we continue to use essentialist language in criminal justice, immigration, or general health. Let's look at criminal justice in more detail.

The noun 'criminal', as defined in the *Oxford English Dictionary* (*OED*), has two distinct senses: (1) a person guilty or convicted of a crime; (2) a person with a *tendency* to commit crime. Only the second of these senses identifies a disposition to offend, but its essentialist connotations seep into all our uses of the term 'criminal'. Scholars and legislators who are more careful with their terminology use the less loaded but nonetheless classificatory term 'offender', which is defined in the *OED* as: (1) a person who offends, who infringes a rule or regulation; a transgressor or sinner, as well as a person who gives offence, displeases, or causes resentment, upset, etc.; and (2) a person who breaks the law, one who commits an offence. These definitions do not highlight a disposition to offend, but the term 'offender' nonetheless has such connotations.

In July 2015, then UK Justice Secretary Michael Gove used heartening rhetoric in a lecture to the Prisoners' Learning Alliance on 'The Treasure in the Heart of Man: Making Prisons Work'.

> Our streets will not be safer, our children will not be properly protected and our future will not be more secure unless we change the way we treat

offenders and offenders then change their lives for the better. There is a treasure, if only you can find it, in the heart of every man, said Churchill. It is in that spirit we will work.[7]

Yet, unsurprisingly, as this quote confirms, Gove uses the essentialist label 'offenders' to refer to people who have committed crimes.[8]

Even before someone is convicted, we use essentialist language. We refer to people who are suspected of committing a crime as 'suspects' rather than as 'people suspected of committing a crime'. This identifies the person with the suspected offence and puts some pressure on our commitment to the presumption of innocence. (Indeed, historically, a person suspected of committing a crime was referred to as a 'criminal', i.e. 'the criminal in the dock'.[9]) Thankfully, the term 'suspect' is temporally constrained; the person carries this label for a period, not for life. But the person who is convicted of a criminal offence carries the official label 'offender', as well as all other unofficial labels, for a long time, sometimes for life.

Moreover, we often call people who have completed their sentence 'ex-offender', 'ex-convict', and 'ex-con'. And, during their punishment—if it includes incarceration—we brand them as a 'jailbird' or a 'yardbird'. Additionally, in many prisons, officials refer to the people in their care by their surname only, as 'Smith' and never as 'Mr Smith', which is a demeaning form of address in this context that fits with broader, reductive, dehumanizing practices in criminal justice.

In addition to these broad classificatory terms, we have a host of subtler terms, which we apply to people who have committed particular offences. In ordinary speech, we refer to certain people as 'murderers', 'rapists', 'thieves', 'psychopaths', or 'serial killers'. Even reputable, language-conscious newspapers such as *The New York Times* and *The Guardian* have headlines such as 'To Catch a Rapist', 'Rapist Who Came to UK with Fake ID Jailed for "Sadistic" Sex Attacks', and 'How Not to Raise a Rapist'.

In a related vein, Nicola Lacey observes that we have a host of classificatory labels for people who are suspected or convicted of criminal wrongs that pertain to the particular social and political challenges that we face as a society today. We describe these people with such bad-apple terms as 'terrorist', 'sex offender', 'irregular migrant', 'anti-social youth', and 'paedophile'.[10] Sample *New York Times* and *Guardian* headlines on these themes include: 'Sex Offender Village', 'Sex Offenders Gain Right to Appeal against Registration', and 'Why Giving Polygraph Tests to Sex Offenders Is a Terrible Idea'.

This appeal to character as probative or constitutive of guilt has been prominent at other times in history, Lacey notes, such as in the Victorian era, where political and social anxieties led to the rise of various status classifications. The ostensible 'bad apples' then included the 'fallen woman', the 'inebriate', and the 'feeble-minded'. Lacey suggests that we tend as a society to resort to these kinds of shortcut approaches to identifying criminal responsibility when our society is confronting particularly pressing perceived or genuine security risks. That may be true for any specific buffet of bad-apple labels, but our general selection of epithets remains on prominent display in our everyday language even when our society is not gripped by genuine or induced anxieties.

Our use of epithets in criminal justice parallels our use of them in other segregating institutions like healthcare and immigration. In healthcare, our generic terms of 'patient' 'victim', and 'sufferer' not only cast the people receiving care in a passive role, but also put an unequivocally negative valence on people's experience of illness or injury. We put this gloss on ourselves too when we to refer to ourselves, and each other, by essentialist health-related labels. We say things like: 'I'm an asthmatic', 'I'm an anorexic', 'I'm a diabetic, a dyslexic, an epileptic, a manic depressive, or a schizophrenic'—or, famously, at the start of AA meetings, 'Hello, I'm John. I'm an alcoholic'—thereby making that feature of our lives highly prominent, if not definitive of who we are. (For some people, a particular label is life-defining in a positive, stigma-defying way; one woman told me that she happily identified herself as 'an autistic'.)

More strikingly, medical professionals are known to reduce the people they treat to their ailments. Doctors and nurses often speak of such people not only as 'cases', but also more specifically as 'the heart attack in Room 3', or 'the third-degree burn in Room 9'. Some people become labelled more explicitly by a disease, such as Mary Mallon, an asymptomatic carrier of the pathogen for typhoid fever, who became known as 'Typhoid Mary'.

Concerning immigration, we use reductive labels all the time to describe people who immigrate, but we use them most eagerly when we are in the throes of genuine or induced anxieties. During the Trump presidency, for instance, many people have given full-throated voice to xenophobic rhetoric about the 'alien', 'stranger', 'outsider', and 'foreigner'.[11] These labels do not cast their targets in a passive role, but instead dehumanize them as strange, foreign, separate, unfamiliar, threatening, and unacceptable.

8.1.2 Why Do We Use Essentialist Language?

Given that we have conscientiously woken up to how important our language is in domains such as disability, sex, socio-economic income, and ethnicity, why do we still speak in essentialist terms of people who have committed offences, are ill or injured, or seek to migrate? (Concerning crime, I fully acknowledge the seriousness of the acts that lead people to be convicted. Nonetheless, I doubt we respond acceptably by describing such people in the terms just outlined.)

One reason that we continue to use essentialist language in these areas might be that people who are convicted of offences, are ill or incapacitated, or are migrating are less politically empowered and, hence, less able to advocate that we collectively undergo a process of self-re-education about the language we use to describe them.[12]

A second, ostensible reason—most notably related to crime—concerns apparent responsibility. Whereas some other socially salient groups, such as people with disabilities, women, and ethnic minorities, are not blameworthy or liable for the traits and experiences by which they came to be labelled, people who have committed crimes are responsible, blameworthy, and liable for their conduct, and hence are not treated with prejudice when classified by that conduct, so the argument goes.

But of course, moral blameworthiness, criminal responsibility, and criminal liability can diverge, such as when people are held strictly liable even though they are not culpable and not thought to be culpable for the offence; and conversely, when people are morally blameworthy for actions that fall outside the proper scope of the law, such as infidelity. Also, even when moral blameworthiness and criminal liability do coincide, there is invariably more to each person's story than the simple fact that he committed a criminal offence.[13]

Moreover, some of the people who are members of the social groups noted above, such as people with disabilities, are indeed responsible for the properties by which we no longer classify them. The reckless surfer who sustains a traumatic spinal injury while testing out rough waters, and the football star who becomes severely cognitively impaired after continuing to play with a concussion, are responsible to some extent at least for having the disability by which we now recognize it would be derogatory to classify them. (When we use reductive language in healthcare, we imply, intentionally or not, that people who are ill or injured are somehow responsible for being less than healthy. Similarly, when we use reductive language in immigration, we imply that people who need to flee have some control over their plight, and that people who wish to emigrate are self-indulgent or disloyal.)

Focusing still on offending, once a person commits a crime, it does become a feature of his life-story. But how much should the crime define who he is? Unless we are relentlessly consequentialist about punishment, we imply, through punishment practices like life imprisonment without parole and execution, that the person's offence defines him so completely that he is irredeemable, beyond the pale, or incapable of change. This is a heavy, indefensible judgement to make of any human being. Bracketing the fact that Avishai Margalit uses language that I am challenging, Margalit observes credibly on this point:

> Even if there are noticeable differences among people in their ability to change, they are deserving of respect for the very possibility of changing. Even the worst criminals are worthy of basic human respect because of the possibility that they may radically reevaluate their past lives and, if they are given the opportunity, may live the rest of their lives in a worthy manner...Even though it is likely that she will continue living this way, this likelihood should not be turned into a presumption, because in principle an evildoer has the capacity to change and repent. This capacity implies that she deserves basic respect as a human being who should not be 'given up on', precisely because there is a chance, no matter how small, that she will repent.[14]

To a lesser degree, other punishments also convey that a person who has offended seriously is irredeemable or, at least, forever under suspicion. In some jurisdictions, if a person is given a prison sentence of four or more years, he then acquires a criminal record that he can never spend, but must always disclose on employment applications, volunteering applications, insurance papers, education courses, and immigration papers. In societies like ours that heavily stigmatize past offending, he might as well wear a scarlet letter O (for 'offender') on his chest that casts him permanently in the role of a social threat and all but denies him access to many areas of social life.[15] Of course, this is a contingent consequence. If we viewed past criminal records with less aversion, the requirement to disclose one would not be so isolating. (Analogously, a person with a pre-existing medical condition living in the US, with its private healthcare system, may well feel stigmatized by a feature that he must disclose in many settings which then deny him access to resources, often including insurance cover.)

A critic might still ask: Shouldn't a person *sometimes* be judged, and classified, by a single act or feature? In the opening paragraph of his novel *How to Be Good*, Nick Hornby's protagonist, Dr Katie Carr, reflects on this question:

Even though I am, apparently, and to my immense surprise, the kind of person who tells her husband that she doesn't want to be married to him anymore, I really didn't think that I was the kind of person to say so in a car park, on a mobile phone. That particular self-assessment will now have to be revised, clearly. I can describe myself as the kind of person who doesn't forget names, for example, because I have remembered names thousands of times and forgotten them only once or twice. But for the majority of people, marriage-ending conversations happen only once, if at all. If you choose to conduct yours on a mobile phone, in a Leeds car park, then you cannot really claim it is unrepresentative, in the same way that Lee Harvey Oswald couldn't really claim that shooting presidents wasn't like him at all. Sometimes we have to be judged by our one-offs.[16]

While entertaining, the conclusion of the passage is debatable. First, we can only make sense of statements like 'That act is wholly out of character' if a given one-off action discords with the person's past behaviour, general disposition, tendencies, preferences, commitments, and values. If proposing to divorce her husband by mobile phone from a car park is out of keeping with Katie Carr's character, then it's irrelevant that she hasn't had many moments in her life to act this way. Even in the case of a horrible crime (though probably not a premeditated, carefully orchestrated crime), the act also could be entirely out of keeping with the person's overall character.[17]

Of course, the problem is that much offending is not 'out of character' in the sense of being a one-off. Many people who commit criminal offences go on to re-offend. Indeed, consider the following statistics noted by Michael Gove:

> 45% of adult prisoners re-offend within one year of release. For those prisoners serving shorter sentences—those of less than twelve months—the figure rises to 58%. And, saddest of all, more than two-thirds of offenders under the age of 18 re-offend within twelve months of release.[18]

Recidivism might seem to suggest that the person's criminal conduct becomes part of a pattern of behaviour (that often increases in seriousness over time), and that such a pattern is evidence of a certain disposition. In other words, the conduct might seem to reflect some solidifying of personality that tracks the person's broader behavioural tendencies, attitudes, and beliefs. When a person shows what seems to be a disposition to offend, would it be prejudicial to apply an essentialist status classification to him that reflects that disposition? Would it be prejudicial to require him to declare that criminal record for the rest of his life?

I expect that very, very few people are 'built' to commit crimes regardless of their upbringing, income, social conditions, education, or experiences. Conditions matter, and the people who tend to end up in prison typically grow up and live in conditions far worse than those of the average citizen (being more likely to witness or endure domestic abuse, more likely to have learning difficulties and to drop out of school, more likely to use Class A drugs, more likely to be poor, and more likely to have an absent parent).[19] In other words, the people who tend to offend are those who tend to live in conditions in which many of us would be likely to offend were they our conditions. (Related to this, statistics indicate that people tend to grow out of crime; the usual pattern of criminal behaviour peaks in the person's (or the man's) early 20s, and then tends to tail off as they age.[20])

But, for a few people, it might indeed be probable that they will offend regardless of their conditions. If they live long enough to grow into self-directing agents, they will most likely engage in behaviour that our society has criminalized. (This idea invokes a stronger notion of *essentialism* than that deployed above: not only is the person deemed to be irredeemably an 'offender' in virtue of what he did (or will do), but he is deemed to be, by nature, an 'offender', i.e. someone who in all likelihood will engage in offending and re-offending regardless of his conditions.)

Admittedly, some people do seem impervious to change, such as Leroy Hendricks, who was convicted of fourteen counts of child molestation, who reportedly declared he would molest children again if released, and who was eventually given a civil commitment on the ground of mental abnormality.[21]

For these persons, a life-long criminal record and an essentialist label do not reflect a prejudicial judgement of their dispositions. But the record and the label would still bring injustice with them for two reasons. First, crime-related labels tend to occlude all other identities that people might have such as 'mother', 'father', 'spouse', 'child', 'caregiver', 'teacher', or 'friend'. Second, if indeed people are unable to change because of mental illness, for example, then crime-related labels and records would be unjust, as they would imply a level of self-control that those people lack. For these reasons, we should eschew crime-related essentialist labels or lifelong criminal records for people even if those things accurately characterize their dispositions.

Furthermore, even if we treat a person justly by labelling him by his offences, there are other good reasons—some of which are justice-related—to avoid such labels.

First, according to research cited in the UK Ministry of Justice report *Transforming Rehabilitation* (2014), a person is more likely to desist from crime if he does not identify with being an 'offender' or 'criminal', where *desistance* is understood as the process by which a person who is engaged in a sustained pattern of offending gives up crime:

> People with criminal records who do not define themselves purely as 'offenders' but see themselves as basically good people who made a mistake may find it easier to desist.[22]

Through our essentialist approaches to crime and punishment, we may be setting up the very conditions for people to become 'the *kind* of person who does x'.[23]

Second, as a society, we might benefit from dropping our essentialist approaches regardless of their impact on people's conduct and attitudes toward their own offending, since we might then be less resentful, harsh, and hateful toward people who commit crimes. Third, since we cannot engineer a system of labelling in criminal justice that is sufficiently accurate that it ensures that we only apply essentialist labels to people to whom we would thereby do no injustice, we should dispense with essentialist labels all together.[24]

Fourth, relatedly, philosophers have long distinguished between making correct judgements and appropriately expressing those correct judgements.[25] If we opted for non-essentialist approaches in criminal justice, we would engage not so much in a deception or noble lie as in an optimistic, charitable, friendly, cautious, humble, and respectful gesture that leaves open genuine prospects for redemption, repair, and restoration, whereby a person may *genuinely* disown and disavow the conduct for which he was convicted. Much suffering is endured both by the people who commit crimes and by their families.[26] We needn't add to it by branding them (for life) with a reductive, stigmatized classificatory status. There is some evidence of progress in this regard in the recent shift in the United States away from describing people as 'ex-offenders' and 'ex-cons', to describing them as 'returning citizens'.[27]

Many of the points just made apply *mutatis mutandis* to both healthcare and immigration. First, we do sometimes deem people with particular conditions to be beyond the pale. Consider society's expulsion of people with leprosy to so-called 'leper' colonies, or people's aversion in the 1980s to touching someone with AIDS. Often such treatment is rooted in ignorance and bigotry rather than a commitment to collective well-being. In some cases, such as that of Mary Mallon, who was a contagious but asymptomatic carrier of the pathogen associated with typhoid fever, isolation was a necessary evil, but an evil nonetheless. Second, the ways we perceive someone greatly influence how they perceive themselves. Social psychology studies suggest that 'words can kill'.[28] Third, in softening our language and reconsidering the necessity of certain segregating measures, we can adopt a gentler, more humane approach that potentially benefits not only the people we regrettably must segregate but society as a whole.

One final point on essential language is worth making. Undoubtedly, sometimes people who have been the subjects of derogatory language can take charge of the terms applied to them and reconceive of them in ways that remove the sting. The essentialist term *queer* is one example. But, other terms, such as *criminal*, *crook*, *offender*, and *sex offender* are not co-optable in that way because, roughly, outside totalitarian regimes where 'disobedient', if not 'criminal', can be a badge of honour, these labels track wrongdoing. These are not labels that a person usually can, or should wish to, co-opt and redefine to wear proudly. So too in the domains of immigration and healthcare, the labels of *alien*, *stranger*, *foreigner*, *patient*, and *sufferer* are not intuitively co-optable even though, in principle, they should be, since the life experiences they track can be positive. Indeed, migrating people are often fundamentally important to, and actively sought by, societies for their labour, expertise, and resource; for reproductive purposes; to redress demographic imbalances, including age and gender imbalances, and so on. Concerning healthcare, illnesses and injuries can have considerable instrumental value as vehicles through which to expand knowledge and understanding. They can be experiences that force people to adopt new perspectives. For instance, Henri Matisse became a painter during a period of convalescence following an attack of appendicitis.

Let me sum up this discussion of metaphorical segregation through branding language. When we publicly brand a person with a label that he cannot reconceive or abandon, we severely diminish his ability to shape how he is perceived. We deny him the chance to define for himself and others who he is. Changing the language we use to describe people who have committed offences, who are ill or injured, or who are seeking to migrate, is only one step—but an important step—in overcoming our prejudices against such people.

Abandoning other ways that we brand and, thereby, publicly shame people who fall into certain social categories is another step. In criminal justice, we have historically used vicious punitive markers to identify and stigmatize people who have offended. Consider the prisoner's tattooed serial number, the amputated hand of the person who stole, the stocks in the public square, or the red letter *A* for 'adulterer' worn by Hester Prynne in Nathaniel Hawthorne's famous novel *The Scarlet Letter*.[29] Nowadays, such badges of shame are out of favour or illegal, but we nonetheless use 'perp walks' (i.e. walking a suspect through a public place in front of the media), prison uniforms, and trial by internet to brand and isolate people who allegedly offend. In healthcare, the hospital patient is distinguished by the flimsy nightgown. In many immigration centres, the people in custody wear uniforms, whose colours distinguish those who have offended from those who have not.[30] In the US, most immigration detention facilities are run by the same for-profit companies that administer many prisons, and hence bring with them all the tropes of punitive incarceration including the handcuffs (on display at the entrance to the detention facility), the cell-like rooms, and the reductive, dehumanizing language. In the UK, immigration detention centres, though external to the criminal justice system, are similar to prisons in many ways, being either converted former prisons or designed along the same lines as Category B prisons.[31]

8.2 The People We Incarcerate

Our prejudicial attitudes toward people who have offended are made vivid by the statistics on whom we incarcerate. According to the Howard League for Penal Reform, as of January 2016, 85,260 people are being held in prison or young-offender institutions in England and Wales. Of that population, 81,443 are male and, 3,817 are female: women represent 4.5% of the prison population. The Howard League also states: 'The child custody population at the end of November 2015 was 991. This a decrease of 9 since the last month and a fall of 64 compared to the same point last year. There are 37 girls in custody.'[32] According to the US Bureau of Justice Statistics, by the end of 2014, there were over 1,500,000 people in federal prisons. Of that, 7% were women, i.e. 105,000.

Anglo-American prison sentences are often long. Prisons are highly repellent places (prisons tend to repel outsiders). Given those facts, these statistics expose a societal prejudice against men as contributors to others' survival and well-being. Specifically, the fact that we are willing to lock up people—mostly men—for extended periods in these repellent institutions regardless of the negative impact on them, their families, friends, and dependants reflects a general, societal judgement about men, or certainly about men who have committed crimes, that they do not contribute meaningfully to others' survival or well-being in ways that we should protect. (Similarly, if we imprisoned the most useful doctors, nurses, and teachers in privative settings that threatened their competence, we would display the attitude that we do not value their continued usefulness as doctors, nurses, and teachers. We would be saying that we don't value the services they can offer enough to ensure that they retain their skills.[33]) We undervalue men within family settings anyway (awarding them little or no paternity leave in their own right, and sometimes questioning their choices when they prioritize family over work), and consequently we tend to locate their recognized opportunities to contribute in public, political, and economic settings. When a man offends and thereby shows that he is disregarding the norms of those public settings, he loses his footing to show that he is a meaningful social contributor in other spheres such as his family.[34]

We exhibit a similar, indeed stronger prejudice toward young black men, who are over-represented among prison populations, and who endure multiple, intersecting forms of discrimination and disadvantage. These include, first, the prejudicial judgement that young black men fail to contribute as much as they should either within families or within the more public spheres in which men are viewed as key contributors and, second, the suspicion that young black men are actively socially threatening.

Our prejudicial attitudes about the social contribution potential of people who have offended come out in the concrete ways we treat these people both during and after incarceration. Many of our behavioural forms of social contribution injustice toward these people are mirrored in our treatment of people we segregate in other settings including healthcare and immigration.

8.3 The Harms of Segregation

In his speech 'The Treasure in the Heart of Man', Michael Gove made an obvious observation that is nonetheless worth highlighting:

> While individuals are in custody the state is responsible for every aspect of their welfare. We can determine who prisoners see, how they eat, wash

and sleep. We can decide how they spend their day, what influences they are exposed to, what expectations we will hold them to, what they can watch, read and hear, what behaviour is rewarded and what actions punished, who we expect them to admire and what we hope they will aspire to.[35]

In short, people in prison are rendered utterly dependent on their custodians. So too are many people in hospitals, immigration facilities, and other institutional settings, especially if they're immobile. We decide how much privacy they get, how they spend their day, whom they see, how they eat, wash, and sleep, what they can watch, read, or hear, and so on. Some of this dependency is unavoidable, but could be managed much more humanely than it often is.

The following is an indicative list of the kinds of social harms that we often do to people in prisons, hospitals, and immigration centres, which compromise their social resources, deny them social-contribution opportunities, and rob them of appropriate autonomy in their social interactions. (For now, I shall stipulate that, since the things listed below are among the most serious injuries we can do to people as social beings, these are genuine social wrongs against confined people, rather than goods to which these people have forfeited their rights-claims. In the next section, I consider which rights, including social rights, people might forfeit through serious wrongdoing or have justifiably infringed for public good reasons.)

1. *Juvenile institutionalization.* Holding a child in any institutional setting long-term, such as an orphanage or immigration centre, let alone a juvenile detention centre or prison, robs him of needed social resources (and much else) both in the present and in the future. Institutional settings often deny a child the close, personalized contact and care he requires to develop well. In immigration centres, a child might get nurturing care if he is detained with his family, but, since adult men are often held separately, a child will most likely be robbed of that connection with his father. Additionally, in holding a child in custody, we as a society convey a prejudicial judgement about that child's present and future prospects, signalling that we do not value the child's potential as a contributor sufficiently to ensure that he retains and cultivates his social abilities.

2. *No privacy.* In many ordinary, Anglo-American prisons, people lack privacy, and have little control over their living space. Someone can walk into their cell at any moment. Relatedly, they have little or no control over their living arrangements, i.e. whether they'll be housed with others and who those others will be. Also, they must perform all of their private

functions in the presence of their cellmates. Although freedom of dissociation is lexically secondary to positive associational claim rights, it is nonetheless fundamentally important, and is wholly disregarded in these kinds of forced living arrangements.

Similarly, in hospital wards, the person immobilized in the bed cannot control the curtain that other people swing open and closed to expose her or protect her privacy. Doctors, nurses, and visitors can enter her room without knocking. That room is often shared with other people whom she hasn't chosen. The same is true in many immigration centres whose prison-like environments bring with them the same group-housing and lack of privacy that typify prisons.

3. *Lack of decent social opportunities.* Ordinary prison conditions give people opportunities to contribute to others' survival or well-being, but often not *decent* opportunities. In both segregating and overcrowded prisons, marked by brutality or neglect, people may well be systematically denied conditions conducive to cultivating decent social connections marked by joint narratives, mutual investment, and trusting relations.

Similarly, ordinary prisons usually give people some opportunities to stay connected with their families, but those opportunities lack meaning if the person is housed in a prison far away or if he is rarely given meeting privileges. Roy Baumeister and Mark Leary hold that 'relationships characterized by strong feelings of attachment, intimacy, or commitment but lacking regular contact will…fail to satisfy the need [to belong]'.[36] So, even if a person maintains family connections while they are in prison, their need to belong will go unmet if they are unable to have regular, direct contact with their family. The same complaints can be made, to a lesser degree, against hospitalization and immigration detention, which bring with them both forced proximity and relative isolation.

4. *Grieving.* Segregating persons from their families can complicate, if not compromise, the grieving process. When a person is in detention, his family may not stay close to him to grieve together for the loss of family member. The person in detention cannot help or support his family fully. He also cannot know whether he might have saved the person who died or eased their pain; he cannot be present with that person when they die. He may also be refused permission to attend the funeral, especially if doing so requires an escort to make an overnight stay.

5. *Solitary confinement.* Isolated detention conditions vary, but typically they are intensely physically straining, sensorily privative, and socially privative. They deny people the *hope* of connecting, which comes from being in the proximity of other people. And they risk eroding a person's basic abilities to lead a socially integrated life. They also convey a prejudicial judgement that the person is not, and possibly never again can be, a meaningful contributor to others' survival and well-being. Instead, he is a persistent social threat or nonentity.

Now, some prisons, hospitals, or immigration facilities differ from those just described. Weekend prisons, prisons that allow for conjugal visits and family stays, hospitals that allow family members to stay, as well as institutions that have norms of etiquette that require officials to address people respectfully, differ significantly from the kinds of institutions just described. In the settings just described, we positively deny people the space to honour whatever moral responsibilities they have to play their part in ensuring that certain others' social needs are met; specifically, we prevent them from discharging duties they have to care for dependants and affiliates.[37]

8.4 Forfeited Rights and Infringed Rights

8.4.1 Forfeiting Rights in Prison

Which rights does a person legitimately forfeit when he engages in serious wrongdoing that warrants (let's stipulate) some form of incarceration? If a person forfeits rights other than his freedom of movement, do those rights include his social rights even though this denies him meaningful ways to show that he's interested in reintegrating, that he can assume responsibilities, and that he can be someone on whom others could depend? Does he forfeit his rights to have opportunities to try to contribute meaningfully to others' survival or well-being? Does he forfeit his rights to retain his social resources (i.e. social abilities, opportunities, and existing connections) while in prison? Does he forfeit his right to exercise any meaningful control over his associations in prison? And if the answer to any of these questions is yes, the next question is: Does he forfeit the rights only temporarily, or permanently?

Some of these questions I have answered in Chapters 2 and 3, where I explained why our core social rights, and notably the right against social deprivation, cannot be denied to us as a legitimate form of punishment.

In brief, they are (a) too fundamental and (b) preconditions for the meaningful exercise of many other rights. My claim here is that, even if a person who is sentenced to prison were to forfeit all of the rights just noted, the issue would remain unsettled, since other rights are also at stake.

First, we must consider the social impact of prison on indirect victims, namely, the particular people—notably children and other dependants—and non-human animals who would otherwise benefit from the incarcerated person's use of his social resources, as well as the wider community that would otherwise enjoy the ripple effects of his and his associates' contributions to each other's survival and well-being. Second, we must consider the residual impact of prison on the person's rights *upon release*, in a spirit akin to *jus post bellum*, which is the responsibility of victorious parties even when their *ad bellum* cause was just and *in bello* behaviour legitimate.

Segregation both into prison and within prison threatens, stretches, and breaks social bonds. The longer that a person stays in prison, the more likely it is that his social bonds will deteriorate, since his friends and family members (if he has them) may die, move, or abandon him. This is noteworthy both in itself and for its impact on him when he is released, because lacking accommodation, employment, a non-criminal social group, and family are all factors correlated with re-offending.

To take rehabilitation seriously, our society must invest in the post-prison transition. This means doing more than requiring that a person report regularly to his parole officer. It means helping him to set up a new social network: helping him in those initial days and months to secure a home and a supportive, law-abiding group.[38] These provisions are vital to mitigate the damage done to his social connections during his time in prison.

The severing of a person's social bonds is salient both for its effect on the person after release and for its effect on society as a whole. According to research cited in the report *Transforming Rehabilitation* (2014), numerous factors linked to desistance turn on having non-criminal social bonds.[39] One such factor is having something to give to others:

> [People who have offended] who find ways to contribute to society, their community or their families appear to be more successful at giving up crime. If these achievements are formally recognised, the effect may be even stronger.

If correct, this point about recognition is particularly noteworthy. It signals that, when we fail to acknowledge that people who have been incarcerated can be social contributors, we both do them an injustice and make desistance harder for them. Another set of factors associated with desistance are intimate relationships:

> There is evidence that forming strong and supportive intimate bonds with others appears to help desistance from crime, although more contemporary research is needed on this subject. Such relationships can reduce the amount of time spent in groups of same-age, same-sex friends (a known risk factor for young male offending). Strong partnerships and relationships with his or her children also provide an individual with something to lose if there is a return to prison. Living with non-offending parents can have the same sort of effect on ex-offenders who have returned to the family home. Finally, family and intimate attachments may give offenders a sense of purpose, meaning and direction. Individuals who devote themselves to raising their children or caring for older parents may find that crime and imprisonment are incompatible with such roles.

A third set of factors is hope and motivation:

> Research suggests that individuals who desist from crime are usually very motivated and confident that they can change their lives: offenders who clearly say they want to stop offending are the most likely to desist. The impact of these motivational factors has even been found in long-term studies up to ten years after release from prison.

A fourth factor is having a place within a non-criminal social group:

> Those who feel connected to others in a (non-criminal) community are more likely to stay away from crime. Social networks that help desistance include extended family, mutual aid groups, clubs and cultural or religious groups.

A fifth factor is being believed in:

> Research with desisters has identified that having someone believe in them is important and that desistance can be supported by interactions with others who communicate a belief that they can and will change, that they are good people, and that they have something to offer society or other people.[40]

All of these factors reinforce the claim of this chapter that we are deeply social, that we wish to make social contributions, and that we are better able to establish or re-establish ourselves socially when we are given meaningful opportunities to contribute.[41]

8.4.2 Overriding Rights in Institutional Settings

Similar questions to those asked above apply to other segregation institutions, such as hospitals and immigration centres, even though, here, the people segregated retain their rights. Their rights are, at most, justifiably overridden (infringed). We must ask: Which of a person's social rights may we justifiably override when we segregate him for public-good reasons, because he is contagious, dangerous, undocumented, or unverified?

First, can we justify denying someone access to his dependants and affiliates, especially if they wish to take the risks that go with being in contact with him? A story that brings out this issue comes from Hong Kong. In 2014, a father and mother tried to leave Queen Elizabeth Hospital with their 2-year-old son after the three of them were ordered to spend 10 days separated from each other in isolated quarantine—each in separate room. The order came after the hospital discovered that a girl being treated in the same ward as the boy was infected with a deadly strain of bird flu. Hospital staff stopped the family from leaving. They then adjusted their plans for the family and put them in two adjacent rooms, rather than in three rooms as originally planned. The father was held in isolation and the mother and son were quarantined together. The father, Tam Ming-wah, said that he would accept the consequences of his conduct (which can include a HK$5,000 fine and six months in jail for attempted escape), but he believed the hospital had mishandled the case: 'I hope there are other ways that allow the three of us to stay together...Our boy is so young and it is very lonely for me not to be able to see my family for so long.'[42] When the hospital staff originally sought to isolate the father, mother, and son from each other, they tried to deny them meaningful opportunities to contribute to each other's well-being. The parents might reasonably have preferred that one of them take the risk of being infected rather than that both be separated from their very young child.

Second, can we justify denying a person the conditions necessary for him to retain his social resources, including most importantly his social abilities? Someone like Mary Mallon poses a life-threatening to risk to all non-immune people who come in contact with her. But she poses no risk to anyone who is immune. Isolating her indefinitely is only justifiable if no less severe response could suffice to protect others from the life-threatening disease she carries.

Third, can we justify denying someone meaningful control of their associations or lack of associations? It's unlikely we can justify denying someone *all* control. Instead, we have a duty to mitigate as much as possible the loss of control the person suffers, by providing mediated contact or social surrogates where that is a defensible measure. It's also worth noting that when we infringe rather than violate people's rights by segregating them, we nonetheless owe them an apology for this treatment.

8.5 Objections

8.5.1 The Corrective System as a Place to Contribute

Focusing on punishment, one possible objection is that the correction system itself is the avenue through which a person who has committed a serious offence makes his social contributions. He does this by being open to re-education, by being responsive to societal expectations, and by genuinely seeking to repair, repent, and reintegrate socially.

In reply, first, this objection feeds into and from our prejudice about people who have committed offences. It sees them as 'offenders' first and last; their other identities have been suspended or eliminated. They must reform themselves first and then, once reformed, they might seek again to contribute socially through the various roles they once held, if they are able.

Alternatives to long-term incarceration such as weekend prison, very short custodial sentences, non-custodial sentences such as fines, community service, and mandatory victim restitution, as well as non-punitive restorative justice, mediation, and healing rituals would allow people who have offended to retain some of their other social identifies, rather than be 'offenders' first and last until they have somehow reformed themselves.

Second, if indeed we can view long-term incarceration as providing a person who has committed a crime with a forum through which to contribute socially, we can see it this way only in an attenuated sense (at least in Anglo-American systems). Moreover, even if we could legitimately view prison in this way, we should still be uneasy about the justness of our practices. We could say only that we do not compromise the person's social resources (i.e. abilities, opportunities, connections). We would have to do more to say we recognize the person as a potential social contributor in other contexts and forums.

8.5.2 Genuine Social Threats

A second possible objection, which applies not only to prisons but to all segregating institutions, is that our society is right to view at least some contagious, undocumented, dangerous, or offending people as social threats.

The cause of their threateningness may well come from their being mistreated, but the fact remains that they are permanently compromised in their social abilities and are regrettably genuinely 'intolerable', so the argument goes. Related to this, we ask too much of victims in particular when we propose to regard the people who have wronged them as more than their offences, but as individuals whose social bonds should be protected from the assault of certain punishments. Allowing the man who has raped a woman to return to his parents' home next door to her, allowing him to move freely and without social stigma, is too onerous for her, so the argument goes.

In reply, there are admittedly great costs in abandoning some of the typical ways that we respond to people who have committed serious offences. But we can grant that we should temporarily change the ways that we relate to a person who has committed offences, to reorient his attention to his wrongdoing, without granting that these changes must include denying him minimally adequate access to decent social contact, inclusion, and contribution opportunity. The alternatives to long-term prison sentences noted above—such as weekend prison, short custodial sentences, non-custodial sentences, and non-punitive restorative justice measures—are all ways to signal that our relations with the person have temporarily changed, without denying him access to social connections.

Moreover, although we cannot guarantee that a person will make good social contributions, particularly if the evidence is that he has a disposition to do otherwise, we still have good reasons to ensure that his social resources are secured to enable him meaningful opportunities both *to try* to contribute and to learn from others how to contribute.

Conclusion

This chapter has shown that we engage in forms of social injustice when we represent as social threats people who have committed offences, people who are migrating, or people who are ill or injured. This tendency is reflected in our continuing use of classificatory terms that essentialize people's wrongdoing, migratory status, or health condition. In addition, we engage in a more concrete, visible form of injustice through many of our social arrangements within prisons, hospitals, and immigration centres, which include solitary confinement, lack of variety in contact, lack of decent contact, forced contact with the same one or two unchosen roommates, non-repeated contact, and severed contact. We also do injustices to indirect victims, and we do injustices to people upon release from confinement when we fail to help them to reintegrate. Much of this injustice is contingent on our practices, policies, and attitudes toward the people who find themselves in the position of being segregated. Their experience contrasts sharply with the non-judgemental acceptance, safety, and indeed love that we glimpsed in the vignette between Pooh Bear and Piglet which opened this book. Pooh and Piglet's hand-holding moment in the woods is an ideal. But it is an approximable ideal that highlights the reality of our situation: we are non-contingently, fundamentally social creatures who need our society and its members, as well as our associates, to assure and reassure us that we are accepted, valued, and needed. Even when we have acted egregiously or we frighten others just by being who we are, we need to know that we can nonetheless be *sure* of a few specific people and sure of our acceptance within the wider social world. Indeed, as this book has shown, we have secure human rights to these constitutive parts of a minimally decent life.

Notes

Introduction

1. A. A. Milne (2009 [1928]), *The House at Pooh Corner* (Penguin), ch. 7: "In Which Tigger Is Unbounced."
2. See Martha Nussbaum (2011), *Creating Capabilities* (Harvard University Press); and Jonathan Wolff and Avner de-Shalit (2007), *Disadvantage* (Oxford University Press).
3. A substantial literature exists on the ethics of care, which often eschews the language of *rights*, *duties*, and *justice* and highlights the role that women tend to play as caregivers. Some care ethicists consider how to integrate the concerns of *justice* with those of *care*. See e.g. Virginia Held (2006), *The Ethics of Care: Personal, Political, and Global* (Oxford University Press), ch. 4; and Daniel Engster (2007), *The Heart of Justice* (Oxford University Press).
4. Michael Ignatieff (2001), *Human Rights as Politics and Idolatry* (Princeton University Press), 173. Cited from Joshua Cohen (2004), 'Minimalism About Human Rights: The Most We Can Hope For?', *Journal of Political Philosophy* 12(2): 190–213.
5. Joshua Cohen notes that one argument for human rights minimalism which stresses the value of *universal assent* reveals a dilemma for more expansive conceptions of *human rights*: 'we can be tolerant of fundamentally different outlooks on life or we can be ambitious in our understanding of what human rights demand, but we cannot—contrary to the aims of many human rights activists—be both tolerant and ambitious' (Cohen 2004: 192). My project is ambitious in that it seeks to revise our general attitudes about which rights-grounding interests are elemental priorities. But if my arguments are credible, they show that prioritizing our core social needs is necessary to secure the protections for 'any life at all' (to borrow Cohen's phrase) that is recognizable as a human life.
6. In his book *Social*, Matthew Lieberman observes that we should invert Abraham Maslow's famous pyramid of the *hierarchy of needs*. Maslow puts at the bottom, most basic level of the pyramid our physiological needs for food, water, and sleep. On the level above that, he puts our safety needs for physical shelter, bodily security, and health. Above that come the needs that he regards as something of a luxury, such as our social needs, then our needs for esteem, and finally at the top our needs for self-actualization. Noting that infants cannot meet their

physiological or safety needs themselves, Lieberman points out that we must move social needs to the bottom of the pyramid. 'Without social support, infants will never survive to become adults who can provide for themselves. Being socially connected is a need with a capital N... Love and belonging might seem like a convenience we can live without, but our biology is built to thirst for connection because it is linked to our most basic survival needs.' Matthew Lieberman (2013), *Social: Why Our Brains Are Wired to Connect* (Oxford University Press), 41–3.
7. We also seek out interspecies connections, both when we are in a pinch and cannot find safe connections within our own species and when we want them for their own sake. Many non-human animals display interspecies sociality, not only with us but also with other species—a topic I hope to explore another day.
8. For another example of work that considers specific political and social implications of taking our core social needs seriously, see Kathleen Lynch, John Baker, and Maureen Lyons (2009), *Affective Equality: Love, Care, and Injustice* (Palgrave). Drawing on feminist philosophy that exposes how much our affective, caring domains of life are discrete spheres of social action that nonetheless interweave with the economic, political, and cultural spheres, Lynch, Baker, Lyons, and their co-authors argue that society should pay more attention to the affective domain and to the absence of affective equality. Using empirical analyses, they examine specific inequalities in the distribution of both love and caring labour and the receipt of that labour.
9. Joseph Raz (1986), *The Morality of Freedom* (Oxford University Press).

Chapter 1

1. Elif Batuman (2018), 'Japan's Rent-a-Family Industry', *New Yorker*, 30 Apr.
2. Many philosophers restrict their focus to our personal relationships. One aim of this book is to take a broader view of our social world, to explore our interactional lives with strangers as well as our associational lives. On relationships, Niko Kolodny argues that the non-instrumental reason we have to love someone lies in our relationship with her, that is to say, in the ongoing history we share with her. Indeed, it is the final value of our relationship that gives us reason to love. 'Love is both a final valuation of a relationship, from the perspective of a participant in that relationship, and a nonfinal, noninstrumental valuation of one's "relative".' Niko Kolodny (2003), 'Love as Valuing a Relationship', *Philosophical Review* 112(2): 135–89. Jonathan Seglow argues that our associative duties to our family, friends, colleagues, and even fellow citizens are grounded in the non-instrumental value of our relationships: Jonathan Seglow (2013), *Defending Associative Duties* (Routledge). See also Anca Gheaus (2018), 'Personal Relationship Goods', *Stanford Encyclopedia of Philosophy*, ed. Edward N. Zalta:

https://plato.stanford.edu/archives/fall2018/entries/personal-relationship-goods/.
3. Social connections are distinguished by certain qualities. For instance, decent human interactions, although they tend to be momentary, goal-oriented, and unemotional, are nonetheless typically marked by mutual consideration, respect, courtesy, and a context-specific acknowledgement of each other's needs and wishes. Associations are, of course, richer than this. Most intimate associations, and all loving relationships, are marked by mutual concern, shared activity, trust, intimacy, and a joint narrative that is conditional on certain (perceived) merits of the parties, and such associations are pursued typically through direct interactions for each other's sake.
4. Soran Reader and Gillian Brock (2004), 'Needs, Moral Demands and Moral Theory', *Utilitas* 16(3): 251–66.
5. Unless we adopt a deeply subjectivist account of well-being, we do *need* to survive—we have a fundamental interest in surviving—even if we do not *want* to survive.
6. Harry G. Frankfurt (1984), 'Necessity and Desire', *Philosophy and Phenomenological Research* 45(1): 1–13, at 3.
7. Ibid. 2.
8. In my analysis here, *morally important needs* cover roughly the same conceptual territory as morally important *interests*, i.e. the interests that are sufficiently weighty to ground duties in others and thereby generate rights.
9. On this point, Reader and Brock note: 'the ongoing agency, life, harm-avoidance or flourishing of a wicked being will not normally be treated as a moral demand. I may need all sorts of help in order to carry on as a child-abuser, but moral agents connected to me may not take these needs to be morally demanding. Similarly, short-lived non-contingent needs, such as the requirements for continuing the operatic diva phase of a teenager's life, are not usually taken to be very demanding by those around the diva.' Reader and Brock (2004: 255).
10. James Nickel (2006), *Making Sense of Human Rights*, 2nd edn (Blackwell), 62ff.; and James Nickel (2005), 'Poverty and Rights', *Philosophical Quarterly* 55: 385–402, at 391ff.
11. Ibid. 392.
12. Ibid. 393.
13. Ibid. 394.
14. Ibid.
15. One richer conception of the conditions for a minimally good life is Martha Nussbaum's list of ten central capabilities: life; bodily health; bodily integrity; sense, imagination, and thought; emotions; practical reason; affiliation; other species; play; and control over one's environment. See Martha Nussbaum (2011), *Creating Capabilities* (Harvard University Press), 33–4.
16. Henrik Ibsen [1882], *An Enemy of the People* (various edns).

17. As a retired military carpenter, Proenneke built himself a log cabin at remote Twin Lakes, Alaska, and lived there alone for close to 30 years. He received supplies from a bush pilot during warm months, but spent the winters entirely isolated in this remote, inaccessible area. (The bush pilot was a friend of Proenneke's, and his presence in Proenneke's life aligns with my comment, in the Introduction to this book, that we need to be persistently sure of at least one other person in order to survive.) Proenneke documented his life at Twin Lakes in video footage that later became the documentary *Alone in the Wilderness* (2004). Even in his mid-80s, he seemed to glow with contentment in the life he'd chosen. There are, however, a few points to note about Proenneke. Although he did indeed live alone for much of this time, he had a sophisticated, socially acquired set of skills—in carpentry and military training—that helped him to make this way of life possible. Also, he opted for a tough but beautiful wilderness, and had many animal companions. See also Sam Smith and Richard Proenneke (1999), *One Man's Wilderness: An Alaskan Odyssey* (Alaska Northwest Books).
18. See e.g. Eva Kittay (1999), *Love's Labor* (Routledge); M. Fineman (2008), 'The Vulnerable Subject: Anchoring Equality in the Human Condition', *Yale Journal of Law & Feminism* 20(1): 1–23, at 10–12. M. Fineman (2010), 'The Vulnerable Subject and the Responsive State', *Emory Law Journal* 60: 251–75, at 266–7; and Daniel Engster (2007), *The Heart of Justice* (Oxford University Press).
19. Nussbaum (2011: 34ff.).
20. Ibid. 39.
21. Ibid. 40.
22. Jonathan Wolff and Avner de-Shalit (2007), *Disadvantage* (Oxford University Press).
23. For defences of this claim, see Kittay (1999); Engster (2007).
24. According to social neuroscientist John T. Cacioppo, not only do we have the longest period of abject dependency from birth of any species, but we are dependent on conspecifics throughout our lives for survival and prosperity. See John T. Cacioppo and William Patrick (2008), *Loneliness* (Norton).
25. Roy F. Baumeister and Mark R. Leary (1995), 'The Need to Belong: Desire for Interpersonal Attachments as a Fundamental Human Motivation', *Psychological Bulletin* 117(3): 497–529, at 499ff.
26. *The Oxford English Dictionary* (current online edn).
27. For a related discussion, see George Monbiot (2017), *Out of the Wreckage: A New Politics for an Age of Crisis* (Verso).
28. Examples such as 'apple pie and ice cream' and 'apple pie and motherhood' show two things. First, a single entity can be part of more than one two-party belonging-relation. Two-party belonging-relations are not unique and mutually exclusive. Second, they are also not transitive: motherhood and ice cream do

not belong together simply because apple pie belongs with both ice cream and motherhood.
29. Marlene Goldman (2018), 'Forgotten: Narratives of Age-Related Dementia', paper presented at 'Living a Good Life in Older Age' symposium, University of Warwick, July 2018: https://www.youtube.com/watch?v=C-m_L6ksFQA&index=12&t=0s&list=PLwiglpnV-9XGRr-YYzxte1bN6w6DPv9dq&frags=pl%2Cwn.
30. L. M. Montgomery [1908], *Anne of Green Gables* (various edns), ch. 2 (emphasis added).
31. On the importance of place, see Elizabeth Brake (2019), 'Rebuilding in the Wake of Disaster: The Political Importance of Place', *Social Theory and Practice* 45(2): 179–204.
32. I thank Zofia Stemplowska for this example.
33. In her historical novel *Snow Flower and the Secret Fan*, Lisa See tells the story of two unrelated Chinese girls of good standing who form a lifelong, intimate, non-sexual relationship called a *laotong* (the word *laotong* means 'old same' or kindred spirit), which was formalized by oaths and a written contract. See says that such relationships were more intimate for the women involved than their marriages were since, unlike marriages, the women voluntarily entered into these connections. See Lisa See (2005), *Snow Flower and the Secret Fan* (Random House).
34. Sherry Richert Belul (2018), 'When a Boyfriend Joins the Marriage', *New York Times*, 7 Dec. 2018: https://www.nytimes.com/2018/12/07/style/modern-love-when-a-boyfriend-joins-the-marriage.html. For a discussion of different ways that a state might regulate personal relationships, see Clare Chambers (2016), 'The Limitations of Contract: Regulating Personal Relationships in a Marriage-Free State', in Elizabeth Brake (ed.), *After Marriage: Rethinking Marital Relationships* (Oxford University Press).
35. See Michael Walzer (2004), 'Involuntary Association', in *Politics and Passion: Toward a More Egalitarian Liberalism* (Yale University Press), 18–37, at 5ff.
36. See e.g. Mavis Biss (2011), 'Aristotle on Friendship and Self-Knowledge: The Friend Beyond the Mirror', *History of Philosophy Quarterly* 28(2): 125–40.
37. While close caring connections are chronologically prior to, and necessary to, developing social abilities, their value in this ordering is instrumental: they have instrumental value in ensuring that we can cultivate social abilities. (Social connections have non-instrumental value, but that value is not what informs their chronological priority.)
38. There is a burgeoning literature on the philosophy of childhood and the philosophy of the family. See e.g. Adam Swift and Harry Brighouse (2014), *Family Values: The Ethics of Parent–Child Relationships* (Princeton University Press); Anca Gheaus (2018), 'Children's Vulnerability and Legitimate Authority Over Children', *Journal of Applied Philosophy* 35(1): 60–75; Elizabeth Brake and

Lucinda Ferguson (eds) (2018), *Philosophical Foundations of Children's and Family Law* (Oxford University Press); and Françoise Baylis and Carolyn McLeod (2014), *Family-Making: Contemporary Ethical Challenges* (Oxford University Press).

39. Joel Feinberg [1980] (1994), 'The Child's Right to an Open Future', in *Freedom and Fulfillment: Philosophical Essays* (Princeton University Press).
40. Anca Gheaus (2015), 'Unfinished Adults and Defective Children: On the Nature and Value of Childhood', *Journal of Ethics and Social Philosophy* 9(1): 1–21.
41. For references to empirical studies on the effects of social isolation upon children, see fn. 10ff. in S. Matthew Liao (2006), 'The Right of Children to Be Loved', *Journal of Political Philosophy* 14(4): 420–40. For a more recent list of such references, see S. Matthew Liao (2015), *The Right to Be Loved* (Oxford University Press).
42. Ibid. 76.
43. Liao (2006).
44. M. Cowden (2012), 'What's Love Got to Do with It? Why a Child Does Not Have a Right to Be Loved', *Critical Review of International Social and Political Philosophy* 15(3): 325–45. See also S. Matthew Liao (2012), 'Why Children Need to Be Loved', *Critical Review of International Social and Political Philosophy* 15(3): 347–58.
45. See e.g. Baumeister and Leary (1995); Jean Decety and John T. Cacioppo (2011), *Handbook of Social Neuroscience* (Oxford University Press); M. Seligman (2011), *Flourish* (Random House); and C. Nathan DeWall (2013), *The Oxford Handbook of Social Exclusion* (Oxford University Press).
46. See Cacioppo and Patrick (2008).
47. Baumeister and Leary (1995: 501ff.) survey a substantial literature that supports this claim. They conclude (p. 502): 'Friendships and group allegiance seem to arise spontaneously and readily, without needing evidence of material advantage or inferred similarity. Not only do relationships emerge quite naturally, but people invest a great deal of time and effort in fostering supportive relationships with others. External threat seems to increase the tendency to form strong bonds.'
48. According to Baumeister and Leary (ibid. 498), the conditions for a *primary human motivation*, which I will not dispute here, are that it '(a) produce effects readily under all but adverse conditions, (b) have affective consequences, (c) direct cognitive processing, (d) lead to ill effects (such as on health or adjustment) when thwarted, (e) elicit goal-oriented behavior designed to satisfy it (subject to motivational patterns such as object substitutability and satiation), (f) be universal in the sense of applying to all people, (g) not be derivative of other motives, (h) affect a broad variety of behaviors, and (i) have implications that go beyond immediate psychological functioning.' They then test the need to belong against these criteria and find that it satisfies them.

49. Ibid. 497.
50. Ibid.
51. George Vaillant (2012), *Triumphs of Experience: The Men of the Harvard Grant Study* (Belknap Press).
52. Baumeister and Leary say that the *belongingness hypothesis* entails that people should strive to achieve a certain minimum quantity and quality of social contacts, but once this level is surpassed, the motivation to connect should diminish. The need is, thus, for a certain minimum number of bonds and quantity of interaction, but not for a maximum number of such bonds. Anca Gheaus has pointed out to me that Baumeister and Leary's claim may be true if we consider how social bonds affect our health, but may not be true if we consider how social bonds affect other aspects of our well-being such as our economic security: when it comes to trying to get financial support in a situation of economic deprivation, having many, fairly shallow social bonds might be more beneficial than having few, close friends.
53. Baumeister and Leary (1995: 500).
54. Ibid. They also state (p. 506): 'More generally, happiness in life is strongly correlated with having some close personal relationships. Research suggests that it does not seem to make a great deal of difference what sort of relationship one has, but the absence of close social bonds is strongly linked to unhappiness, depression, and other woes.'
55. Ibid. 500.
56. In making this point, I rely on conversations with psychologists Pamela Qualter, Rebecca Nowland, and Luc Goossens.
57. The Harvard Grant Study indicates that the men who were happiest in retirement were those who actively sought to replace past colleagues with new friends and companions.
58. Baumeister and Leary specify *affiliation* in more modest terms than Nussbaum does. They describe affiliation in terms of 'frequent contacts with nonsupportive, indifferent others'. Such contacts 'can go only so far in promoting [our] general well-being and would do little to satisfy the need to belong.' Baumeister and Leary (1995: 500).
59. Ibid. 511.
60. Ibid. 499.
61. Ibid. 519.
62. For a critique of the *belongingness hypothesis*, see Mariana Bockarova (2016), 'Does One Truly Need to Belong? A Case for the Need to Meaningfully Exist', *Semiotica* 210: 251–7.
63. See Sara Maitland (2008), *A Book of Silence* (Granta). Sara Maitland is one of the many people interviewed in the 2016 BBC documentary *The Age of Loneliness*. She lives alone in the Scottish Highlands and does not self-report as feeling lonely. While she does spend much time in solitude, she does have

animal companions, attends church regularly, is a respected writer, and is linked to two universities.
64. Bertrand Russell [1967] (2000), 'Prologue', *Autobiography* (Routledge), 9.
65. Louise C. Hawkley et al. (2010), 'Loneliness Predicts Increased Blood Pressure: 5-Year Cross-Lagged Analyses in Middle-Aged and Older Adults', *Psychology and Aging* 25(1): 132–41.
66. John T. Cacioppo et al. (2006), 'Loneliness as a Specific Risk Factor for Depressive Symptoms: Cross-sectional and Longitudinal Analyses.' *Psychology and Aging* 21(1): 140–51.
67. Pamela Qualter et al. (2013), 'Trajectories of Loneliness during Childhood and Adolescence: Predictors and Health Outcomes', *Journal of Adolescence* 36: 1283–93.
68. Baumeister and Leary (1995: 511). In my terminology, this 'need' is a morally important need and most likely a non-contingent, fundamental need.
69. See H. T. Stelfox, D. W. Bates, and D. A. Redelmeier (2003), 'Safety of Patients Isolated for Infection Control', *Journal of the American Medical Association* 290(14): 1899–1905; and A. Zuger (2010), 'Isolation, an Ancient and Lonely Practice, Endures', *New York Times*, 30 Aug.: http://www.nytimes.com/2010/08/31/health/31essay.html
70. B. A. Arrigo et al. (2008), 'The Psychological Effects of Solitary Confinement on Prisoners in Supermax Units', *International Journal of Offender Therapy and Comparative Criminology* 52(6): 622–40; C. Haney (2003), 'Mental Health Issues in Long-Term Solitary and "Supermax" Confinement', *Crime and Delinquency* 49: 124–56; and A. Gawande (2009), 'Hellhole', *New Yorker*, 30 Mar. For a discussion of sensory deprivation as torture, see David Luban and Henry Shue (2012), 'Mental Torture: A Critique of Erasures in U.S. Law', *Georgetown Law Journal* 100: 823–63.
71. Gawande (2009).
72. Shane Bauer (2012), 'Solitary in Iran Nearly Broke Me. Then I Went Inside America's Prisons', *Mother Jones*, Nov./Dec.: http://www.motherjones.com/politics/2012/10/solitary-confinement-shane-bauer.
73. Gawande (2009).
74. See Report of the Commission on Safety and Abuse in America's Prisons (2006): prisoncommission.org/. Michael Jackson (2002), *Justice Behind the Walls* (Douglas & McIntyre); and Sharon Shalev (2008), *Sourcebook on Solitary Confinement* (Nuffield Foundation Report: http://www.solitaryconfinement.org/uploads/sourcebook_web.pdf).
75. See the numerous references to empirical studies in Liao (2015).
76. For a summary of relevant studies on this point, see Baumeister and Leary (1995: 503ff.).
77. Matthew Lieberman (2013), *Social: Why Our Brains Are Wired to Connect* (Oxford University Press), 16–23.

78. Baumeister and Leary (1995: 503).
79. See e.g. James L. McClelland, Julie A. Fiez, and Bruce D. McCandliss (2002), 'Teaching the /r/-/l/ Discrimination to Japanese Adults: Behavioral and Neural Aspects', *Physiology & Behavior* 77(4–5): 657–62.
80. Studies indicate that orchestra members' brainwaves synchronize when they play together: Max-Planck Institute for Human Development (2012), 'Making Music Together Connects Brains: When Guitarists Play Together, Networks of Nerve Cells Are Formed Between Their Brains', 29 Nov.: https://www.mpg.de/6634785/music-connects-brains. See also Cass Sunstein (2003), *Why Societies Need Dissent* (Harvard University Press), for a discussion of various studies that show how our brain activity changes when we are in group settings (such as staff meetings).
81. See e.g.Catriona Mackenzie and Natalie Stoljar (eds) (2010), *Relational Autonomy: Feminist Perspectives on Autonomy, Agency, and the Social Self* (Oxford University Press); Joseph Raz (1986), *The Morality of Freedom* (Oxford University Press), chs 14, 15; Marina Oshana (1998), 'Personal Autonomy and Society', *Journal of Social Philosophy* 29: 81–102; Charles Taylor (1989), *Sources of the Self: The Making of the Modern Identity* (Cambridge University Press), chs 10, 11; Andrea Westlund (2009), 'Rethinking Relational Autonomy', *Hypatia* 24: 26–49; and S. Buss (1994), 'Autonomy Reconsidered', in P. A. French, T. A. Uehling, and H. K. Wettstein (eds), *Midwest Studies in Philosophy* 19: 95–121.
82. In *The Metaphysics of Morals*, pt II: 'Metaphysical First Principles of the Doctrine of Virtue', Kant speaks about an obligation to develop friendships and to participate in social intercourse (6: 469–74). See also Stephanie Collins (2013), 'Duties to Make Friends', *Ethical Theory & Moral Practice* 16: 907–21.
83. I thank Andy Mason for highlighting this point. See Andrew Mason (2000), *Community, Solidarity and Belonging* (Cambridge University Press). See also Charles Taylor (1995), 'Irreducibly Social Goods', in *Philosophical Arguments* (Harvard University Press), ch. 7.
84. In 2019, *The Guardian* reported that, in the UK, over 400 mental health patients presently live in locked rehabilitation wards, including one person who has been held in a locked ward for over 21 years. The average length of time in a locked ward at Sussex partnership NHS trust (which means that the person may not leave the ward as and when they wish) is two years. Most of these people are housed in wards far from their homes. Sarah Marsh (2019), 'Mental Health Patients Detained in Hospital Wards for up to 21 Years', *The Guardian*, 23 Apr. 2019.
85. On the right to be loved, see Liao (2015, 2006); Cowden (2012); on family values, see Swift and Brighouse (2014); on the ethics of care, see Virginia Held (2006), *The Ethics of Care* (Oxford University Press); Engster (2007); on relational theories of autonomy, see Mackenzie and Stoljar (2010); on theories of vulnerability, embodiment, and intimacy, see Fineman (2008); and D. Ornish (1998), *Love and Survival: The Scientific Basis for the Healing Power of Intimacy*

(HarperCollins); on communitarianism, see Taylor (1989); and Charles Taylor (1985), *Philosophy and the Human Sciences: Philosophical Papers 2* (Cambridge); on affiliation, see Nussbaum (2011); on integration, see E. Anderson (2010), *The Imperative of Integration* (Princeton University Press).
86. Aristotle, *Nicomachean Ethics*, bk VIII.
87. Daniel Schwartz states: 'It is almost customary in treatments of pre-modern ideas of friendship to point out that Aristotelian *philia* and Thomistic *amicitia* significantly differ from what we now understand as friendship. One element of *philia–amicitia* that is often considered to be at odds with modern friendship is its wide reach. In the Aristotelian tradition, fellow soldiers, fellow travellers, and fellow citizens are friends, as are those who interact with a view to utility and those whose bond is founded on erotic love. Indeed, it would seem that almost anyone who is not an enemy, and is in some way engaged in a more or less stable and mutually beneficial relationship, is a friend.' Daniel Schwartz (2007), *Aquinas on Friendship* (Oxford University Press), 2.
88. Aristotle, *Nicomachean Ethics*, bk VIII.
89. Cited from Jeremy Waldron (1992), 'Minority Cultures and the Cosmopolitan Alternative', *University of Michigan Journal of Law Reform* 25: 751–92.
90. John Rawls (1999), *A Theory of Justice* (Harvard University Press), 155–6, 386ff.
91. Ibid. 441. I thank Tom Parr for highlighting these quotations.
92. Frankfurt (1984) makes this point when he notes that our volitional needs may not be voluntary; our desires may not be voluntary.
93. Just as it is true of us that we have five fingers on each hand, it is equally true of us that, during the periods of adolescence and healthy adulthood, we have an important, but not vital, need for sexual intimacy.

Chapter 2

1. John Watkins (2016), 'The Invisible Aged: The People Politics Forgot', *The Guardian*, 16 May: https://www.theguardian.com/commentisfree/2016/may/16/the-invisible-aged-the-people-politics-forgot.
2. Sue Bourne (2016), *The Age of Loneliness*, BBC One, 7 Jan.: http://www.bbc.co.uk/programmes/b06vkhr5.
3. Parts of this chapter build on material in Kimberley Brownlee (2013), 'A Human Right Against Social Deprivation', *Philosophical Quarterly* 63(251): 199–222.
4. The cases of Natascha Kampusch and of Amanda Berry, Michelle Knight, and Gina DeJesus involve both the first form of social deprivation—coercive isolation—and the third—persistent brutality.
5. Atul Gawande (2009), 'Hellhole: The United States Holds Tens of Thousands of Inmates in Long-Term Solitary Confinement. Is This Torture?' *New Yorker*, 30 Mar.

6. Brian Barry (2002), 'Social Exclusion, Social Isolation, and the Distribution of Income', in *Understanding Social Exclusion*, ed. John Hills, Julian Le Grand, and David Piachaud (Oxford University Press), 13–29.
7. See Report of the Commission on Safety and Abuse in America's Prisons (2006): prisoncommission.org/. Michael Jackson (2002), *Justice Behind the Walls* (Douglas & McIntyre); and Sharon Shalev (2008), *Sourcebook on Solitary Confinement* (Nuffield Foundation): http://www.solitaryconfinement.org/uploads/sourcebook_web.pdf.
8. Journalist Terry Anderson reports believing that he would find solitary confinement as a political prisoner bearable, but then found his mind breaking down into a black mass of misery. So too, others who have endured solitary confinement in prison report afterward that they would rather have the worst companion than no companion at all. See Gawande (2009).
9. Baumeister and Leary note that 'the belongingness hypothesis can be distinguished from a hypothesized need for mere social contact in terms of whether interactions with strangers or with people one dislikes or hates would satisfy the need'. Roy F. Baumeister and Mark R. Leary (1995), 'The Need to Belong: Desire for Interpersonal Attachments as a Fundamental Human Motivation', *Psychological Bulletin* 117(3): 497–529, at 500.
10. Jane Taber (2012), 'Elderly American Caregiver Being Deported Has Been Granted Temporary Visa', *Globe and Mail*, 15 Nov.: http://www.theglobeandmail.com/news/national/elderly-american-caregiver-being-deported-has-been-granted-temporary-visa/article5328771/. I thank Elizabeth Brake for highlighting this case.
11. Henry Shue (1996), *Basic Rights: Subsistence, Affluence, and US Foreign Policy*, 2nd edn (Princeton University Press), 24–5.
12. See Shalev (2008). See David Luban and Henry Shue (2012), 'Mental Torture: A Critique of Erasures in U.S. Law', *Georgetown Law Journal* 100: 823–63. My comments here pertain to Shue's discussion in *Basic Rights*. In new work in progress that responds to my critique, Shue turns his attention to social human rights and argues that, when it comes to social inclusion, two distinguishable goods are at stake. One is the good of initially developing social abilities through social contact in childhood. The other is the good of maintaining those social abilities through social contact in adulthood. While both goods are vital interests that deserve the protection of human rights, our interest in initially developing social abilities 'seems to be as fundamental an interest as there can be. In effect, it is an interest in becoming human', and as such it is a basic right ('Interlocking Rights, Layered Protections', draft manuscript). I comment on this development in Shue's account in Section 2.4.2.
13. James Nickel (2005), 'Poverty and Rights', *Philosophical Quarterly* 55: 385–402, at 386. Emphasis added.

14. At the time of writing, the Committee on the Rights of Persons with Disabilities is producing a General Comment on Article 19.
15. Article 28, Section 1 states: 'States Parties recognize the right of persons with disabilities to an adequate standard of living for themselves and their families, including adequate food, clothing and housing, and to the continuous improvement of living conditions, and shall take appropriate steps to safeguard and promote the realization of this right without discrimination on the basis of disability.'
16. *European Social Charter Explanatory Report* (1996) (rev. edn): https://rm.coe.int/16800ccde4.
17. United Nations Standard Minimum Rules for the Treatment of Prisoners (the Nelson Mandela Rules), adopted 17 December 2015: https://undocs.org/A/RES/70/175.
18. James Nickel (2006), *Making Sense of Human Rights* (Blackwell), 70–1.
19. Cf. Laura Valentini (2016), 'What's Wrong with Being Lonely? Justice, Beneficence, and Meaningful Relationships', *Proceedings of the Aristotelian Society Supplementary Volume* 90(1): 49–69, for a critical discussion of these kinds of proposals.
20. As Baumeister and Leary observe, 'The need to belong entails that relationships are desired, so interactions with strangers would mainly be appealing as possible first steps toward long-term contacts (including practicing social skills or learning about one's capacity to attract partners')' (1995: 500).
21. No sharp line separates interpersonal social connections from community membership. Our negative social rights can protect us against forced displacement, exile, abandonment, or other denials of political, legal, or cultural community membership. For such protection to be meaningful, it must include both negative claims against interference and positive claims to the resources necessary to guarantee us access to community membership.
22. I thank Virginia Mantouvalou for drawing my attention to this point. In her response to my paper at the 2010 Royal Holloway 'Margins of Citizenship' conference, she observed that the European Court of Human Rights has considered one dimension of social deprivation in prison, namely, whether lengthy solitary confinement in prison violates Article 3 of the European Convetion on Human Rights (ECHR), which prohibits inhuman and degrading treatment. She observed that, whereas the ECHR does not protect so-called 'second-generation' socio-economic human rights, it does protect so-called 'first-generation' human rights and thus the court could afford legal protection to applicants through a civil- and political-rights procedure.
23. Will Kymlicka (2017), 'Human Rights Without Human Supremacism', *Canadian Journal of Philosophy*: doi: 10.1080/00455091.2017.1386481.
24. See Nickel (2006; 2005); Shue (1996).

25. According to one account, 'the resource debt that individuals acquire as children and adolescents is not paid off until around [age] 50': Kim Sterelny (2012), *The Evolved Apprentice: How Evolution Made Humans Unique* (MIT Press), 30. Cited from Neil Levy (2016), 'Neuroethics and Responsibility', in *The Blackwell Companion to Applied Philosophy*, ed. Kasper Lippert-Rasmussen, Kimberley Brownlee, and David Coady (Wiley).
26. Shannon Vallor offers a nice brief description of reciprocity as one of the goods internal to caring in 'Robots at War and at Home' in her 2016 book *Technology and the Virtues: A Philosophical Guide to a Future Worth Wanting* (Oxford University Press), 223ff.
27. The next three paragraphs are drawn from Kimberley Brownlee (2015), 'Do We Have a Human Right to the Political Determinants of Health?' in *Philosophical Foundations of Human Rights*, ed. Rowan Cruft, Matthew Liao, and Massimo Renzo (Oxford University Press), 502–14.
28. Article 26 (2), *Universal Declaration of Human Rights* (1948) (emphasis added).
29. Joseph Raz (2015), 'Human Rights in the Emerging World Order', in *Philosophical Foundations of Human Rights*, ed. Rowan Cruft, Matthew Liao, and Massimo Renzo (Oxford University Press), ch. 11.
30. Compare this with Shue's claims quoted above on physical security and basic subsistence: 'No one can fully…enjoy any right that is supposedly protected by society if he or she lacks the essentials for a reasonably healthy and active life….Any form of malnutrition, or fever due to exposure, that causes severe and irreversible brain damage, for example, can effectively prevent the exercise of any right requiring clear thought' (1996: 24–5).
31. As we saw in Ch. 1, James Nickel articulates four abstract, secure moral claims that persons have upon others: (a) a secure claim to have a life; (b) a secure claim to lead a life; (c) a secure claim against severely cruel or degrading treatment; and (d) a secure claim against severely unfair treatment. Nickel argues that these four abstract rights are 'secure' in the sense that they do not have to be earned through membership or good behaviour and their availability does not depend on that person's ability to generate utility or other good consequences. Cf. Nickel (2008: ch. 9; 2005).
32. Shue (draft manuscript).
33. For critical discussions of Henry Shue's notion of 'basic rights', see Thomas Pogge (2009), 'Shue on Rights and Duties', in *Global Basic Rights*, ed. C. Beitz and R. Goodin (Oxford University Press), ch. 6; James Nickel (2008), 'Rethinking Indivisibility', *Human Rights Quarterly* 30: 984–1001; and Nickel (2006: 88–9).
34. In a different idiom, Martha Nussbaum maintains that two of the central capabilities to which we all have a claim of justice are the capabilities for affiliation and emotion. See Martha Nussbaum (2001), *Women and Human Development* (Cambridge University Press); and Martha Nussbaum (2011),

Creating Capabilities (Harvard University Press), 33–4. As Anca Gheaus puts the point, 'If, indeed, being affiliated and capable to become attached to others are preconditions for achieving other capabilities—such as for bodily health, practical reasoning or play—then the former are more basic.' Anca Gheaus (2018), 'Personal Relationship Goods', in *The Stanford Encyclopedia of Philosophy*, ed. Edward N. Zalta: https://plato.stanford.edu/archives/fall2018/entries/personal-relationship-goods/. As Gheaus notes, Jonathan Wolff and Avner de-Shalit defend a similar point, namely, that some kinds of functionings are *fertile* in that they have good effects for other kinds of functionings. In their view, there is strong evidence to suggest that affiliation is a very fertile functioning, and that being disadvantaged in terms of our affiliation is corrosive. Jonathan Wolff and Avner de-Shalit (2007), *Disadvantage* (Oxford University Press), ch. 8.

35. For her discussion of claimability, see Onora O'Neill (2005), 'The Dark Side of Human Rights', *International Affairs* 81(2): 427–39.
36. John Tasioulas (2007), 'The Moral Reality of Human Rights', in *Freedom from Poverty as a Human Right: Who Owes What to the Very Poor?*, ed. T. Pogge (Oxford University Press), ch. 3.
37. Ibid.
38. Valentini (2016).
39. I thank David Miller for formulating the objection in these terms (personal correspondence).
40. Cf. Michael Sandel (1982), *Liberalism and the Limits of Justice* (Cambridge University Press), 15–56. Cited from John Tomasi (1991), 'Individual Rights and Community Virtues', *Ethics* 101(3): 521–36.
41. Ibid. 525.
42. Valentini (2016).
43. Peter Jones (1994), *Rights* (Palgrave).
44. The paragraphs in this subsection on conceptual redundancy are drawn from Kimberley Brownlee (2012), 'Social Deprivation and Criminal Justice', in *Rethinking Criminal Law Theory*, ed. François Tanguay-Renaud and James Stribopoulos (Hart), 217–30.
45. Nickel (2005; 2008).
46. Cf. Joseph Raz (1999), *Practical Reason and Norms* (Clarendon Press).
47. I consider the intolerability problem in relation to violent offences, and offer somewhat different replies from those discussed here, in Brownlee (2012).
48. For an assessment of the alienating effect of our technologically savvy, social-media-driven world, see Sherry Turkle (2011), *Alone Together* (Basic Books).
49. The next three paragraphs reproduce material in Kimberley Brownlee (2018), 'Dwelling in Possibility', in *Human Rights: Moral or Political*, ed. Adam Etinson (Oxford University Press) 313–26.
50. Amartya Sen (2004), 'Elements of a Theory of Human Rights', *Philosophy and Public Affairs* 32: 315–56, at 329. Cited from John Tasioulas (2011), 'The Nature

of Human Rights", in *The Philosophy of Human Rights: Contemporary Controversies*, ed. G. Ernst and J.-C. Heilinger (de Gruyter), 17–59. Sen's condition of social influenceability excludes, for example, a right to tranquillity from qualifying as a human right. As a feasibility test, it is less demanding than others, since all it asks is that it be possible in practice for people to make some difference by paying attention to a putative right.

51. Sen (2004: 348).
52. Pablo Gilabert (2009), 'The Feasibility of Basic Socioeconomic Human Rights: A Conceptual Exploration', *Philosophical Quarterly* 59(237): 559–81; and Pablo Gilabert (2012), *From Global Poverty to Global Equality: A Conceptual Exploration* (Oxford University Press), chs. 4 and 7.
53. Nickel (2006: 78–81). This test can be understood, at least partly, as specifying the framing of human rights, rather than as a strict condition on the existence of certain rights. Nickel says that human rights need to be selected and formulated so that they can be effectively implemented: 'Neither morality nor law is advanced by rights that are stated so idealistically that most of their addressees will be excused most of the time on grounds of inability' (p. 81).
54. James Nickel (1982), 'Are Human Rights Utopian?' *Philosophy & Public Affairs* 11: 246–64, at 261.
55. Ibid. 262.
56. Sen (2004).
57. Tasioulas (2011: 42).
58. Raymond Geuss (2001), *History and Illusion in Politics* (Cambridge University Press), 138–46.
59. In this chapter, I use the terms *realizable* and *feasible* interchangeably and the terms *unrealizable* and *infeasible* interchangeably. *Unrealizability* is perhaps a broader notion than *infeasibility*; the latter has specific connotations in human rights debates of implementation, enforcement, and workability. But, even so, the term *infeasible* is synonymous with *unattainable* and *unachievable*, which are synonymous with *unrealizable* as I am using it.
60. I thank an anonymous referee for highlighting this worry.
61. For a compelling case for the claim that our emotions are sufficiently under our control to be the object of duties, see S. M. Liao (2006), 'The Right of Children to Be Loved', *Journal of Political Philosophy* 14(4): 420–40. This view is corroborated in the psychology and neuroscience literature. See e.g. D. Siegel (2010), *Mindsight* (Oxford University Press); and R. Hanson and R. Mendius (2009), *Buddha's Brain: The Practical Neuroscience of Happiness, Love and Wisdom* (Oakland).
62. See e.g. Christopher Bennett (2008), *The Apology Ritual* (Cambridge University Press). It is worth noting that this idea of suspending ordinary relations with a person who has offended until she assumes her restorative responsibilities is not exclusive to retributivist accounts like Bennett's. See e.g. Victor Tadros (2011),

The Ends of Harm (Oxford University Press). Tadros defends an instrumental argument for punishment from within a non-consequentialist moral framework. He calls this the 'Duty View' of punishment. It says that a person who has offended has certain restorative and reparative duties (other than compensation) that flow from his wrongdoing, and in light of this, when a person who has offended is unwilling to honour those duties, it is permissible to suspend ordinary relations and impose burdens on him in the name of those duties.

Chapter 3

1. Although 'sustaining' implies that we do everything for someone and do it successfully, I use the term more lightly to mean that we contribute non-negligibly to someone's survival or well-being.
2. Parts of this chapter develop material in Kimberley Brownlee (2016), 'The Lonely Heart Breaks', *Proceedings of the Aristotelian Society Supplementary Volume* 90, 27–48.
3. Aristotle, *Nicomachean Ethics*, bk IX (trans. W. D. Ross): 'Do we need friends more in good fortune or in bad? They are sought after in both; for while men in adversity need help, in prosperity they need people to live with and to make the objects of their beneficence; for they wish to do well by others.'
4. This analysis of the self-preservation needs behind contributing is simplistic. Just as some people can appear to contribute, and be secure within a group based on that appearance, so too some people can contribute significantly, but be less secure than others for various reasons, one being that they are members of a group that is stereotyped as being less contributory. And, of course, many people contribute largely through productive labour rather than through interpersonal connections. The point is that our deep inclination to contribute socially sits atop our need to feel secure within a reciprocity-based social group.
5. Joseph Raz distinguishes *biological self-interest*, which depends on longevity, from *well-being*, which does not. 'A person's well-being is not reduced by the shortening of his life, nor by frustrating his biological needs, when this is the means of or the accepted by-product of his pursuit of a valuable goal. A person who undergoes great deprivations in order to bring medical help to the victims of an epidemic is sacrificing his interest in favour of that of others, but his life is no less successful, rewarding or accomplished because of that.' Joseph Raz (1986), *The Morality of Freedom* (Oxford University Press), 296.
6. Elizabeth von Arnim (2015 [1922]), *The Enchanted April* (Vintage Classics) 99.
7. Laura Valentini specifies the contrast between matters of *political justice* and matters of *personal* or *private justice* in terms of enforceability; the duties of political justice may be rightfully enforced by appropriately placed agents. She further distinguishes private injustice from duties of beneficence. 'Duties of

beneficence are unlike duties of justice in that they are not correlative to rights, that is, not directed.' Laura Valentini (2016), 'What's Wrong with Being Lonely?' *Proceedings of the Aristotelian Society Supplementary Volume* 90(1): 46–69.
8. W. H. Auden (1960), 'The More Loving One', in *Homage to Clio* (Random House).
9. Alfred, Lord Tennyson (1850), *In Memoriam A. H. H.* Accessed from The British Library: https://www.bl.uk/works/in-memoriam-ahh.
10. See e.g. Sue Gerhardt (2015), *Why Love Matters: How Affection Shapes a Baby's Brain*, 2nd edn (Routledge). For numerous references to the psychological and neuro-scientific literature, see S. Matthew Liao (2015), *The Right to Be Loved* (Oxford University Press).
11. Virginia Held observes: 'To be a caring person requires more than the right virtues or dispositions. It requires the *ability* to engage in the practice of care, and the *exercise* of this ability.' Virginia Held (2006), *The Ethics of Care: Personal, Political, and Global* (Oxford University Press), 51 (emphasis added).
12. See Chris Rogers (2009), 'What Became of Romania's Neglected Orphans?' *BBC News*, 22 Dec.: http://news.bbc.co.uk/1/hi/world/europe/8425001.stm.
13. Now, although a mistreated child endures undeniable injustice, child neglect is excusable in extreme circumstances where there is social resource scarcity and, consequently, insufficient numbers of able carers who can ensure that each child receives care and socialization. This may happen in a society where the healthy adult population has been decimated by a disease like AIDS. (That said, although those within the society may be excused for perpetuating this wrong, others outside the society bear the responsibility to ensure that the children receive adequate care and socialization.)
14. Variations of this case might include a person who is severely cognitively impaired; a solitary immigrant who does not speak the local language; or a person released after years in prison who has no family or friends.
15. I thank an anonymous OUP reader for highlighting this point.
16. If her social resources erode to the point where she is unable to contribute socially, then society's judgment would not be unjustly prejudicial. Instead, there would be the historical injustice in rendering her unable to contribute socially.
17. The reciprocity argument applies to a lonely person and not to a mistreated child because, most likely, the mistreated child has far less of a resource debt to repay.
18. I thank an anonymous OUP reader for highlighting that it matters what Sophie's society's reasons are (if they have some) for treating her this way. The expressive nature of the society's treatment of her turns on its *reasons* for treating her this way.
19. The fact that people get paid to perform a role does not necessarily undermine the authenticity of their connection. Actors in the reality TV show are analogous, in principle, to doctors and nurses, whose capacity for compassion is compatible with the fact they receive a salary.

20. First, coercive isolation denies a person all opportunities for social ties. Second, as noted in Ch. 2, people who've endured coercive isolation, notably solitary confinement, tend to report that it is as painful as any physical torture they know, and that any companion is better than no companion. See Kimberley Brownlee (2013), 'A Human Right Against Social Deprivation', *Philosophical Quarterly* 63: 199–222.
21. Sara Forsdyke (2005), *Exile, Ostracism, and Democracy: The Politics of Expulsion in Ancient Greece* (Princeton University Press).
22. Kimberley Brownlee (2012), 'Social Deprivation and Criminal Justice', in *Rethinking Criminal Law Theory: New Canadian Perspectives in the Philosophy of Domestic, Transnational, and International Criminal Law*, ed. François Tanguay-Renaud and James Stribopoulos (Hart), 217–30.
23. This case is similar in many respects to 'Lovely Gertraud' discussed in Valentini (2016).
24. See Gerhardt (2014).
25. I thank Cécile Fabre for highlighting this point.
26. Jonathan Wolff and Avner de-Shalit (2007), *Disadvantage* (Oxford University Press).
27. Rose, Julie (2017), *Free Time* (Princeton University Press), ch. 5.
28. While there's no guarantee that she'd make a good social contribution, it's likely that there would, in principle, be people who could benefit from her use of social resources, since our typical state as human beings is one of social connection. In other words, we can reasonably assume that, given the chance, an isolated person would be socially connected.

Chapter 4

1. We also have interests in asserting interactional control on behalf of our children. 'Don't talk to strangers' is a common injunction from parents to children. Danielle Allen questions the wisdom of this kind of distrustful approach to living alongside each other in *Talking to Strangers: Anxieties of Citizenship since Brown v. Board of Education* (University of Chicago Press, 2004).
2. In this last example, the parties cannot help but associate given their embodiment. Also, depending on how they are conjoined, they may not have the option to separate and thereby reconfigure or terminate their association. They might also disagree about whether to separate, if indeed they could do so safely.
3. Susan Cain (2012), *Quiet: The Power of Introverts in a World That Can't Stop Talking* (Crown), 73ff. Cass Sunstein also cites evidence to indicate that we act more independent-mindedly when we are not deeply embedded within a group. See Cass Sunstein (2003), *Why Societies Need Dissent* (Harvard University Press).
4. Hannah Arendt (2006 [1961]), *Between Past and Future* (Penguin), 237.

5. Sharon Clott Kanter (2011), Interview of Tina Fey in *InStyle* magazine, Apr. 2011.
6. I thank Kartik Upadhyaya for highlighting this point.
7. H. W. Wright (1942), 'The Values of Personal Association', *Ethics* 52(4): 447–62.
8. Barbara Fredrickson (2013), 'Remaking Love', TEDx LowerEastSide, 25 Oct.: https://www.youtube.com/watch?v=Nw9x8MNoCJE. See also Barbara Fredrickson (2013), *Love 2.0: Finding Happiness and Health in Moments of Connection* (Penguin).
9. These three sets of questions are drawn from Kimberley Brownlee (2016), 'Freedom of Association', in *The Blackwell Companion to Applied Philosophy*, ed. Kasper Lippert-Rasmussen, Kimberley Brownlee, and David Coady (Wiley), 356–69.
10. James Dwyer (2014), 'The Moral Basis of Children's Relational Rights', in *The Routledge Handbook of Family Law and Policy*, ed. John Eekelaar and Rob George (Routledge), 275.
11. John Stuart Mill [1859], *On Liberty*, ch. 4 (various edns).
12. When we *interact*, we participate in a reciprocal exchange in which we mutually influence each other. Mutual influence is not the same thing as mutual support. Although our interactions with each other are often decent, progressive, and mutually supportive, they can also be deceptive, manipulative, hostile, vicious, or deadly. Here I focus on interactions that fit under the heading of *social connections*, and hence are at least minimally decent. Interactions that are minimally decent are neither gratuitously offensive nor indefensibly aggressive, cruel, inhumane, or unfair.
13. In Paris, a woman told a man who was sexually harassing her with wolf whistles and animal noises to 'shut up', thereby shutting down his bid for attention. He started to walk away, then came back, threw an ashtray at her, and then violently hit her: Kim Willsher (2018), 'Uproar in France over Video of Woman Hit by Harasser in Paris Street', *The Guardian*, 30 July: https://www.theguardian.com/world/2018/jul/30/uproar-in-france-over-video-of-woman-marie-laguerre-hit-by-harasser-in-paris-street.
14. Emily McTernan (2018), 'Microaggressions, Equality, and Social Practices', *Journal of Political Philosophy* 26(3): 261–81.
15. Firat Akova has observed in correspondence that, after enough trips to the grocery store or visits to the doctor, a person might realize that these non-associative interactions lack the meaning she craves, and hence may come to feel great loneliness, in which case these momentary interactions ultimately harm her by reinforcing how socially malnourished she is. In the main text above, I indicate that 'mere' non-associative interactions are ill-suited to satisfy all our core social needs. But they are a vital source of social support—as a confirmation of our general acceptance—in their own right.
16. Campaign to End Loneliness, survey results (2013), 'Lonely Visits to the GP'. Cited from *A Connected Society: A Strategy for Tackling Loneliness. Laying the Foundations for Change* (London: HMSO, 2018).

17. I do not mean to imply that intimate associations cannot conflict with members' interests. They can. But it's not the case that the animating purpose of such associations is to pursue interests other than those of the member parties. I thank Rob Jubb for prompting me to clarify this point.
18. I am grateful to David Silver for highlighting this distinction.
19. Jane Austen continues: '[The Miss Steeles] declared [Elinor and Marianne] to be the most beautiful, elegant, accomplished, and agreeable girls they had ever beheld, and with whom they were particularly anxious to be better acquainted.— And to be better acquainted therefore, Elinor soon found was their inevitable lot, for as Sir John was entirely on the side of the Miss Steeles, their party would be too strong for opposition, and that kind of intimacy must be submitted to, which consists of sitting an hour or two together in the same room almost every day. Sir John could do no more; but he did not know that any more was required: to be together was, in his opinion, to be intimate, and while his continual schemes for their meeting were effectual, he had not a doubt of their being established friends.' Let me note that, in saying that frequent direct contact tends to lead to associations, I do not mean that nothing more than this is required for friendship. But I do mean that frequent contact can prompt one person to feel more at liberty to impose on the other, as in the case where Lucy burdens Elinor with her secret.
20. Tom Parr has suggested to me that people might be a family in more than name even if they never interact, provided that they are always prepared to interact when a member needs assistance. In reply, I think this might make these people members of a *clan*, but not a *family* in its paradigmatic sense. A *clan* in this sense is not well-characterized as an intimate association; it is at best an abstract association.
21. For interesting discussions of different issues pertaining to the rights of collective associations, see Cécile Laborde (2017), *Liberalism's Religion* (Harvard University Press), ch. 5, which distinguishes two sets of associational interests salient to religious groups' exemption rights: (1) coherence interests and (2) competence interests; see also S. White (1998), 'Trade Unionism in a Liberal State', in *Freedom of Association*, ed. A. Gutmann (Princeton University Press), 330–56; and see Dale Carpenter (2001), 'Expressive Association and Anti-Discrimination Law After Dale: A Tripartite Approach', *Minnesota Law Review* 85: 1515–89.
22. This shows that it would be a mistake to think intimate associations are, by nature, voluntaristic and require that members be able to join and leave at will. A more credible view of intimate associations is akin to that underpinning Dworkin's account of associative or communal obligations, better known as role obligations, which are 'the special responsibilities social practice attaches to membership in some biological or social group, like the responsibilities of family or friends or neighbours'. Ronald Dworkin (1986), *Law's Empire* (Harvard University Press), 196.

23. Jonathan Seglow argues that our relationship-based duties—associative duties—'make up most of the substance of our moral lives. We do things with, to and for our children, parents, friends, colleagues, team members and even...our fellow citizens. We spend most of the time most of our life interacting with people through the medium of the relationships we share with them...Such is the richly complex nature of human social life that the most salient encounters we have with other people tend to be through the medium of the social roles through which they connect with us.' Jonathan Seglow (2013), *Defending Associative Duties* (Routledge), p. 1. He defines *social relationships* as enduring, substantive, mutually affirmed interactions between two or more people (p. 28). They are not brief encounters or episodic collective experiences, such as those that interest me in this chapter. While Seglow is right that our social relationships are a central domain of morality, he is mistaken, in my view, to say they make up *most* of the substance of our moral lives. The non-associative interactional domain I am exploring here is a vital and morally significant site of social connection in its own right, and it is the garden in which associative duties and claims can grow.
24. On 'mandatory rights', see Joel Feinberg (1977), 'Voluntary Euthanasia and the Inalienable Right to Life', The Tanner Lecture on Human Values: http://tanner-lectures.utah.edu/_documents/a-to-z/f/feinberg80.pdf. See also L. W. Sumner (1987), *The Moral Foundation of Rights* (Oxford University Press), 34. Sumner argues that a bare (half-)liberty is a poor candidate for a right.
25. Onora O'Neill (1986), 'The Public Use of Reason', *Political Theory* 14: 523–51. Emphasis added.
26. According to Mill, our core personal freedoms include freedom of thought, conscience, opinion, and feeling, which means that we have complete control over our own inner domain of consciousness; freedom of expression in speech and writing, since expression is so closely linked to thought as to be almost inextricable from it; freedom to shape our own lives according to our tastes and pursuits in line with our character and inclinations; and freedom to unite in combination with other people 'for any purpose not involving harm to others: the persons combining being supposed to be of full age and not forced or deceived' (Mill 1859: ch. 4). Our associational freedom is subject to Mill's 'very simple principle', which we now call the *harm principle*, which states that we are permitted to interfere with someone's conduct only to prevent harm to other people. Our freedoms of thought and expression are largely immune to the harm principle. Protecting harmful free expression is in the interests of humanity as a progressive species. Only through the unfettered collision of opinions—including false opinions and highly damaging opinions—can we hope to arrive at the truth on any matter. We don't need to embrace quite so generous an account of free expression to take the view that our freedom to associate or not as we please is much more limited than our freedom to express offensive, or even harmful, things.

27. I thank Firat Akova for noting that a demandingness objection might rear its head here unless we grant that a person may defensibly ignore others' interactional bids when he has attended to the interactional needs of as many people as he can reasonably be expected to accommodate (whatever number that may be). I thank Simon Gansinger for noting, by contrast, that sometimes a person may *un*reasonably feel depleted when, for instance, he has unreasonably wasted his energies and now has no appetite or competence for social interactions. He has unreasonably incurred the feeling of depletion, but, given that he is feeling depleted, it may be excusable for him not to respond presently to new overtures.
28. Karen Stohr holds that our manners are the ways in which we wear our moral commitments on the outside: they show others what matters to us. Drawing on a distinction from Judith Martin between general, universal principles of manners and the specific, culturally varying rules of etiquette, which attempt to instantiate those general principles, Stohr argues that principles of manners are moral principles that instruct us to be considerate and respectful of people. Specific etiquette rules can do a better or worse job of instantiating those principles and communicating our commitment to them. Karen Stohr (2012), *On Manners* (Routledge), ch. 2.
29. For a range of psychological perspectives on the motivation, nature, and effects of socially excluding people, see C. Nathan DeWall (2013), *The Oxford Handbook of Social Exclusion* (Oxford University Press).
30. Gregory P. Smith (2018), 'After 25 years of Being Homeless, I Learned There's One Simple Thing You Can Do to Help', *The Guardian*, 24 June: https://www.theguardian.com/books/2018/jun/25/after-25-years-of-being-homeless-i-learned-theres-one-simple-thing-you-can-do-to-help-gregory-p-smith.
31. Leslie Green (2010), 'Two Worries about Respect for Persons', *Ethics* 120(2): 212–31.
32. Ibid. 222.
33. I thank Kartik Upadhyaya for this observation.
34. Alternatively, we might see the homeless person's very presence on the street corner as an interactional bid, i.e. a bid to her society and to us who pass by to help her to remedy her situation. I thank Firat Akova for this suggestion.
35. An apparent difference between this rescue case and ordinary interactions is that the former is an emergency and the latter, in any one instance, are not. But chronic denial or absence of minimally adequate access to decent human contact can become an emergency, as demonstrated by the empirical evidence cited in the previous chapters.
36. I thank David Jenkins for highlighting this point.
37. Jonathan Wolff and Avner de-Shalit (2007), *Disadvantage* (Oxford University Press), ch. 2.

38. Deepa Narayan et al. (2000), *Voices of the Poor: Can Anyone Hear Us?* (Oxford University Press and the World Bank), 39. Cited from Wolff and de-Shalit (2007): 48.
39. *Oxford English Dictionary* (current online edn).

Chapter 5

1. Laura Valentini (2016), 'What's Wrong with Being Lonely? Justice, Beneficence, and Meaningful Relationships', in *Proceedings of the Aristotelian Society Supplementary Volume* 90(1): 57.
2. In this discussion, I treat the terms 'associative' and 'associational' as interchangeable. I also treat the terms 'interactive' and 'interactional' as interchangeable.
3. Derek Parfit (2011), *On What Matters*, vol. 1 (Oxford University Press), 302.
4. For a discussion of the distributive justice of relational resources, see Chiara Cordelli (2015), 'Justice as Fairness and Relational Resources', *Journal of Political Philosophy* 23(1): 86–110. By 'relational resources', Cordelli means something different from what I describe here as 'social resources'. By 'relational resources', she means the by-products of healthy relationships such as trust and self-respect.
5. For a survey of the rights that define *freedom of association*—the rights to exclude, to exit, and to exercise organizational autonomy—see Kimberley Brownlee and David Jenkins (2019), 'Freedom of Association', in *The Stanford Encyclopedia of Philosophy*, ed. Edward N. Zalta: https://plato.stanford.edu/entries/freedom-association/.
6. Amy Gutmann (1998), 'Freedom of Association: An Introductory Essay', in *Freedom of Association*, ed. Amy Gutmann (Princeton University Press), 11.
7. Mill (1859: ch. 4).
8. Joseph Raz (1986), *The Morality of Freedom* (Oxford University Press), ch. 7.
9. Mill (1859: ch. 1), emphasis added.
10. Even though *intimate associations* and *collective associations* have distinct argumentative foundations, the conceptual space between them is rough terrain. Indeed, some thinkers deny that the two types of association can be clearly divided. Seana Shiffrin offers plausible reasons to question a sharp dichotomy between intimate associations and collective associations, such as that both are sites in which members' thoughts and ideas are formed and the content of their expressions is generated and germinated rather than merely concentrated and exported. Similarly, Larry Alexander argues that, although associations can be classified as intimate, political, expressive, creedal, hobby-based, recreational, commercial, and so on, nevertheless many, if not most, associations fall into more than one category. For instance, social clubs are venues for close friendships,

recreation, and commerce. Finally, Rob Jubb has suggested in correspondence that it may be better to think of associations as lying along a continuum from more impersonal and instrumental associations to more intimate and affective associations. I grant that these views are credible, but even so, paradigmatically, intimate associations differ from collective associations in that, unlike the latter, they need not have some further purpose beyond associating to motivate their existence. See Seana Shiffrin (2005), 'What Is Really Wrong with Compelled Association?' *Northwestern Law Review* 99(2): 839–88, at 865; and see Larry Alexander (2008), 'What Is Freedom of Association, and What Is Its Denial?' *Social Philosophy and Policy* 25(2): 1–21.

11. Christopher Heath Wellman (2008), 'Immigration and Freedom of Association', *Ethics* 119: 109–41. A competing view of immigration is defended by Chandran Kukathas (2005), 'The Case for Open Immigration', in *Contemporary Debates in Applied Ethics*, ed. A. I. Cohen and C. H. Wellman (Blackwell), 207–20.

12. David Miller holds that this argument—that we have deep interests against being forced into associations with others—applies most clearly in our intimate relationships ('it would clearly be intolerable if I were obliged to share my house or my bed with another person or persons without my consent'). But, it does not apply at the level of political communities the size of nation-states. Those are not intimate associations. David Miller (2008), *National Responsibility and Global Justice* (Oxford University Press), 210–11. Cited from Sarah Fine (2010), 'Freedom of Association Is Not the Answer', *Ethics* 120(2): 338. On related issues, see David Miller (2016), *Strangers in Our Midst: The Political Philosophy of Immigration* (Oxford University Press).

13. Our associations take a range of forms, some more persistent and comprehensive than others. Scholars and practitioners often distinguish our freedom of *intimate* association from our freedom of *collective* association and assembly. The US Supreme Court highlights this distinction in *Roberts v. United States Jaycees* where Justice Brennan, writing for the majority, states: 'Our decisions have referred to constitutionally protected "freedom of association" in two distinct senses. In one line of decisions, the Court has concluded that choices to enter into and maintain certain intimate human relationships must be secured against undue intrusion by the State because of the role of such relationships in safeguarding the individual freedom that is central to our constitutional scheme. In this respect, freedom of association receives protection as a fundamental element of personal liberty. In another set of decisions, the Court has recognized a right to associate for the purpose of engaging in those activities protected by the First Amendment—speech, assembly, petition for the redress of grievances, and the exercise of religion. The Constitution guarantees freedom of association of this kind as an indispensable means of preserving other individual liberties.' *Roberts v. United States Jaycees* 468 U.S. 609, 618 (1984).

14. Stuart White (1997), 'Freedom of Association and the Right to Exclude', *Journal of Political Philosophy* 5: 373–91.

15. Sonu Bedi (2010), 'Expressive Exclusion: A Defense', *Journal of Moral Philosophy* 7(4): 428.
16. See Jacob T. Levy (2014), *Rationalism, Pluralism, and Freedom* (Oxford University Press).
17. Catriona McKinnon (2000), 'Exclusion Rules and Self-Respect', *Journal of Value Inquiry* 34(4): 491–505, at 498. See also Steffen N. Johnson (2001), 'Expressive Association and Organizational Autonomy', *Minnesota Law Review* 85(6): 1639–68.
18. Wellman (2008).
19. See Michael Walzer (2004), 'Involuntary Association', in *Politics and Passion* (Yale University Press), 18–37.
20. For an interesting discussion of the morality of engineering children, see Jonathan Glover (2008), *Choosing Children* (Oxford University Press).
21. White (1997: 383ff.).
22. Fine (2010: 346).
23. Andres Moles (2014), 'The Public Ecology of Freedom of Association', *Res Publica* 20(1): 85–103.
24. Parfit (2011: 14).
25. Ibid. 302.
26. Ibid. 303.
27. Of course, some people seeking social contact may not be able to give social contact that is decent.
28. In negative each-we dilemmas of sociability, the better result for everyone is actually the one in which *not everyone* avoids Jo, rather than the one in which *no one* avoids Jo. This is because everyone seeking Jo's company can generate other dilemmas, as we will see in the positive dilemmas. I thank Matthew Kramer for pressing me to clarify this point.
29. See Sharon Shalev (2008), *Sourcebook on Solitary Confinement* (Nuffield Foundation): http://www.solitaryconfinement.org/uploads/sourcebook_web.pdf.
30. I thank an OUP reader for noting this objection.
31. I thank David Silver for this observation.
32. I thank Jonathan Floyd for highlighting this point about past contributions.
33. I thank Jonathan Floyd for highlighting this idea.
34. The conditions for autonomy that I take for granted here are those outlined by Joseph Raz (1986), *The Morality of Freedom* (Oxford University Press), 369–429. For a discussion of competent-judgment-compromising experiences, see Kimberley Brownlee (2016), 'The Competent Judge Problem', *Ratio* 29(3): 312–26.
35. We become like the terrified person trapped in her house trying to escape the person who wants to kill her, or like the person who is paralysed by a phobia. In such cases, we cannot make use of our options. Our reasoning is diminished such that we cannot decide at all. This *autonomy dilemma* would be resolvable if acts that undermine the possibility for continued autonomy were not really

autonomous, and hence should not be protected as such. But such a resolution would be *ad hoc*.
36. Parfit discusses the egoist in (2011: 15–16).
37. I thank an OUP reader for highlighting this point.
38. I thank Christopher Bennett for highlighting this point.
39. John T. Cacioppo and William Patrick (2008), *Loneliness* (Norton), 19.
40. I thank Daniel Groll for pressing me on this point.
41. In Nathaniel Hawthorne's novel *The Scarlet Letter*, puritanical Boston shuns the protagonist, Hester Prynne, for her act of adultery.

Chapter 6

1. In fact, in such cases it is not even possible for Jo to form an association, since there is no *mutual* attachment but instead active detachment from Andy, and therefore what she is trying to make cannot be created.
2. One argument against compelled association is that it will interfere with the emotionally expressive purposes of the association, i.e. the expression of affection between the parties. This argument, while not trivial, is less forceful than the argument that people require at least minimal access to intimate association even when it lacks the emotional connections we would wish to have in such associations. For a discussion of parents' obligations to enter into a relationship with their children because they are morally responsible for their existence, see Serena Olsaretti (2017), 'Liberal Equality and the Moral Status of Parent–Child Relationships', in *Oxford Studies in Political Philosophy*, vol. 3, ed. David Sobel, Peter Vallentyne, and Steven Wall (Oxford University Press).
3. In the remainder of this chapter and in the next, I offer a variety of real, fictional, and hypothetical cases as (hopefully) useful illustrations. I readily admit that some of these cases are controversial. This chapter develops some ideas in Kimberley Brownlee (2015), 'Freedom of Association: It's Not What You Think', *Oxford Journal of Legal Studies* 35(2): 267–82.
4. Jonathan Seglow defends what he calls the 'relationship goods view', according to which relationship goods such as those cultivated between parents and children, between friends, and even among citizens can ground a person's associative duties regardless of whether she has voluntarily assumed these associative roles and their responsibilities. See Jonathan Seglow (2013), *Defending Associative Duties* (Routledge).
5. Of course, relations between a parent and a child are hierarchical and can pose distinctive risks to the child for that very reason. But that non-egalitarian feature is inescapable for much of childhood and, typically, its risks are vastly outweighed by the benefits of the relation.
6. I thank an OUP reader for this example.

7. I thank Jeremy Waldron for highlighting this point.
8. This notion of *integration* comes from Elizabeth Anderson (2010), *The Imperative of Integration* (Princeton University Press), ch. 6.
9. For an excellent discussion of the fact that we need to have meaningful amounts of *shared* free time if we are to sustain our associations, see Julie Rose (2017), *Free Time* (Princeton University Press), ch. 5.
10. I thank an OUP reader for noting that this case raises issues related to the non-identity problem. Specifically, none of this child's relationships could have existed without the rape. All her relationships have come about as a consequence of this illegitimate process. But we do not want to say that every relationship this child has is *morally wrong*. In order to condemn the rape without condemning all the relationships that the rape made possible, we must highlight that the morally wrong relationship is the *authoritative* relationship between the guilty parent and the child.
11. This example is fictional, but loosely based on Michelle Knight's experience of being kidnapped by Ariel Castro in Cleveland, Ohio, and held captive for close to ten years. She had a son at the time she was captured. After her disappearance, he was taken into foster care and then adopted by his foster family. However, prior to being kidnapped, Michelle Knight had lost custody of her child to the state. I explore this case further in Ch. 7.
12. The conjunction of 'association' with 'assembly' suggests that this article applies in the first instance to non-intimate, collective associations. (Commentaries on the drafting of the *Universal Declaration of Human Rights* confirm that political associations, such as trade unions, were uppermost in the drafters' minds.) But I take it that this unspecified notion of *associational freedom* should be extended, broadly unaltered, to intimate associations, since no other article in the UDHR protects non-familial, intimate connections such as friendships. In subsequent agreements, such as the *International Covenant on Civil and Political Rights*, freedom of assembly and freedom of association are enumerated under different articles, and one explanation given for this is that freedom of association includes private informal contacts. See Martin Scheinin (1999), 'Article 20', in *The Universal Declaration of Human Rights: A Common Standard of Achievement*, ed. Guðmundur Alfreðsson and Asbjørn Eide (Martinus Nijhoff), 417–30.
13. John Rawls (1971), *A Theory of Justice* (Harvard University Press), 205–8, 370.
14. Loren Lomasky (2008), 'The Paradox of Association', *Social Philosophy and Policy* 25: 182.
15. Lomasky (2008: 183).
16. We must proceed cautiously. In the most famous president and intern case between President Bill Clinton and Monica Lewinsky, the relationship and its aftermath proved to be incredibly harmful to Lewinsky. Partly due to the rise of social media, this relationship became a life-shaping and life-shattering event

for her. To hear her speak eloquently of its impact on her, see Monica Lewinsky (2015), 'The Price of Shame': https://www.ted.com/talks/monica_lewinsky_the_price_of_shame?language=en. I return to this case in Ch. 7. In the case of professors and students, we might view these relationships as analogous to those between doctors and patients, with the possibility that a professional might lose their licence or tenure through unprofessional conduct.
17. Of course, Romeo and Juliet's liaison also poses life-threatening risks to their family members, which those people do not willingly assume. Therefore, although it's not Romeo and Juliet's fault that their families are at war, their freedom of association doesn't extend to posing such risks, or it is overridden by the risks it poses to their families.
18. I thank Tom Parr for pressing me to address this objection.

Chapter 7

1. As noted in Ch. 6, this example is fictional, but loosely based on Michelle Knight's experience of being kidnapped by Ariel Castro in 2002 in Cleveland, Ohio, and held captive for over ten years. She had a son, Joey. After her disappearance, he was taken into foster care and then adopted by his foster family. However, prior to being kidnapped, Michelle had lost custody of Joey to the state following an incident where an injury was done to him that was possibly inflicted by her mother's abusive partner. ('Sam' and 'Sara Smith' are fictional names.)
2. These two stories resemble a range of cases in which children are taken from their birth families and given to other people to raise on the ostensible grounds that the biological parents are either incompetent or unable to secure necessary goods for their children. In Canada, over 100,000 aboriginal children were forcibly removed from their families and culture and put into residential schools administered by either the Catholic Church or Anglican Church, in order to sever familial ties and integrate them into the dominant culture. Given the state's complicity in these removals, these were not officially 'kidnappings', but morally speaking they amounted to the same thing. In the United States, many black children have been taken away from their parents on the grounds that the parents are incompetent. In Argentina in the 1970s, many activists were put in jail and their children given to families loyal to the dictator. Now those children are in their 30s and 40s and report very mixed views about their adoptive parents.
3. These three stories describe inegalitarian parent–child relations of care and dependency. I have chosen them, as they are vivid examples of the moral messiness I explore here. But they are not the only kind of relationship in which

moral messiness can arise. It can arise in more voluntaristic relationships such as that between a president and an intern or Beauty and the Beast.
4. Derek Parfit discusses several cases that highlight the differences between *ex ante* and *ex post* moral reasoning. See Derek Parfit (1984), *Reasons and Persons* (Oxford University Press), 357–61 (on a young girl who decides to have a baby and, given her age, gives that baby a bad start in life); 165–7 (on past pain versus future pain); and 181–4 (on past suffering versus future suffering of those we love). An anonymous OUP reader raised the question of whether, in the case of forced marriage, it might be a simple solution for states to nullify such marriages because they were contracted without consent, and then make it easy for spouses to contract a new, morally and legally valid marriage together if they wished. In reply, this might be a viable strategy when the spouses are adequately resourced and empowered to choose whether to renew their contract. If, however, they are resource-deprived or unequally placed in the way that female parties often are, then the state might leave vulnerable parties woefully unprotected if it declared their marriage null and void.
5. This seems to be true even in some of the worst kinds of associations. Consider e.g. Natascha Kampusch, the Austrian girl who was kidnapped at the age of 10 by Wolfgang Přiklopil and held captive for eight years. She reportedly cried inconsolably when told that Přiklopil had committed suicide after she escaped.
6. I focus here on intimate associations, rather than on collective and expressive associations, since intimate associations generate the most pressing examples of moral messiness. Intimate associations are distinguished by their persistence, the quality of the interactions (i.e. they are usually marked by mutual investment, care, and concern), and their comprehensiveness as well as their small size, selectivity, and seclusion.
7. Recall from Ch. 4 that there are five ways an association can be morally wrong: (1) its content, (2) its form, (3) its form and content, (4) its form and likely content, and (5) indirectly. Recall also that some specific sources of wrongness include lack of consent, harm, risk, burdensomeness, and illegitimate exclusivity.
8. In the sequel to *The Face on the Milk Carton*, Janie is returned to her biological family; but when she turns 16 she leaves them in order to return to Frank and Miranda.
9. One could say that, prior to Janie's biological parents being identified, Janie's relationship with Frank and Miranda *should* exist in this same simple sense since she needs a family to care for her.
10. This case differs from one in which Michelle is killed. We might say of her death that 'circumstances should be otherwise', but we would simply express regret for what might have been, not an active expectation that those circumstances change.
11. See Adam Swift and Harry Brighouse (2014), *Family Values* (Princeton University Press).

12. The association among Patrick, Saskia, and Jack is morally messy in that, structurally, Jack is very insecure. By not adopting him, Saskia puts their relationship at risk.
13. Liane Moriarty (2011), *The Hypnotist's Love Story* (Thorndike Press).
14. Of this case, we might say that *ex ante* the woman has duties *ceteris paribus* to do her best to stay connected to her spouse, but *ex post* the husband has to accept that the woman has ended the relationship. A more tragic variant of this case is one in which the abandoned spouse is a child.
15. One of the mothers struggled with the decision to exchange the babies. See Bojan Pancevski (2007), 'Birth Mix-Up Mother Refuses to Swap Babies', *Telegraph*, 11 Oct.: http://www.telegraph.co.uk/news/worldnews/1565861/Birth-mix-up-mother-refuses-to-swap-babies.html.
16. Roy F. Baumeister and Mark R. Leary (1995), 'The Need to Belong: Desire for Interpersonal Attachments as a Fundamental Human Motivation', *Psychological Bulletin* 117(3): 497–529, at 503.
17. Joseph Raz (1986), *The Morality of Freedom* (Oxford University Press), 247–8.
18. For discussions related to piggybacking, see ibid. 179, 247–8; Joseph Raz (1994), 'Rights and Individual Well-Being', in *Ethics in the Public Domain* (Oxford University Press), 149–51, 274–5; Gopal Sreenivasan (2005), 'A Hybrid Theory of Claim Rights', *Oxford Journal of Legal Studies* 25(2): 257–74; Rowan Cruft (2013), 'Why Is It Disrespectful to Violate Rights?' *Proceedings of the Aristotelian Society* 113(2), pt 2: 201–24. On duty-bearing as a ground for holding rights, see Leif Wenar (2013), 'The Nature of Claim-Rights', in Symposium on Rights and the Direction of Duties, *Ethics* 123(2): 202–29.
19. Raz (1986: 253).
20. Kamm observes, 'If the satisfaction of the interests of others is the reason why the journalist gets a right to have his interest protected, his interest is *not sufficient* to give rise to the duty of non-interference with his speech.' Frances Kamm (2002), 'Rights', in *Oxford Handbook of Jurisprudence and Philosophy of Law*, ed. Jules L. Coleman, Kenneth Einar Himma, and Scott J. Shapiro, 476–513 (Oxford University Press), at 485. Cited from Leif Wenar (2005), 'The Nature of Rights', *Philosophy & Public Affairs* 33(3), at 242 n. 34.
21. Ibid. 242.
22. In this discussion, I bracket questions about structural injustice which might lead us to say that ordinary judges, police officers, prosecutors, legislators, and executives are illegitimate occupants of their legitimate social role in virtue of an unfair distribution of positions of authority within society. I thank Fay Niker for highlighting this point.
23. Wenar (2013).
24. Arguably, the wrongdoer's best interests are also to remain in the association, but those best interests are set aside here.

25. We cannot assume that the parent is incompetent simply because he engaged in very serious wrongdoing prior to becoming a parent. In US family law, in cases involving life-generating rape, the default position is that the biological father has parental rights (even though the child was conceived through rape), which seems to concede the point that competence does not depend on the process through which one comes to have (putative) rights that require competence. However, in such cases, the mother can petition a court to terminate the biological father's rights, and such petitions are overwhelmingly likely to succeed. If the biological father fails to exercise his parental rights for a given period of time, the termination of his rights will be even easier. If the biological father attempts to exercise parental rights, e.g. by seeking partial custody over the child, then the mother can argue that his petition for custody should be denied and his rights terminated on grounds that such rulings would be in the best interest of the child. I thank Michelle Dempsey for summarizing the legal position for me.
26. This suggestion is a dangerous one because it cuts both ways. Legitimate expectations do part of the moral work to give parasites their right to act. So we cannot say that legitimate expectations of *performance* by duty-bearers matter but legitimate expectations about *legitimate role-occupancy* do not.
27. Peter Jones (1994), *Rights* (Palgrave Macmillan), 190.
28. Ronald Dworkin (1984), 'Rights as Trumps', in *Theories of Rights*, ed. Jeremy Waldron (Oxford University Press), 153–67.
29. Jones (1994: 192).
30. Alasdair Cochrane summarized the proportionality test along these lines in a recent lecture at All Souls College, Oxford, Apr. 2016.
31. James Nickel (2006), *Making Sense of Human Rights*, 2nd edn (Blackwell), 62ff.; and James Nickel (2005), 'Poverty and Human Rights', *Philosophical Quarterly* 55: 385–402, at 391ff.
32. In morally messy situations, we can see the reasoning behind legislation that requires divorcing people to wait two years if they have kids and less time if they do not.

Chapter 8

1. This chapter develops the account in Kimberley Brownlee (2016), 'Don't Call People "Rapists": On the Social Contribution Injustice of Punishment', *Current Legal Problems* 69(1): 327–52.
2. I take Anglo-American systems as my reference point.
3. There is a substantial literature on equity, justice, and 'social deprivation' where the latter term refers to poverty, not interpersonal social deprivation. See

e.g. Martha Nussbaum (1993), 'Equity and Mercy', *Philosophy & Public Affairs* 22(2): 83; Victor Tadros (2009), 'Poverty and Criminal Responsibility', *Journal of Value Inquiry* 43(3): 391; Barbara Hudson (1998), 'Mitigation for Socially Deprived Offenders', in *Principled Sentencing*, ed. Andrew Ashworth and Andrew von Hirsch (Hart), 205–8; Antony Duff (2001), *Punishment, Communication, and Community* (Oxford University Press), ch. 5; Nicola Lacey (1994), *State Punishment* (Routledge); J. Q. Whitman (2005), *Harsh Justice: Criminal Punishment and the Widening Divide between America and Europe* (Oxford University Press); Antony Duff (2005), 'Punishment, Dignity, and Degradation', *Oxford Journal of Legal Studies* 25(1): 141.

4. Siobhan Fenton (2017), 'UK Prisons "Holding Child Inmates in Solitary Confinement against UN Torture Rules"', *Independent*, 21 Feb.: http://www.independent.co.uk/news/uk/home-news/uk-prisons-child-inmates-solitary-confinement-un-torture-rules-young-offenders-institutes-break-jail-a7591781.html.

5. Canadian Prime Minister Justin Trudeau mandated that the Canadian Minister of Justice implement a series of recommendations to ban the use of long-term solitary confinement in all federal prisons. See Sean Fine and Patrick White (2015), 'Trudeau Calls for Ban on Long-Term Solitary Confinement in Federal Prisons', *Globe and Mail*, 13 Nov.: http://www.theglobeandmail.com/news/national/trudeau-calls-for-implementation-of-ashley-smith-inquest-recommendations/article27256251/.

6. I thank Adrian Blau for stressing this point.

7. Michael Gove (2015), 'The Treasure in the Heart of Man: Making Prisons Work', address to the Prisoners' Learning Alliance, July: https://www.gov.uk/government/speeches/the- treasure-in-the-heart-of-man-making-prisons-work.

8. We do not tend to describe people who have committed regulatory offences as 'offenders'.

9. See *The Oxford English Dictionary* (current online edn).

10. Nicola Lacey (2011), 'The Resurgence of Character: Responsibility in the Context of Criminalisation', in *Philosophical Foundations of Criminal Law*, ed. Antony Duff and Stuart Green (Oxford University Press), ch. 8.

11. Other countries, such as Switzerland, have had terms (now outdated) that assign second-class status to migrants, such as *Papierlischweizer* or 'paper Swiss'.

12. In many jurisdictions, people who are incarcerated are politically powerless; they are often denied the rights to vote, to work, and to stand for office; they are segregated from society in a 'repellent' institution.

13. Psychology studies indicate that we are more lenient in our judgement of a person for his offence when we know the details of his story. See e.g. Mike Hough and Julian V. Roberts (1999), 'Sentencing Trends in Britain: Public Knowledge and Public Opinion', *Punishment and Society* 1(1): 11; Julian V. Roberts et al. (eds)

(2003), *Penal Populism and Public Opinion: Lessons from Five Countries* (Oxford University Press); and Sam Cuthbertson (2013), 'Analytical Summary 2013: Analysis of Complete "You Be the Judge" website experiences'. UK Ministry of Justice: https://www.gov.uk/government/uploads/system/uploads/attachment_data/file/203006/Analysis_of_complete_You_be_the_Judge_website_experiences__web_.pdf. I thank Andrew Neilson for highlighting this point.

14. Margalit Avishai (1996), *The Decent Society* (Harvard University Press), 70–75. Cited in John Tasioulas (2006), 'Punishment and Repentance', *Philosophy* 81: 279. Cited also in Kimberley Brownlee (2012), *Conscience and Conviction* (Oxford University Press), 36.
15. For an analysis of the horrific impact on children's lives when they are put on the sex-offender registry, see Sarah Stillman (2016), 'The List: When Juveniles Are Found Guilty of Sexual Misconduct, the Sex-Offender Registry Can Be a Life Sentence', *New Yorker*, 14 Mar.: http://www.newyorker.com/magazine/2016/03/14/when-kids-are-accused-of-sex-crimes. I thank Avia Pasternak for highlighting this article.
16. Nick Hornby (2001), *How to Be Good* (Viking), 1. I thank John Gardner for directing me to this passage.
17. A critic might argue that a horrible crime, even if it is unpremeditated, must have a partly constitutive impact on a person's character. Put differently, we would be troubled by a person who dismissed his commission of a horrible crime as 'out of character'. I thank an anonymous referee for highlighting this challenge. In reply, his viewing a horrible crime as out of character does not entail that he dismisses it. A person might well react to his crime with disbelief and horror, and the reason for his disbelief and horror is that the act is out of character. Until he committed it, he had every reason to believe he would not act in such a way.
18. Gove (2015).
19. Ibid.
20. I thank an anonymous referee for highlighting this point. For relevant references, see UK Ministry of Justice Report on *Transforming Rehabilitation* (2014): https://www.gov.uk/government/publications/transforming-rehabilitation-a-summary-of-evidence-on-reducing-reoffending.
21. See *Kansas v. Hendricks* (1997) USSC 521 U.S. 346. I thank Walter Sinnott-Armstrong for highlighting this case.
22. UK Ministry of Justice Report (2014).
23. For a discussion of related issues pertaining to desistance, see Helen Brown Coverdale (2018) 'Punishment and Welfare: Defending Offender's Inclusion as Subjects of State Care', *Ethics and Social Welfare* 12(2): 117–32.
24. I thank Laura Valentini for highlighting this point.
25. I thank John Gardner for highlighting this point.

26. See e.g. William Bülow (2014), 'The Harms Beyond Imprisonment: Do We Have Special Moral Obligations Towards the Families and Children of Prisoners?', *Ethical Theory and Moral Practice* 17(4): 775–89.
27. Although this language is less loaded than that of an 'ex-con', it nonetheless mis-describes people who have spent time in prison, since they have not left the society; they remain very much under its control as institutionalized and utterly dependent persons. I thank Jeffrey Howard for noting this point.
28. Matthew Lieberman observes: 'From a young age, we teach children to say, "Sticks and stones will break my bones, but names will never hurt me." But this isn't true. Bullying hurts so much not because one individual is rejecting us but because we tend to believe that the [person bullying us] speaks for others—that if we are being singled out by [that person], then we are probably unliked and unwanted by most. Otherwise, why would all those others watch...rather than [be] stepping in to help support us? Absence of support is taken as a sign of mass rejection.' Matthew Lieberman (2013), *Social: Why Our Brains Are Wired to Connect* (Oxford University Press), 69.
29. I thank Nigel Warburton for highlighting these cases.
30. At the Adelanto Detention Facility in California, 'Red uniforms are worn by "high risk" detainees, who have spent time in state or federal prison. Other immigrants wear blue, meaning they have no criminal convictions, or orange, which signifies a non-felony crime.' Leanna Garfield (2017), 'What Life Is Like Inside California's Largest Immigration Detention Center', *Business Insider*, 9 May: http://uk.businessinsider.com/alifornias-largest-immigration-detention-center-photos-2017-5/#the-adelanto-immigration-detention-center-is-located-about-85-miles-northeast-of-los-angeles-california-1.
31. Mary Bosworth and Blerina Kellezi (2016), 'Getting In, Getting Out and Getting Back: Conducting Long-Term Research in Immigration Detention Centres', in *Reflexivity and Criminal Justice: Intersections of Policy, Practice and Research*, ed. Sarah Armstrong, Jarrett Blaustein, and Alistair Henry (Palgrave Macmillan), 237–62.
32. Statistics provided by the Howard League for Penal Reform: http://www.howardleague.org/weekly-prison-watch/
33. I thank an OUP reader for pressing me on this point.
34. For a discussion of a related issue under the heading of 'hormonal inequality', see Philippe van Parijs (2015), 'Four Puzzles on Gender Equality', *Law, Ethics, and Philosophy* 3: 79–89 . Parijs says: 'Consider the fact that young men are massively overrepresented among perpetrators of violent crimes (partly against women, but to a large extent against other men), and hence...also among prison inmates. Here again, the hormonal story is not implausible...Has an [historical] advantage not thereby be turned into a disadvantage? Can it not be said that men are handicapped relative to women because of their greater propensity to end up in jail as a result of acts they would not have committed had they been women?'

35. Gove (2015).
36. Roy F. Baumeister and Mark R. Leary (1995), 'The Need to Belong: Desire for Interpersonal Attachments as a Fundamental Human Motivation', *Psychological Bulletin* 117(3): 497–529, at 500.
37. I thank Jeffrey Howard for highlighting this issue.
38. Concerning accommodation, a 2015 report from the Australian Institute of Health and Welfare states that 31% of prisoners expect to be homeless upon release. (In the case of indigenous people, it is 38%.) See Australian Institute of Health and Welfare, 'The Health of Australia's Prisoners' (2015): http://www.aihw.gov.au/WorkArea/DownloadAsset.aspx?id=60129553682. In the UK, in 2012, two in five prisoners (37%) stated that they would need help to find a place to live after they were released. Of those, 84% reported needing a lot of help. See Kim Williams, Jennifer Poyser, and Kathryn Hopkins (2012), 'Accommodation, Homelessness and Reoffending of Prisoners: Results from the Surveying Prisoner Crime Reduction (SPCR) Survey'. UK Ministry of Justice: https://www.gov.uk/government/uploads/system/uploads/attachment_data/file/278806/homelessness-reoffending-prisoners.pdf.
39. UK Ministry of Justice Report (2014).
40. I shall bracket the problem of determining whether the supporter is sincere in their belief in the person who has offended. I thank Tom Parr for highlighting this problem.
41. For a discussion that briefly surveys different approaches to rehabilitation in different countries, see Kim Samuel (2017), 'Reimagining Rehabilitation: "A Treasure in the Heart of Every Man"', *Huffington Post*, 7 July: https://www.huffingtonpost.com/entry/reimagining-rehabilitation-a-treasure-in-the-heart_us_596fd948e4b0d72667b05e2d.
42. Emily Tsang (2014), 'Police Called After Family Defies H7N9 Quarantine Order'. *South China Morning Post*, 7 Mar.: https://www.scmp.com/news/hong-kong/article/1442074/police-called-after-family-defies-h7n9-quarantine-order.

Bibliography

Ideas in several chapters first came to life in journal articles, but since then have been substantially revised and integrated with new material to form parts of this book. The articles that underlie sections of the book are:

Kimberley Brownlee, 'Ethical Dilemmas of Sociability', *Utilitas* 28(1): 54–72, Copyright © 2016, Cambridge University Press, doi: 10.1017/S0953820815000175. Reproduced under the terms of the Creative Commons Attribution 3.0 Unported License (CC-BY-3.0): https://creativecommons.org/licenses/by/3.0/.

Kimberley Brownlee, 'Freedom of Association: It's Not What You Think', *Oxford Journal of Legal Studies* 35(2): 267–82, Copyright © 2015, doi: 10.1093/ojls/gqu018. Reprinted by permission of Oxford University Press: https://academic.oup.com/ojls.

Kimberley Brownlee, 'A Human Right Against Social Deprivation', *Philosophical Quarterly* 63(251): 199–222. Copyright © 2013, The Editors of *The Philosophical Quarterly*, doi: 10.1111/1467-9213.12018. Reprinted by permission of Oxford University Press: https://academic.oup.com/pq.

Kimberley Brownlee, 'Don't Call People "Rapists": On the Social Contribution Injustice of Punishment', *Current Legal Problems* 69(1): 327–52, Copyright © 2016, doi: 10.1093/clp/cuw009. Reprinted by permission of Oxford University Press: https://academic.oup.com/clp.

Kimberley Brownlee, 'The Lonely Heart Breaks', *Proceedings of the Aristotelian Society Supplementary Volume* 90(1): 27–48, Copyright © 2016, doi: 10.1093/arisup/akw008. Reprinted by courtesy of the Editor of the Aristotelian Society: https://academic.oup.com/aristotelian.

Kimberley Brownlee, 'Freedom of Association', in *A Companion to Applied Philosophy*, ed. Kasper Lippert-Rasmussen, Kimberley Brownlee, and David Coady, 356–69, Copyright © 2016, John Wiley and Sons, Inc., doi: 10.1002/9781118869109. Reprinted with permission.

Kimberley Brownlee, 'Getting Rights out of Wrongs', in *Oxford Studies in Political Philosophy, Volume 6*, ed. David Sobel, Peter Vallentyne, and Steven Wall, 3–31, Copyright © 2020. Reprinted by permission of Oxford University Press: https://global.oup.com/academic.

* * * * * * *

Alexander, Larry (2008), 'What Is Freedom of Association, and What Is Its Denial?', *Social Philosophy and Policy* 25(2): 1–21.
Anderson, Elizabeth (2010), *The Imperative of Integration*. Princeton University Press.
Arendt, Hannah (2006 [1961]), *Between Past and Future*. Penguin.
Aristotle, *Nicomachean Ethics* (various edns).

von Arnim, Elizabeth (2015 [1922]), *The Enchanted April*. Vintage Classics.
Arrigo, Bruce A., and Jennifer Leslie Bullock (2008), 'The Psychological Effects of Solitary Confinement on Prisoners in Supermax Units', *International Journal of Offender Therapy and Comparative Criminology* 52(6): 622–40.
Australian Institute of Health and Welfare (2015), 'The Health of Australia's Prisoners', http://www.aihw.gov.au/WorkArea/DownloadAsset.aspx?id=60129553682.
Barry, Brian (2002), 'Social Exclusion, Social Isolation, and the Distribution of Income', *Understanding Social Exclusion*. ed. John Hills, Julian Le Grand, and David Piachaud. Oxford University Press, 13–29.
Batuman, Elif (2018), 'Japan's Rent-a-Family Industry', *New Yorker*, 30 Apr.
Bauer, Shane (2012), 'Solitary in Iran Nearly Broke Me. Then I Went Inside America's Prisons', *Mother Jones*, Nov./Dec.
Baumeister, Roy F., and Mark R. Leary (1995), 'The Need to Belong: Desire for Interpersonal Attachments as a Fundamental Human Motivation', *Psychological Bulletin* 117(3): 497–529.
Baylis, Françoise, and Carolyn McLeod (eds) (2014), *Family-Making: Contemporary Ethical Challenges*. Oxford University Press.
Bedi, Sonu (2010), 'Expressive Exclusion: A Defense', *Journal of Moral Philosophy* 7(4): 427–40.
Bennett, Christopher (2008), *The Apology Ritual*. Cambridge University Press.
Biss, Mavis (2011), 'Aristotle on Friendship and Self-Knowledge: The Friend Beyond the Mirror', *History of Philosophy Quarterly* 28(2): 125–40.
Bockarova, Mariana (2016), 'Does One Truly Need to Belong? A Case for the Need to Meaningfully Exist', *Semiotica* 210: 251–7.
Bosworth, Mary, and Blerina Kellezi (2016), 'Getting In, Getting Out and Getting Back: Conducting Long-Term Research in Immigration Detention Centres', in *Reflexivity and Criminal Justice: Intersections of Policy, Practice and Research*, ed. Sarah Armstrong, Jarrett Blaustein, and Alistair Henry. Palgrave Macmillan, 237–62.
Bourne, Sue (2016), *The Age of Loneliness*. Documentary aired on BBC One on 7 Jan. 2016: http://www.bbc.co.uk/programmes/b06vkhr5.
Brake, Elizabeth (2019), 'Rebuilding in the Wake of Disaster: The Political Importance of Place', *Social Theory and Practice*: https://www.pdcnet.org/soctheorpract/content/soctheorpract_2019_0999_4_29_56.
Brake, Elizabeth, and Lucinda Ferguson (eds) (2018), *Philosophical Foundations of Children's and Family Law*. Oxford University Press.
Brown Coverdale, Helen (2018), 'Punishment and Welfare: Defending Offender's Inclusion as Subjects of State Care', *Ethics and Social Welfare* 12(2): 117–32.
Brownlee, Kimberley (2012), 'Social Deprivation and Criminal Justice', in *Rethinking Criminal Law Theory*, ed. François Tanguay-Renaud and James Stribopoulos. Hart, 217–32.
Brownlee, Kimberley (2012), *Conscience and Conviction*. Oxford University Press.
Brownlee, Kimberley (2013), 'A Human Right Against Social Deprivation', *Philosophical Quarterly* 63(251): 199–222.
Brownlee, Kimberley (2015), 'Do We Have a Human Right to the Political Determinants of Health?' in *Philosophical Foundations of Human Rights*, ed. Rowan Cruft, Matthew Liao, and Massimo Renzo. Oxford University Press, 502–14.

Brownlee, Kimberley (2015), 'Freedom of Association: It's Not What You Think', *Oxford Journal of Legal Studies* 35: 356–69.
Brownlee, Kimberley (2016), 'The Lonely Heart Breaks', *Proceedings of the Aristotelian Society Supplementary Volume* 90: 27–48.
Brownlee, Kimberley (2016), 'Freedom of Association', in *The Blackwell Companion to Applied Philosophy*, ed. Kasper Lippert-Rasmussen, Kimberley Brownlee, and David Coady. Wiley, 356–69.
Brownlee, Kimberley (2016), 'The Competent Judge Problem', *Ratio* 29(3): 312–26.
Brownlee, Kimberley (2016), 'Don't Call People "Rapists": On the Social Contribution Injustice of Punishment', *Current Legal Problems* 69(1): 327–52.
Brownlee, Kimberley (2018), 'Dwelling in Possibility', in *Human Rights: Moral or Political*, ed. Adam Etinson. Oxford University Press, 313–26.
Brownlee, Kimberley, and David Jenkins (2019), 'Freedom of Association', in *Stanford Encyclopedia of Philosophy*, ed. Edward N. Zalta. Stanford University Press. https://plato.stanford.edu/entries/freedom-association/.
Bülow, William (2014), 'The Harms Beyond Imprisonment: Do We Have Special Moral Obligations Towards the Families and Children of Prisoners?' *Ethical Theory and Moral Practice* 17(4): 775–89.
Buss, Sarah (1994), 'Autonomy Reconsidered', in *Midwest Studies in Philosophy*. University of Minnesota Press, 95–121.
Cacioppo, John T., and William Patrick (2008), *Loneliness*. Norton.
Cacioppo, John T., Mary Elizabeth Hughes, Linda J. Waite, Louise C. Hawkley, and Ronald A. Thisted (2006), 'Loneliness as a Specific Risk Factor for Depressive Symptoms: Cross-sectional and Longitudinal Analyses.' *Psychology and Aging* 21(1): 140–51.
Cain, Susan (2012), *Quiet: The Power of Introverts in a World That Can't Stop Talking*. Crown Publishing.
Carpenter, Dale (2001), 'Expressive Association and Anti-Discrimination Law After Dale: A Tripartite Approach', *Minnesota Law Review* 85: 1515–89.
Chambers, Clare (2016), 'The Limitations of Contract: Regulating Personal Relationships in a Marriage-Free State', in *After Marriage*, ed. Elizabeth Brake. Oxford University Press, 51–83.
Clott Kanter, Sharon (2011), Interview of Tina Fey in *InStyle* magazine, April issue.
Cohen, Josh (2004), 'Minimalism About Human Rights: The Most We Can Hope For?' *Journal of Political Philosophy* 12(2): 190–213.
Collins, Stephanie (2013), 'Duties to Make Friends', *Ethical Theory & Moral Practice* 16(5): 907–21
Cordelli, Chiara (2015), 'Justice as Fairness and Relational Resources', *Journal of Political Philosophy* 23(1): 86–110.
Cowden, Mhairi (2012), 'What's Love Got to Do with It? Why a Child Does Not Have a Right to Be Loved', *Critical Review of International Social and Political Philosophy* 15(3): 325–45.
Cruft, Rowan (2013), 'Why Is It Disrespectful to Violate Rights?' *Proceedings of the Aristotelian Society* 113(2): 201–24.
Cuthbertson, Sam (2013), 'Analytical Summary 2013: Analysis of Complete "You Be the Judge" Website Experiences'. UK Ministry of Justice.

Decety, Jean, and John T. Cacioppo (eds) (2011), *The Oxford Handbook of Social Neuroscience*. Oxford University Press.
DeWall, C. Nathan (ed.) (2013), *The Oxford Handbook of Social Exclusion*. Oxford University Press.
Duff, Antony (2001), *Punishment, Communication and Community*. Oxford University Press.
Duff, Antony (2005), 'Punishment, Dignity, and Degradation', *Oxford Journal of Legal Studies* 25(1): 141.
Dworkin, Ronald (1984), 'Rights as Trumps', in *Theories of Rights*, ed. Jeremy Waldron. Oxford University Press, 153–67.
Dworkin, Ronald (1986), *Law's Empire*. Harvard University Press.
Dwyer, James (2014), 'The Moral Basis of Children's Relational Rights', in *The Routledge Handbook of Family Law and Policy*, ed. John Eekelaar and Rob George, ch. 4. Routledge.
Engster, Daniel (2007), *The Heart of Justice*. Oxford University Press.
European Social Charter Explanatory Report (1996) (revised edn): http://conventions.coe.int/Treaty/EN/Reports/Html/163.htm.
Feinberg, Joel (1977), 'Voluntary Euthanasia and the Inalienable Right to Life', The Tanner Lecture on Human Values: https://tannerlectures.utah.edu/_documents/a-to-z/f/feinberg80.pdf.
Feinberg, Joel [1980] (1994), 'The Child's Right to an Open Future', in *Freedom and Fulfillment: Philosophical Essays*. Princeton University Press, ch. 3.
Fenton, Siobhan (2017), 'UK Prisons "Holding Child Inmates in Solitary Confinement Against UN Torture Rules"', *The Independent*, 21 Feb.
Fine, Sarah (2010), 'Freedom of Association Is Not the Answer', *Ethics* 120(2): 338–56.
Fine, Sean, and Patrick White (2015), 'Trudeau Calls for Ban on Long-Term Solitary Confinement in Federal Prisons', *Globe and Mail*, 13 Nov.
Fineman, Martha Albertson (2008), 'The Vulnerable Subject: Anchoring Equality in the Human Condition', *Yale Journal of Law & Feminism* 20(1): 1–23.
Fineman, Martha Albertson (2010), 'The Vulnerable Subject and the Responsive State', *Emory Law Journal* 60: 251–75.
Forsdyke, Sara (2005), *Exile, Ostracism, and Democracy: The Politics of Expulsion in Ancient Greece*. Princeton University Press.
Frankfurt, Harry G. (1984), 'Necessity and Desire', *Philosophy and Phenomenological Research* 45(1): 1–13.
Fredrickson, Barbara (2013), 'Remaking Love', TEDx LowerEastSide, 25 Oct.: https://www.youtube.com/watch?v=Nw9x8MNoCJE.
Fredrickson, Barbara (2013), *Love 2.0: Finding Happiness and Health in Moments of Connection*. Penguin.
Garfield, Leanna (2017), 'What Life Is Like Inside California's Largest Immigration Detention Center', *Business Insider*, 9 May.
Gawande, Atul (2009), 'Hellhole', *New Yorker*, 30 Mar.
Gerhardt, Sue (2015), *Why Love Matters: How Affection Shapes a Baby's Brain*, 2nd edn. Routledge.
Geuss, Raymond (2001), *History and Illusion in Politics*. Cambridge University Press.

Gheaus, Anca (2015), 'Unfinished Adults and Defective Children: On the Nature and Value of Childhood', *Journal of Ethics and Social Philosophy* 9(1): 1–21.
Gheaus, Anca (2018), 'Personal Relationship Goods', in *The Stanford Encyclopedia of Philosophy*, ed. Edward N. Zalta: https://plato.stanford.edu/archives/fall2018/entries/personal-relationship-goods/.
Gilabert, Pablo (2009), 'The Feasibility of Basic Socioeconomic Human Rights: A Conceptual Exploration', *Philosophical Quarterly* 59(237): 559–81.
Gilabert, Pablo (2012), *From Global Poverty to Global Equality: A Conceptual Exploration*. Oxford University Press.
Glover, Jonathan (2008), *Choosing Children*. Oxford University Press.
Goldman, Marlene (2018), 'Forgotten: Narratives of Age-Related Dementia', 'Living a Good Life in Older Age' Symposium, University of Warwick, July: https://www.youtube.com/watch?v=C-m_L6ksFQA.
Gove, Michael (2015), 'The Treasure in the Heart of Man: Making Prisons Work', address to the Prisoners' Learning Alliance, July: https://www.gov.uk/government/speeches/the-treasure-in-the-heart-of-man-making-prisons-work.
Green, Leslie (2010), 'Two Worries about Respect for Persons', *Ethics* 120(2): 212–31.
Gutmann, Amy (ed.) (1998), *Freedom of Association*. Princeton University Press.
Haney, Craig (2003), 'Mental Health Issues in Long-Term Solitary and "Supermax" Confinement', *Crime and Delinquency* 49: 124–56.
Hanson, Rick, and Richard Mendius (2009), *Buddha's Brain: The Practical Neuroscience of Happiness, Love, and Wisdom*. Oakland.
Hawkley, Louise C., et al (2010), 'Loneliness Predicts Increased Blood Pressure: 5-Year Cross-lagged Analyses in Middle-aged and Older Adults', *Psychology and Aging* 25(1): 132–41.
Held, Virginia (2006), *The Ethics of Care: Personal, Political, and Global*. Oxford University Press.
Hornby, Nick (2001), *How to Be Good*. Viking.
Hough, Mike, and Julian V. Roberts (1999), 'Sentencing Trends in Britain: Public Knowledge and Public Opinion', *Punishment and Society* 1(1): 11–26.
Hudson, Barbara (1998), 'Mitigation for Socially Deprived Offenders', in *Principled Sentencing*, 2nd edn, ed. Andrew Ashworth and Andrew von Hirsch, 205–8. Hart.
Ibsen, Henrik [1882], *An Enemy of the People* (various edns).
Jackson, Michael (2002), *Justice Behind the Walls*. Douglas & McIntyre.
Johnson, Steffen N. (2001), 'Expressive Association and Organizational Autonomy', *Minnesota Law Review* 85(6): 1639–68.
Jones, Peter (1994), *Rights*. Palgrave.
Kamm, Frances (2002), 'Rights', in *The Oxford Handbook of Jurisprudence and Philosophy of Law*, ed. Jules Coleman, Scott J. Shapiro, and Kenneth Himma. Oxford University Press, 476–513.
Kansas v. Hendricks (1997) USSC 521 U.S. 346.
Kant, Immanuel (1996 [1797]), *The Metaphysics of Morals*. Cambridge University Press.
Kittay, Eva (1999), *Love's Labor*. Routledge.
Kolodny, Niko (2003), 'Love as Valuing a Relationship', *Philosophical Review* 112(2): 135–89.

Kukathas, Chandran (2005), 'The Case for Open Immigration', in *Contemporary Debates in Applied Ethics*, ed. Andrew I. Cohen and Christopher Heath Wellman, 207–20. Blackwell.
Kymlicka, Will (2017), 'Human Rights without Human Supremacism', *Canadian Journal of Philosophy*: doi: 10.1080/00455091.2017.1386481.
Laborde, Cécile (2017), *Liberalism's Religion*. Harvard University Press.
Lacey, Nicola (1994), *State Punishment*. Routledge.
Lacey, Nicola (2011), 'The Resurgence of Character: Responsibility in the Context of Criminalisation', in *Philosophical Foundations of Criminal Law*, ed. Antony Duff and Stuart Green. Oxford University Press, 151–78.
Levy, J. T. (2014), *Rationalism, Pluralism, and Freedom*. Oxford University Press.
Levy, Neil (2017), 'Neuroethics and Responsibility', in *The Blackwell Companion to Applied Philosophy*, ed. Kasper Lippert-Rasmussen, Kimberley Brownlee, and David Coady. Wiley, 270–83.
Lewinsky, Monica (2015), 'The Price of Shame', TED Talk, Mar.: https://www.ted.com/talks/monica_lewinsky_the_price_of_shame?language=en.
Liao, S. Matthew (2006), 'The Right of Children to Be Loved', *Journal of Political Philosophy* 14(4): 420–40.
Liao, S. Matthew (2012), 'Why Children Need to Be Loved', *Critical Review of International Social and Political Philosophy* 15(3): 347–58.
Liao, S. Matthew (2015), *The Right to Be Loved*. Oxford University Press.
Lieberman, Matthew (2013), *Social: Why Our Brains Are Wired to Connect*. Oxford University Press.
Lomasky, Loren (2008), 'The Paradox of Association', *Social Philosophy and Policy* 25(2): 182.
Luban, David, and Henry Shue (2012), 'Mental Torture: A Critique of Erasures in U.S. Law', *Georgetown Law Journal* 100: 823–63.
Lynch, Kathleen, John Baker, and Maureen Lyons (2009), *Affective Equality: Love, Care, and Injustice*. Palgrave Macmillan.
Mackenzie, Catriona, and Natalie Stoljar (eds) (2010), *Relational Autonomy: Feminist Perspectives on Autonomy, Agency, and the Social Self*. Oxford University Press.
Maitland, Sara (2008), *A Book of Silence*. Granta.
Margalit, Avishai (1996), *The Decent Society*. Harvard University Press.
Mason, Andrew (2000), *Community, Solidarity and Belonging*. Cambridge University Press.
Max-Planck Institute for Human Development (2012), 'Making Music Together Connects Brains: When Guitarists Play Together, Networks of Nerve Cells Are Formed between Their Brains', 29 Nov.: https://www.mpg.de/6634785/music-connects-brains.
McClelland, James L., Julie A. Fiez, and Bruce D. McCandliss (2002), 'Teaching the /r/–/l/ Discrimination to Japanese Adults: Behavioral and Neural Aspects', *Physiology & Behavior* 77(4–5): 657–62.
McKinnon, Catriona (2000), 'Exclusion Rules and Self-Respect', *Journal of Value Inquiry* 34: 491–505.
Mill, John Stuart (1859), *On Liberty* (various edns).

Miller, David (2008), *National Responsibility and Global Justice*. Oxford University Press.

Miller, David (2016), *Strangers in Our Midst: The Political Philosophy of Immigration*. Oxford University Press.

Milne, A. A. (2009 [1928]), *The House at Pooh Corner*. Penguin.

Moles, Andres (2014), 'The Public Ecology of Freedom of Association', *Res Publica* 20(1): 85–103.

Monbiot, George (2017), *Out of the Wreckage: A New Politics for an Age of Crisis*. Verso.

Narayan, Deepa, Raj Patel, Kai Schafft, Anne Rademacher, and Sara Koch-Schulte (2000), *Voices of the Poor: Can Anyone Hear Us?* Oxford University Press and the World Bank.

Nickel, James (1982), 'Are Human Rights Utopian?' *Philosophy & Public Affairs* 11(3): 246–64.

Nickel, James (2005), 'Poverty and Rights', *Philosophical Quarterly* 55(220): 385–402.

Nickel, James (2006), *Making Sense of Human Rights*, 2nd edn. Blackwell.

Nickel, James (2008), 'Rethinking Indivisibility', *Human Rights Quarterly* 30: 984–1001.

Nussbaum, Martha (1993), 'Equity and Mercy', *Philosophy and Public Affairs* 22(2): 83–125.

Nussbaum, Martha (2001), *Women and Human Development*. Cambridge University Press.

Nussbaum, Martha (2011), *Creating Capabilities*. Harvard University Press.

Olsaretti, Serena (2017), 'Liberal Equality and the Moral Status of Parent–Child Relationships', in *Oxford Studies in Political Philosophy, Volume 3*, ed. David Sobel, Peter Vallentyne, and Steven Wall, Oxford University Press.

O'Neill, Onora (1986), 'The Public Use of Reason', *Political Theory* 14(4): 523–51.

O'Neill, Onora (2005), 'The Dark Side of Human Rights', *International Affairs* 81(2): 427–39.

Ornish, Dean (1998), *Love and Survival: The Scientific Basis for the Healing Power of Intimacy*. HarperCollins.

Oshana, Marina (1998), 'Personal Autonomy and Society', *Journal of Social Philosophy* 29: 81–102.

Pancevski, Bojan (2007), 'Birth Mix-Up Mother Refuses to Swap Babies', *The Telegraph*, 11 Oct.

Parfit, Derek (1984), *Reasons and Persons*. Oxford University Press.

Parfit, Derek (2011), *On What Matters*, vol. 1. Oxford University Press.

van Parijs, Philippe (2015), 'Four Puzzles on Gender Equality', *Law, Ethics, and Philosophy* 3: 79–89.

Pogge, Thomas (2009), 'Shue on Rights and Duties', in *Global Basic Rights*, ed. Charles R. Beitz and Robert E. Goodin. Oxford University Press, 113–30.

Qualter, Pamela, et al. (2013), 'Trajectories of Loneliness during Childhood and Adolescence: Predictors and Health Outcomes', *Journal of Adolescence* 36(6): 1283–93.

Rawls, John (1999 [1971]), *A Theory of Justice*. Harvard University Press.

Raz, Joseph (1986), *The Morality of Freedom*. Oxford University Press.
Raz, Joseph (1994), *Ethics in the Public Domain*. Oxford University Press.
Raz, Joseph (1999), *Practical Reason and Norms*. Clarendon Press.
Raz, Joseph (2015), 'Human Rights in the Emerging World Order', in *Philosophical Foundations of Human Rights*, ed. Rowan Cruft, Matthew Liao, and Massimo Renzo. Oxford University Press, 217–31.
Reader, Soran, and Gillian Brock (2004), 'Needs, Moral Demands, and Moral Theory', *Utilitas* 16(3): 251–66.
Report of the Commission on Safety and Abuse in America's Prisons (2006): prisoncommission.org/.
Richert Belul, Sherry (2018), 'When a Boyfriend Joins the Marriage', *New York Times*, 7 Dec.
Roberts v. United States Jaycees 468 U.S. 609, 618 (1984).
Roberts, Julian V., Loretta J. Stalans, David Indermaur, and Mike Hough (eds) (2003), *Penal Populism and Public Opinion: Lessons from Five Countries*. Oxford University Press.
Rogers, Chris (2009), 'What Became of Romania's Neglected Orphans?' *BBC News Romania*: 22 Dec.
Rose, Julie (2017), *Free Time*. Princeton University Press.
Russell, Bertrand [1967] (2000), *Autobiography*. Routledge.
Samuel, Kim (2017), 'Reimagining Rehabilitation: "A Treasure in the Heart of Every Man"', *Huffington Post*, 7 July: https://www.huffingtonpost.com/entry/reimagining-rehabilitation-a-treasure-in-the-heart_us_596fd948e4b0d72667b05e2d.
Sandel, Michael (1982), *Liberalism and the Limits of Justice*. Cambridge University Press.
Scheinin, Martin (1999), 'Article 20' in *The Universal Declaration of Human Rights: A Common Standard of Achievement*, ed. Guðmundur Alfreðsson and Asbjørn Eide. Martinus Nijhoff.
Schwartz, Daniel (2007), *Aquinas on Friendship*. Oxford University Press.
Seglow, Jonathan (2013), *Defending Associative Duties*. Routledge.
Seligman, Martin (2011), *Flourish*. Random House.
Sen, Amartya (2004), 'Elements of a Theory of Human Rights', *Philosophy & Public Affairs* 32(4): 315–56.
Shalev, Sharon (2008), *Sourcebook on Solitary Confinement*. Nuffield Foundation: http://www.solitaryconfinement.org/uploads/sourcebook_web.pdf.
Shiffrin, Seana (2005), 'What Is Really Wrong with Compelled Association?' *Northwestern Law Review* 99(2): 839–88.
Shue, Henry (1996), *Basic Rights: Subsistence, Affluence, and US Foreign Policy*, 2nd edn. Princeton University Press.
Siegel, Dan (2010), *Mindsight*. Oxford University Press.
Smith, Sam, and Richard Proenneke (1999), *One Man's Wilderness: An Alaskan Odyssey*. Alaska Northwest Books.
Sreenivasan, Gopal (2005), 'A Hybrid Theory of Claim Rights', *Oxford Journal of Legal Studies* 25(2): 257–74.

Stelfox, H. T., D. W. Bates, and D. A. Redelmeier (2003), 'Safety of Patients Isolated for Infection Control', *Journal of the American Medical Association* 290(14): 1899–1905.
Sterelny, Kim (2012), *The Evolved Apprentice: How Evolution Made Humans Unique*. MIT Press.
Stillman, Sarah (2016), 'The List: When Juveniles Are Found Guilty of Sexual Misconduct, the Sex-Offender Registry Can Be a Life Sentence', *New Yorker*, 14 Mar.
Stohr, Karen (2012), *On Manners*. Routledge.
Sumner, Wayne (1987), *The Moral Foundation of Rights*. Oxford University Press.
Sunstein, Cass (2003), *Why Societies Need Dissent*. Harvard University Press.
Swift, Adam, and Harry Brighouse (2014), *Family Values: The Ethics of Parent–Child Relationships*. Princeton University Press.
Taber, Jane (2012), 'Elderly American Caregiver Being Deported Has Been Granted Temporary Visa', *Globe and Mail*, 15 Nov.
Tadros, Victor (2009), 'Poverty and Criminal Responsibility', *Journal of Value Inquiry* 43: 391–413.
Tadros, Victor (2011), *The Ends of Harm*. Oxford University Press.
Tasioulas, John (2006), 'Punishment and Repentance', *Philosophy* 81(2): 279–322.
Tasioulas, John (2007), 'The Moral Reality of Human Rights', in *Freedom from Poverty as a Human Right: Who Owes What to the Very Poor?*, ed. Thomas Pogge. Oxford University Press, 75–101.
Tasioulas, John (2011), 'On the Nature of Human Rights', in *The Philosophy of Human Rights: Contemporary Controversies*, ed. Gerhard Ernst and Jan-Christoph Heilinger. Berlin: de Gruyter, 17–59.
Taylor, Charles (1985), *Philosophy and the Human Sciences: Philosophical Papers 2*. Cambridge.
Taylor, Charles (1989), *Sources of the Self: The Making of the Modern Identity*. Cambridge University Press.
Taylor, Charles (1995), 'Irreducibly Social Goods', in *Philosophical Arguments*. Harvard University Press, 127–45.
Tomasi, John (1991), 'Individual Rights and Community Virtues', *Ethics* 101(3): 521–36.
Tsang, Emily (2014), 'Police Called After Family Defies H7N9 Quarantine Order', *South China Morning Post*, 7 Mar.
Turkle, Studs (2011), *Alone Together*. Basic Books.
UK Ministry of Justice (2014), *Transforming Rehabilitation*: https://www.gov.uk/government/publications/transforming-rehabilitation-a-summary-of-evidence-on-reducing-reoffending.
Vaillant, George (2012), *Triumphs of Experience: The Men of the Harvard Grant Study*. Belknap Press.
Valentini, Laura (2016), 'What's Wrong with Being Lonely? Justice, Beneficence, and Meaningful Relationships', *Proceedings of the Aristotelian Society Supplementary Volume* 90(1): 49–69.

Vallor, Shannon (2016), *Technology and the Virtues: A Philosophical Guide to a Future Worth Wanting*. Oxford University Press.
Vitrano, Christine (2013), 'Love and Resilience', *Ethical Perspectives* 20(4): 591–604.
Waldron, Jeremy (1992), 'Minority Cultures and the Cosmopolitan Alternative', *University of Michigan Journal of Law Reform* 25(3): 751–92.
Walzer, Michael (2004), 'Involuntary Association', in *Politics and Passion: Toward a More Egalitarian Liberalism*. Yale University Press, 1–37.
Watkins, John (2016), 'The Invisible Aged: The People Politics Forgot', *Guardian*, 16 May.
Wellman, Christopher H. (2008), 'Immigration and Freedom of Association,' *Ethics* 119: 109–41.
Wenar, Leif (2005), 'The Nature of Rights', *Philosophy & Public Affairs* 33(3): 242.
Wenar, Leif (2013), 'The Nature of Claim-Rights', Symposium on Rights and the Direction of Duties, *Ethics* 123(2): 202–29.
Westlund, Andrea (2009), 'Rethinking Relational Autonomy', *Hypatia* 24(4): 26–49.
White, Stuart (1997), 'Freedom of Association and the Right to Exclude', *Journal of Political Philosophy* 5(4): 373–91.
White, Stuart (1998), 'Trade Unionism in a Liberal State', in *Freedom of Association*, ed. Amy Gutmann. Princeton University Press, 330–56.
Whitman, J. Q. (2005), *Harsh Justice: Criminal Punishment and the Widening Divide between America and Europe*. Oxford University Press.
Williams, Kim, Jennifer Poyser, and Kathryn Hopkins (2012), 'Accommodation, Homelessness and Reoffending of Prisoners: Results from the Surveying Prisoner Crime Reduction (SPCR) Survey'. UK Ministry of Justice.
Willsher, Kim (2018), 'Uproar in France over Video of Woman Hit by Harasser in Paris Street', *The Guardian*, 30 July.
Wolff, Jonathan, and de-Shalit, Avner (2007), *Disadvantage*. Oxford University Press.
Wright, H. W. (1942), 'The Values of Personal Association', *Ethics* 52: 447–62.
Zuger, A. (2010), 'Isolation, an Ancient and Lonely Practice, Endures', *New York Times*, 30 Aug.

Index

For the benefit of digital users, indexed terms that span two pages (e.g., 52–53) may, on occasion, appear on only one of those pages.

acquaintanceship 102–5; *see also* friendship
Akova, Firat 213n.15
Alexander, Larry 217n.10
Anderson, Elizabeth 63–4, 203n.85, 221n.8
Anderson, Terry 205n.8
animals 1, 15, 25–6, 30–2, 54–5, 68, 188, 197n.15, 198n.17, 201n.63
 and interspecies sociality 197n.7
Arendt, Hannah 96
Aristotle 21, 34, 76
Arnim, Elizabeth von 39, 79–80
associational freedom 145–7
 and interactional freedom 105–9
 in contrast to freedom of expression 108–9, 146–7
 in contrast to freedom of religion 146–7
 liberal defence of 118–22
 limits of 135–41, 147–51, 222n.17
associations 3–4, 12, 19, 31–2, 51–2, 66–7, 96, 99, 101, 103–8, 162, 212n.2, 214n.20, 217nn.5,10, 218n.13, 220n.2, 221n.12, 224nn.12,24; *see also* associational freedom, freedom to dissociate
 and consent 147–52
 and the state 139–41
 morally messy 154–60, 163–6; *see also* parasite problem
 ways in which associations can be wrong 141–5
Auden, W. H. 80, 92
Austen, Jane 102–4, 112, 214n.19
Australian Institute of Health and Welfare 229n.38
autonomy 32–4, 58, 62, 65, 83, 96, 120–2, 128–9, 144–5, 166, 185–6, 220n.38

Baby M surrogacy case 164
Baker, John 196n.8

Barry, Brian 42
Batuman, Elif 7–8, 15, 31–2
Bauer, Shane 29
Baumeister, Roy F. 24–9, 117, 159–60, 186, 197n.9, 200nn.47–48, 201nn.52,58, 206n.20
belonging; *see* need to belong
Ben Franklin Effect 102–3
Berlin, Isaiah 34
Bolt, Robert 138
Boycott, Charles 113–15
Brock, Gillian 10–11, 197n.9
Buddhism 35, 132
bystander effect 27, 117

Cacioppo, John T. 28, 132, 198n.24
capabilities 1–2, 14, 45, 197n.15, 207n.34; *see also* functionings
Ceaușescu, Nicolae 23, 81
childhood 1–2, 8, 13–15, 17–19, 21–4, 26, 30–1, 36–7, 44, 52, 56, 58, 65, 67, 78, 81–2, 91–2, 107–8, 111, 116, 121, 127–8, 136–7, 142–4, 146–9, 151, 154–9, 161–8, 183, 185, 189–90, 205n.12, 211n.13, 212n.1, 220nn.2,5,221n.10, 222n.2, 225n.25, 227n.15, 228n.28; *see also* family
Cohen, Joshua 195n.5
Collins, Stephanie 203n.82
commons dilemma 27, 117
consent 12, 118–22, 136–8, 142, 147–52, 218n.12, 223n.4
consequentialism 119, 166, 177–8, 207n.31, 209n.62
Cooney, Caroline B. 154
Cordelli, Chiara 217n.4
criminal justice 4–5, 29, 33–4, 65–6, 72–3, 107, 172–92
Crusoe, Robinson 13, 28

de-Shalit, Avner 1–2, 14, 26, 90, 113, 207n.34
democracy 60–1, 120, 135
deportation 43, 83
desires 10, 16–17, 122, 162
  in contrast to needs 36–8
dignity 46, 54–5
disabilities 15, 22–4, 41, 47–9, 70, 83, 113, 173–4, 177, 206n.15
duties 5, 11–12, 56, 58, 63–4, 66–7, 79–80, 118–19, 123, 132–3, 136–8, 140–1, 152, 158, 162–3, 165, 187, 196n.2, 197n.8, 209n.61, 209n.62, 210n.7, 215n.23, 220n.4, 224n.20
  and duty-bearers 59–61
  and feasibility 69–73
  duties of governments 5–6, 60–1, 69, 89–90
  duty to rescue 112–13, 216n.35
  indeterminacy 59–60
  interactional duties 109–13
  Kantian account 32–4
  undue burdens 66–9, 136–8, 149
Dworkin, Ronald 214n.22

each-we dilemmas 116–17, 123–4
each-we dilemmas of sociability 77, 117–18, 124–5, 131–2; *see also* prisoner's dilemma, commons dilemma
  animosity dilemma 131–2
  autonomy dilemma 128–9, 219n.35
  egoist's dilemma 129
  misanthrope's dilemma 117–18, 128
  popular people dilemma 117–18, 130
  popular person dilemma 117–18, 129–30
  rejected people dilemma 117–18, 126–8
  rejected person dilemma 117–18, 125–9, 131
  social butterfly dilemma 117–18, 130–1
economic-welfare rights 1–2, 11, 34, 44–5, 57–8, 78, 195–6n.6; *see also* education, freedom from poverty, health
education 2, 46–7, 56–9, 64–5, 79, 81–2, 90, 146, 191
etiquette 90, 98, 110–11, 187, 216n.28
emotions and sociability 8, 23–5, 31, 63, 71–2, 83–4, 97–8, 139–40, 207n.34, 209n.61, 220n.2; *see also* love
essentialist language 4–5, 173–83
  and criminal justice 174–83

European Convention on Human Rights 206n.22
European Social Charter 47–8

family 9–10, 17–19, 21, 25–6, 36–7, 39, 46, 63, 81–2, 89, 91, 104–5, 137, 143–4, 154, 156–7, 162–3, 167, 185–90, 196n.2, 214nn.20,22, 225n.25; *see also* parenting
  rent-a-family industry, Japan 7–8, 15, 21, 31–2, 63, 84, 142
Feinberg, Joel 22, 107
feminism 14, 197n.8
Fine, Sarah 122
Foot, Philippa 154–5
Forster, E. M. 95
Frankfurt, Harry G. 10, 36, 204n.92
Fredrickson, Barbara 97–8
free-riding 77, 112, 133
freedom of association; *see* associational freedom
freedom of expression 4, 53, 90–1, 99, 108–9, 119–21, 135, 145–7, 152, 215n.26, 217n.10, 220n.2
freedom of religion 4, 53, 91, 119–21, 135, 145–7, 152, 214n.21, 218n.13
freedom of speech; *see* freedom of expression
freedom to dissociate 4, 107, 109, 116–18, 124–8, 132–3, 136–7, 141–2, 146–7, 152, 154–5, 157–9, 164, 170–1, 185–6
friendship 21, 25–6, 31–4, 39, 43, 50–2, 63–4, 80, 84, 88–90, 103, 111–13, 120, 137–8, 144–5, 149–52, 164, 183–4, 188–9, 198n.17, 200n.47, 201nn.52,57, 203n.82, 204n.87, 210n.3, 214n.19, 221n.12
functionings; *see also* capabilities 14, 90, 207n.34

Gansinger, Simon 216n.27
Gawande, Atul 41–2, 205n.8
Geuss, Raymond 71
Gheaus, Anca 22–3, 201n.52, 207n.34
Gilabert, Pablo 69
Goldman, Marlene 17–18
Gosford Park 75, 78–80
Gove, Michael 174–5, 179, 184–5
Green, Leslie 111–12
Gutmann, Amy 118

harm principle 119, 215n.26
Hawthorne, Nathaniel 183
health 28, 65, 68, 77, 98, 192–3
  healthcare 29, 33–4, 41, 62, 88–9, 172, 176–8, 182–3
  mental health 28, 41–2, 46–7, 57
  right to health 11, 44–7, 56–7, 59, 62, 65, 114
Held, Virginia 211n.11
hierarchy of needs 195–6n.6
homelessness 111–12, 216n.34, 229n.38
Hornby, Nick 178–9
Howard League for Penal Reform 183
human rights 1–6, 8–9, 35, 39–40, 89, 118, 145–6, 205n.12, 209n.59, 221n.12; *see also* economic-welfare rights, political rights, social rights
  basic rights 44, 58–9, 114, 205n.12
  civil and political rights 1–2, 39–40, 44–6, 53–4, 57, 59–60, 72, 114, 206n.22, 221n.12
  concept of human rights 49–50, 54–5
  duty-bearers; *see* duties
  feasibility 69–73
  right against social deprivation 39–40, 50–9, 61–73
  neglect of 44–50
  right to sustain others 51, 62, 68–9, 75
  socio-economic rights 44, 53–4, 59–60, 64, 71
  standard and recurrent threats 49–50

imprisonment 2–5, 12, 15, 40, 42, 48–9, 59–61, 65–6, 73, 84, 86–7, 89, 91, 96, 106–8, 114, 128, 140–1, 172–5, 177–80, 183–7, 191–2, 205n.8, 206n.22, 226n.5, 228nn.27,30,34, 229n.38
  and forfeiture of rights 187–90
  and prejudice; *see* essentialist language
  statistics 183
infants; *see* childhood
integration 57, 140
interactions 2, 9, 14, 17, 20, 24–5, 27, 33, 95, 99–101, 103–5, 131, 196n.2, 197n.3, 201n.52, 205n.9, 206n.20, 213nn.12,15, 214n.20, 215n.23, 216n.35, 223n.6
  interactional duties 96, 112–14, 139–40
  interactional overtures 3–4, 80, 86, 98–100, 102–3, 107–12, 216nn.27,34

interactional freedom 3–4, 61, 67, 96–9, 105–10, 185, 212n.1
interactional inclusion 3–4, 51, 88–9, 98, 117
micro-moments 2, 97–8
non-associative interactions 16, 21, 97–8, 101–3
virtual interactions 49–51, 68
interest
  self-interest 16–17, 27, 76, 93, 117, 159–60, 213n.5
  self-and-group-interests 16–17, 27, 77, 93
International Covenant on Civil and Political Rights 45–6, 221n.12
International Covenant on Economic, Social, and Cultural Rights 45–7
interpersonal freedom 99, 107–9, 136
isolation 2–5, 13, 15, 26–9, 33–4, 39–44, 47, 50–1, 60–2, 65–8, 72–3, 84, 87–9, 96, 107, 111, 113–14, 125–6, 128–9, 173, 181–3, 187, 190, 198n.17, 212n.20, 212n.28; *see also* segregation, solitary confinement

Jenkins, David 217n.5
Jones, Peter 64, 166–7
justice 1–3, 34–5, 45, 62, 79–80, 83, 181, 207n.34, 210n.7, 225n.3; *see also* social contribution injustice
  and friendship 34

Kamm, Frances 161, 224n.20
Kant, Immanuel 33, 123, 203n.82, *see also* 'What if everyone did that?' problem
Kolodny, Niko 196n.2
Kukathas, Chandran 218n.11
Kymlicka, Will 54–5

Lacey, Nicola 175–6
Leary, Mark R. 24–9, 117, 159–60, 186, 200nn.47–48, 201nn.52,58, 205n.9, 206n.20
Lewinsky, Monica 221n.16
Lewis, C. S. 116
Liao, S. Matthew 23–4, 209n.61
liberalism 118–20
Lieberman, Matthew 228n.28
Lomasky, Loren 146–7
loneliness 1, 7–8, 26, 28–9, 39, 41–2, 80, 82, 101, 144–5, 190, 201n.63, 211n.17

love 8, 20, 23–4, 28, 51–2, 63, 75, 79–81, 89–90, 92–3, 98, 104–5, 132, 154, 157, 196n.2, 204n.87
Lynch, Kathleen 196n.8
Lyons, Maureen 196n.8

Maitland, Sara 28, 201n.63
Mallon, Mary 176, 181–2, 190–1
Mandela, Nelson 51–2, 89
Margalit, Avishai 177–8
marriage 8, 19, 46–7, 79–80, 120–1, 136–7, 148–9, 154, 173–4, 179, 199n.33, 223n.4; *see also* family, moral messiness
 child marriage 4, 142–3, 158–9, 163–6, 171
Maslow, Abraham; *see* hierarchy of needs
mental illness; *see* health
micro-aggressions 100
Mill, John Stuart 118–19, 146, 215n.26
Miller, David 218n.12
Milne, A. A. 1
Moles, Andres 122
Montgomery, Lucy Maud 18, 90–1
moral messiness 9–10, 144, 148, 154–60, 163–8, 171, 222n.3, 223n.6, 225n.32; *see also* parasite problem, piggybacking problem
 ex ante versus *ex post* standards of moral judgment 52, 144, 154–7, 165, 223n.4, 224n.14
Moriarty, Liane 43, 154

Narayan, Deepa 113
need to belong 14, 17–20, 24–8, 34, 56, 76–7, 101, 159–60, 186, 200n.48, 201n.58, 205n.9, 206n.20; *see also* segregation
 belongingness hypothesis 19–21, 24–8, 159–60, 201n.52, 205n.9
need to sustain others 75–9, 81, 83, 92–3, 172, 183–4, 186–8, 190, 210nn.1,5
needs; *see also* desires, need to belong, need to sustain others, social needs
 contingent and non-contingent 2, 10–14, 16–17, 26, 35, 37–8, 62, 197n.9, 202n.68
 needs for a minimally good life 10–11
 volitional needs 36–7, 204n.92
Nelson Mandela Rules 48–9
Nickel, James 11–13, 44, 49–50, 69–70, 169, 207n.31, 209n.53
non-ideal theory 5–6
Nussbaum, Martha 1–2, 14, 45, 197n.15, 201n.58, 207n.34

obligations; *see* duties
O'Neill, Onora 59–60, 108–10

parasite problem 155–8, 160–70, 228n.26
parenting; *see also* family 17–19, 36–7, 81–2, 97, 120–1, 136–7, 142–6, 148–9, 154–8, 161–70, 180, 189–90
 fathers 8, 17, 89, 91–2, 142–3, 164, 180, 185, 190, 227n.25
Parfit, Derek 116–17, 123–4, 223n.4
van Parijs, Philippe 228n.34
Patrick, William 132, 198n.24
phenomenology 30–2, 55
piggybacking problem 155–6, 160–5
politeness; *see also* etiquette, 102, 110
poverty 90, 113, 174, 225n.1
 freedom from poverty 2, 44, 47–8, 51, 66, 79
prison; *see* imprisonment
prisoner's dilemma 27, 123–4
Proenneke, Richard 13, 28, 198n.17
psychology of sociability 17–18, 23–9, 59, 68, 72–3, 76–7, 79, 98, 102–3, 117, 132–3, 159–60, 181–2, 186, 200n.48, 226n.13
punishment 4–5, 12, 15, 40, 46, 48–9, 59, 72–3, 87–9, 173, 175, 177–8, 181, 184–5, 187–8, 191–2, 209n.62; *see also* imprisonment

quarantine 29, 33–4, 40, 65, 68, 92, 190; see also *Mary Mallon*

rape; *see* sexual offences
Rawls, John 34–5, 146
Raz, Joseph 56–7, 160–1, 210n.5, 219n.34
Reader, Soran 10–11, 197n.9
recognition 3–4, 53, 66–7, 72–3, 188–9; *see also* interactional duties, respect
relationships; *see also* need to belong
 instrumental and non-instrumental value of relationships 8–9, 33–4, 196n.2, 199n.37
 quality, not quantity 25–6
reproductive rights 36, 52, 139–40
respect 3–4, 14, 32–5, 54–5, 57–8, 64, 68, 72–3, 76, 96, 98, 105, 110–13, 121–2, 174, 178, 181, 216n.28, 217n.4
responsibilities; *see* duties
rights; *see also* human rights, social rights
 as trumps 127–8, 166–8
 conditionality 168–9

defeasibility 166–8
ex ante and ex post rights; see moral messiness
forfeiture of rights 11–13, 59, 113–14, 144, 169, 173, 185, 187–90, 207n.31
group rights 169–70
interest-based account
language of rights 1–3, 54, 61–6
moral rights 11
to be exclusive 104–5, 118–22
right to education; see education
Rose, Julie 91
Rubens, Bernice 39
Russell, Bertrand 28

Sandel, Michael 63
Sartre, Jean-Paul 87
Schwartz, Daniel 204n.87
See, Lisa 199n.33
Seglow, Jonathan 196n.2, 215n.23, 220n.4
segregation 2–5, 33–4, 40, 47, 92, 172–3, 176, 181–2, 184–8, 190, 192, 226n.12; see also essentialist language, imprisonment, need to belong
self-determination 120–2
self-preservation (reasons of) 76, 210n.4; see also self-interest
Sen, Amartya 69–71, 208n.50
sexual harassment 100, 213n.13
sexual identity 14, 35–7, 103, 175
sexual offences 12, 42, 77, 142–4, 162–5, 192, 221n.10, 225n.25, 227n.15
sexual relations 137–8, 149–50, 204n.93
Shawshank Redemption 42
Shiffrin, Seana 217n.10
Shue, Henry 44, 49–50, 58–9, 205n.12, 207n.30, 207n.33
Smith, Gregory P. 111
sociability 3, 8, 10–11 see also each-we dilemmas of sociability and sociality 9
social abilities 3, 8, 11–12, 20–3, 58, 75–6, 81–3, 88–90, 93–4, 185, 187, 190–2, 199n.37, 205n.12
social connections 8–10, 15–16, 20–3, 29–31, 35, 42, 44–6, 57, 60–1, 63, 68, 83, 86–91, 95, 105, 109, 124–5, 128–30, 139–41, 186, 188, 197n.3, 199n.37, 206n.21, 212n.28, 213n.12, 215n.23
social contribution 50–1, 68, 81–3, 85–9, 91–2, 127–8,
in prisons 173, 184–5, 191–2, 212n.28

social contribution injustice 3, 75–6, 81–4, 88, 91–4, 184
social-contribution needs; see social needs
social deprivation 8–9, 40–50, 53, 56–61, 64–6, 72, 128, 206n.22, 225n.3; see also quarantine, right against social deprivation, segregation, solitary confinement
as a human rights violation; see right against social deprivation
in contrast to isolation 41–2
social inclusion 33–4, 37, 46, 97, 99, 129–30, 205n.12; see also interactions, social deprivation
social injustice 39–40, 86–7, 92, 172–3, 192–3
social injustices versus social bads 61–2; see also social contribution injustice
social loafing 27, 117
social needs; see also desires, needs
and age 13–16
core social needs 8–22, 35, 37–8, 40, 45–50, 58–61, 65–6, 98, 101, 123, 139, 213n.15
in contrast to social desires 36–8
social-access needs 16–17
social-contribution needs 16–17
social opportunities 8, 20–2, 51, 62, 75–6, 81–2, 84–8, 113, 127–8, 186–7; see also social abilities, social connections
social rights 1–2, 5, 11–12, 44–50, 62, 67–9, 71–3, 94, 114, 116–18, 127–8, 135, 173, 185, 187–91, 206n.21; see also human rights, rights
solitary confinement 2–3, 29, 42–3, 48–9, 54, 65–6, 73, 87–8, 92, 107, 173, 187, 205n.8, 206n.22, 211n.14, 212n.20, 226n.5; see also imprisonment, segregation
solitude 13, 26–7, 41–2, 62, 95–7, 129, 201n.63
Stohr, Karen 216n.28
Sunstein, Cass 212n.3

Tadros, Victor 209n.62
Tasioulas, John 60, 70–1
Lord Tennyson, Alfred 81
Thoreau, Henry David 13
Tomasi, John 63
torture 15, 46, 48–9, 65–6, 107, 166–7, 212n.20

UK Ministry of Justice 181, 188–9
UN Basic Principles for the Treatment of Prisoners; *see* Nelson Mandela Rules
Universal Declaration of Human Rights 45–7, 49, 56–7, 70–1, 118, 145, 221n.12
Urzúa, Luis 135
US Supreme Court
 Kansas v. Hendricks 180
 Roberts v. United States Jaycees 120, 145, 218n.13

Valentini, Laura 63–4, 66–7, 116
Vallor, Shannon 207n.26

vulnerability 11–14, 26, 30–1, 54, 58, 60–1, 64–8, 79, 90, 97, 112–13, 137–8, 143–4, 150, 159, 164–5, 223n.4

Watkins, John 39
well-being 16–17, 23, 27–8, 36, 46, 56, 96, 98, 120, 144, 197n.5, 201n.52, 201n.58; *see also* need to sustain others
Wellman, Christopher H. 120–1
Wenar, Leif 157, 161–2
'What if everyone did that?' problem 3, 116–17, 122–5
Wolff, Jonathan 1–2, 14, 26, 90, 113, 207n.34
Wordsworth, William 95–6
Wright, H. W. 97–8